Due Return	Due Return
Date Date	Date Date

THE TETHERED PRESIDENCY

THE TETHERED PRESIDENCY

*Congressional Restraints on
Executive Power*

EDITED BY
THOMAS M. FRANCK

1981

New York University Press

New York & London

Library of Congress Cataloging in Publication Data
Main entry under title:

The Tethered presidency.
Includes bibliographical references and index.
1. Presidents—United States.   2. United States—
Congresses.   3. United States—Foreign relations.
I. Franck, Thomas M.
JF570.T38   353.03′22   81-1441
ISBN 0-8147-2567-8   AACR2

Manufactured in the United States of America

Acknowledgment

The editor and authors gratefully acknowledge the
generous assistance of the Law Center Foundation
and the Law School of New York University.

I dedicate this book to my co-authors, who, embarking on this venture as colleagues, arrived as friends, an altogether edifying excursion.

T. M. F.

Introduction

BOOKS WRITTEN BY a committee are subject to fabled hazards their editors sometimes seek to assuage by writing an "integrative" introduction. No such literary device accompanies this volume. If it were needed, our effort would have failed.

The authors have made diligent efforts to avoid such failure, culminating in a three-day conference in November 1979 at the Law School of New York University, in the company of a small number of additional specialists. As a result of such interactions and the subsequent redrafting of chapters, all authors can be said to have a role in each chapter.

The authors were drawn to this cooperative task by shared assumptions which are eloquently set out in the chapter by Theodore Sorensen. We continue to be troubled by the long, if fading shadow of the "imperial presidency." Yet all are increasingly disturbed by newer dangers: the excessive fragmentation of the foreign policy process, growing power of special-interest lobbies, internecine warfare between those who legislate and those who execute. We sense a loss of flexibility without commensurate gains in accountability. We see opportunities for mischief by those, including foreign governments, who play off the branches of government against each other, or who would gamble on our inability to transcend domestic stalemate.

The authors have searched diligently for a middle ground, examining the requisites and prospects for a creative foreign policy codetermined by both Congress and president. To such a codeterminative system, each branch would bring special skills exhibiting a healthy skepticism toward the pretensions of the other. Struggle is not eliminated; neither, of course, is good judgment guaranteed. There would be, however, a moratorium on the feckless turf wars that benefit none but the nation's ill-wishers.

Our Constitution, which invites struggle between the branches, also implicitly ordains its limits, not in specific words, but by constituting chaos and stalemate the sole alternatives to residual cooperation. As we enter the century's dangerous eighth decade, the nation's leaders cannot afford to dissipate our strained capacity to endure stress. Reflexive, unproductive confrontations between Congress and the president will leave us a benighted land, with a cynical population of diminished resolve. The tethered presidency is no remedy for past sins of *imperium*.

This study examines the historical origins of the foreign relations conflict between the branches, as well as its most recent antecedents. It examines costs and benefits of congressional resurgence and symptoms and causes of breakdown; and it recommends procedures for peaceful adjustment. The dawn of a new presidential mandate is the propitious moment for creative reconsideration and rapprochement. No less is demanded by the American people of their elected leaders.

Thomas M. Franck

Contents

PART III
Prescriptions for Partnership between President and Congress

Part I
The Tethered Presidency in Perspective

I

Political Perspective: Who Speaks for the National Interest?

Theodore C. Sorensen

Who speaks for the national interest?
"I," said the President,
"Under historical precedent,
I speak for the national interest."

Who speaks for the American people?
"We," said the Congress,
"Our ties are the strongest,
We speak for the American people."

Who speaks for America abroad?
"We," said the Foreign Service,
"These amateurs make us nervous,
We speak for America abroad."

Who speaks for future generations?
"We," said the press, intellectuals and youth,
"We alone know Ultimate Truth,
We speak for future generations."

Then each of these centers of power elite
Renewed its long struggle in anger and heat;
Each pressing its claim of true representation—
And no one spoke out for the American nation.

O NCE UPON A TIME long, long ago, in a republic between the seas, there lived a contented people called the Americans. They had faith in the future, confidence in their system, and respect for their president. Energy was cheap, doctors made house calls, and the president spoke for the national interest. He alone defined it; he alone interpreted it; he alone articulated it. The secretary of state was the president's principal lieutenant in the conduct of foreign affairs, and the president's views were faithfully communicated and uniformly applied by his ambassadors to foreign capitals and in the United Nations. The Congress responded to the president's lead; the public accepted the president's wisdom; and our allies knew that the president could fulfill any commitments he made.

No one doubted that the conduct of foreign affairs was the prerogative of the president and only the president. "His is the only voice," wrote Professor Woodrow Wilson long before he entered political life, ". . . representative . . . of the whole people."

"In this vast external realm," wrote Mr. Justice Sutherland for a practically unanimous Supreme Court in the 1936 case of *U.S.* v. *Curtiss-Wright Export Corp.,* "with its important, complicated, delicate and manifold problems, the President alone has the power to speak as a representative of the nation."

In short, the answer to the question now assigned to me was then clear, in law and in fact. The conduct of American foreign policy was all very orderly. In that area, at least, the president dominated the executive branch; the executive branch dominated the U.S government; and the United States dominated the world. Overseas, only the "Sino-Soviet bloc" and, among Americans, only a few extremists on the radical Left and militant Right took issue with the clear-cut central thesis of American foreign policy: namely, containment of a monolithic communist threat to tyrannize the globe. The president of the United States was the unquestioned leader of the free world; and that role was perfectly suited to the global role and strength of the American dollar and to the prosperity and contentment of the American people.

Unfortunately, they did not live happily ever after. That era of orderly American foreign policymaking (which even then was not as orderly or simplistic as some people now remember) started crumbling more than twenty years ago and is now gone forever. Forever. The formulation of American foreign policy today is unavoidably and immeasurably more complex, more confused, and more contentious than it was in that earlier, more innocent time.

That era will not come back. No president, however strong, determined, or decisive, can ever bring it back. No president today or tomorrow should in fairness be measured by the standards of that earlier era. No current analysis or recommendation regarding U.S. foreign policy decision making can be validly based on those patterns of an earlier era. I begin with that basic reminder because these are facts too often forgotten by hawks and doves, liberals and conservatives, scholars, journalists, politicians, and laymen, in their definitions, promises, and memories of presidential leadership.

I

What happened in the last fifteen to thirty years to alter so drastically this country's way of handling world affairs? It began with a change in the very nature of world affairs—with a rapid and monumental change in America's ability to shape, predict, accept, or even understand developments in the international community. The United States no longer has a nuclear monopoly, a conscript army, an invulnerable currency, a United Nations majority, an unblemished history, or limitless energy. Foreign policy debates now cut across East versus West divisions with intersecting conflicts pitting North versus South, Black Africa versus Southern Africa, producing countries versus consuming countries, and disputes both with and among fifty-seven varieties of the nonaligned, the unaligned, the misaligned, and the badly maligned. U.S. foreign policymakers can no longer take for granted our next-door neighbors; our allies can no longer take for granted our willingness to defend them; and our perception of the "communist world" is confused by the sight of communist Russia threatening communist China for invading communist Vietnam because it invaded communist Cambodia to the dismay of communist Yugoslavia (with none of them trusting Albania).

It is highly doubtful, whether we wish it or not, that the United States will ever again dominate the world militarily, economically, or politically. No matter how zealously and diligently the advocates of a mightier American war machine spend dollars in pursuit of military superiority over the U.S.S.R., their counterparts in the Kremlin have the resources, the will, and the scientific and industrial base to make certain that their nation also is never forced to accept military inferiority. Neither side is willing to be second best, and each is determined to retain at all costs the capacity to inflict unacceptable damage upon the other.

In this unclear and uncomfortable "no win" context, the maintenance in this country of a single set of foreign policy views under a single national leader was already becoming increasingly difficult by early 1965. During the preceding quarter of a century, cracks had already started to appear in the broad policy consensus within this country's foreign affairs "establishment"—those officials, opinion makers, and citizens who were most influential and informed on world events—which had backed virtually all principal presidential foreign policy initiatives, including those involving World War II, the cold war, and the Korean War. But that consensus fell apart as Americans fought and failed in Vietnam; and that bitterly divisive experience shattered any prospect for a new consensus, even among the establishment, for a long time to come.

Then came the revelations of malfeasance in the Nixon presidency collectively called Watergate. These new shocks to the body politic, particularly because they followed fast upon Vietnam's impairment of presidential credibility, dealt a lethal blow to that intangible aura of reverence and sagacity surrounding the White House that had previously caused the public, to a large extent the Congress and the press, and even the courts to defer to the president's judgment in most national security matters. The combination of Vietnam and Watergate created a wholly different atmosphere in Washington. The evils of the "imperial presidency" were exposed and attacked. New restrictions were placed on the president's use of troops, his use of funds, his use of the CIA and trade agreements and foreign economic and military assistance. New restrictions were placed on presidential powers, appointments, agreements, and secrecy. The Congress was determined to check the president more forcefully. The press was determined to challenge the president more frequently. Presidential invocation of formerly magic phrases like "national interest" and "national security" no longer sufficed to silence critics. Invocations of the legal doctrines of "executive privilege" or "inherent and implied powers," and citations of the expansive language of Mr. Justice Sutherland's obiter dicta in the *Curtiss-Wright* case no longer sufficed to satisfy the courts.

The fracture of the national consensus and the failure of presidential credibility were mutually reinforcing. Neither Jimmy Carter nor his predecessor nor his sucessor could be expected any longer to monopolize the center stage of U.S. foreign policy with a solo performance bringing nothing but cheers from the public, press, and Congress seated respectfully in the audience. Now there were many voices and many actors, often speaking at the same time.

Even within the executive branch, the president's word is no longer final, and the secretary of state is no longer his sole instrument. Various presidential advisers and special emissaries have their own political and press contacts. The secretary of the treasury, the secretary of defense, the secretary of commerce, the secretary of agriculture, the chairman of the Federal Reserve Board, the attorney general, and other agency heads all make decisions affecting U.S. relations with other nations; and each has his own set of considerations, constituents, and congressional committees that are not always identical to those motivating the secretary of state and the president. In any major embassy, the president's ambassador finds most of his support team consisting of representatives from half a dozen or more federal agencies outside the Department of State, including, of course, the CIA and the military; and it is not surprising that an ambassador will occasionally be emboldened to pursue his own course of action. As the national security bureaucracy over the last twenty years grew larger, slower, more diverse, more divided and thus less responsive to his wishes, each president created his own ever larger, ever more powerful national security apparatus in the White House, trying to solve the problem by increasing it.

This proliferation of foreign policy voices within the executive branch has been matched by a proliferation of congressional committees and subcommittees on Capitol Hill. No longer does a single Committee on Foreign Relations serve as the channel for each house. More than a dozen committees, each staffed with its own array of professionals to challenge the administration, now exercise jurisdiction in this area. Nearly every senator and congressman considers himself an expert in world affairs. As the pendulum of political power after Vietnam and Watergate swung away from the presidency and back to the legislative branch, Congress has not hesitated to asert this power in foreign affairs as well as domestic. The authority to legislate, appropriate, and educate, if effectively used, can have a powerful role in shaping America's course in the world; and the increasing tendency in recent years to expand Congress' role through legislative vetoes, riders, mandates, and investigations has placed the executive branch on the defensive much of the time.

Outside government, private lobbies—representing ethnic, economic, ideological, and other particular points of view of U.S. foreign policy—now bring pressure to bear on Congress even more than they do on the executive branch. Even outside the United States the former monolith of presidential leadership is no more. Once both law and custom confined international negotiations to the president and his designated representatives. Now the custom has changed if the law has not; and various congressmen, candidates, and even private citizens—ranging in recent times from Jesse Jackson to Jesse Helms, and from Billy Graham to Billy Carter—have undertaken publicly to carry their versions of the national interest to foreign shores as well. Foreign embassies and emissaries, in turn, make representations not only to the executive branch but also to congressmen and private interest groups.

The participation of Congress, moreover, cannot be limited, as it once was, to a few key leaders who speak for or deliver the rest. President Eisenhower could strike a bargain with Senate Majority Leader Lyndon Johnson, Speaker of the House Sam Rayburn, and at most a small handful of others, and know that all of Congress would uphold that bargain. That is no longer possible. President Nixon could inform a few Armed Services Committee members of the secret bombing of Cambodia and assume that he had fulfilled any constitutional requirement. That is no longer possible. Today power in the legislative branch is widely dispersed; party loyalty is virtually nonexistent; far fewer members are willing to risk the displeasure of substantial contributors of newspapers or a substantial number of constituents; and every member speaks for himself on foreign affairs. A president's pledge to other nations of foreign aid, or most-favored-nation status, or economic sanctions, or treaty ratification thus means far less today than it did a generation ago when he could be more certain of congressional approval.

II

So, today, who speaks with the authority for the national interest on U.S. foreign policy questions? Sometimes no one, and that is unfortunate. Sometimes everyone, all at once, and that is equally unfortunate.

Perhaps, when this topic was given to a former presidential counsel, the answer expected was an assertion that only the president truly speaks for the national interest in world affairs. But the facts fly in the face of that assertion—and the president, our allies, and our adversaries all know that the president cannot meaningfully speak alone on these issues.

Our primary objective in this symposium, therefore, the most constructive use to which we can put the brainpower focused on this subject, should not be one of pretending that the president alone holds the reins, or asserting that he alone should hold the reins, or offering hopelessly doomed statutory or constitutional amendments that would restore his sole control of the reins. Our responsibility instead should be not only to recognize that a new balance of power exists in Washington but, more important, to analyze how best any occupant of the White House, regardless of his party and philosophy, can cope with it. Facing the drastically altered situation described above, recognizing that he will not have the wide range of discretion in foreign affairs exercised, for example, by Franklin Roosevelt in his third term or Richard Nixon in his first, what should a president do?

Once all the ambiguous political rhetoric about harmonious cooperation and interdependence between the two coequal branches of government is cleared away, a president facing up to this new climate for foreign policy decision making in Washington has a choice of essentially two roads to follow: the path of submission or the path of leadership.

There exists in theory, of course, a third path, defiance and domination. But that path, in my view, is not in fact open any longer and appears unlikely to be open for another generation at least. To be sure, a president who shared Richard Nixon's view (as recorded for posterity on tape) that Congress is "irrelevant" might be tempted to try international actions not dependent on new legislation or appropriations, acting on his own say-so without making the slightest effort to bring the Congress or public opinion along except through an occasional "If you only knew what I know, you would see that I am right." But such a course of action would not long succeed.

Congress today possesses not only a new determination to cut down to size a president who acts alone internationally, but also the power to make that determination stick—including the power to transfer unexpended funds; abolish agencies; repeal laws; withhold confirmation of the president's appointees; extract promises from them before they are confirmed; subpoena them after they are confirmed; imprison them for contempt if they refuse to testify; and, whether they are subject to confirmation or not, limit their salaries and staffs and perquisites if they do not cooperate. Congress can also block treaties, executive agreements, and deployments of the armed services, demand the disclosure of most secrets, and if necessary impeach and remove the president.

Recognizing this legislative power, the president's own employees in the executive branch—of whom he in fact appoints less than twenty out of every one hundred thousand—have their own weapons with which to block unauthorized presidential actions, including "leaks" to the press; complaints to the Congress; and indifference, delay, or resistance to presidential orders—just as the Internal Revenue Service, for example, refused to investigate Nixon's "enemies list."

Finally, a president who contemplates ignoring the restrictions of the new War Powers Act, Executive Agreements Act, Freedom of Information Act, or other curbs knows that the federal judiciary in the present atmosphere is far more likely to block such plans than previously. No longer do the courts automatically defer to the president's invocation of national security or executive privilege, or to his treatymaking powers; his powers as commander in chief; his emergency powers; his inherent powers; or his powers over trade, spending, secrets, and appointees.

It would therefore be unrealistic for any president to believe that he could turn back the clock with impunity—that this nation in our lifetime could return to an absolute presidential monopoly of power in foreign affairs decision making, the kind of monopoly that reached its peak when President Nixon's 1971 "Christmas bombing" of Vietnam caused Arthur Schlesinger, Jr., to observe that in no other major country in the world, including China and the Soviet Union, could a single leader order so drastic a step in consultation with so few other officials in his own government. At least some degree of democratization and demystification of American foreign policy is here to stay. Whatever the defects of the new climate, it is unavoidably more open, more responsive, more accountable, and less likely to lead the American people into any prolonged course of action without their full and knowing approval.

III

If the "defiance and domination" alternative is out, then the president's options are limited to "submission" and "leadership."

The course of submission is not as totally lacking in justification as its label would indicate. There is much to be said for the argument that Congress is closer to the people, the most representative branch of government, and therefore the most appropriate seat in a democracy of all policymaking power, foreign as well as domestic; that the president should be merely the agent of Congress, a vehicle for administering the law, disbursing funds, and managing the civilian and military departments. Let Congress take the lead, it is said, instead of the president constantly quarreling with its members. If their judgment is wrong too often, the voters will soon set them straight; and in fact their collective wisdom may well be superior to that of those self-designated experts who are isolated in the executive branch and obsessed with their classified documents. Inasmuch as congressional deference to the president in foreign affairs is now consistently lagging, a greater presidential deference to Congress may be the only way to achieve the harmony the American public prefers. The president should "go along in order to get along," as the old political adage advises.

But what a price for harmony! What a distortion of constitutional intent! Members of Congress, by definition and nature, are far more likely to take a parochial view instead of the national view that an effective foreign policy requires. They are, by duty and inclination, less likely than the president to display such executive traits as decisiveness, dispatch, unity, and secrecy—all of which are required for the conduct of foreign affairs in a dangerous, complex, and fast-changing world—and more likely to excel in the functions appropriate to a legislative body: not administration but deliberation, not operations but information, not initiation but approbation or disapprobation through legislation and appropriations.

The years when Congress was in the foreign policy saddle—during the latter third of the nineteenth century and between the two world wars—were not years of renown for America's role in the world. Indeed the post–Civil War Senate rejected and rewrote virtually every treaty submitted to it, resulting in not one major treaty advancing U.S. relations with other countries during the twenty-seven years between 1871 and 1898. "The Secretary of State" in those days, as Henry Adams wrote, "exist[ed] only to recognize the existence of a world which Congress would rather ignore." The post–World War I Congress not only rejected the Versailles treaty but during the years preceding Pearl Harbor imposed a wall of economic isolationism and political neutrality that deepened the depression and hampered the Allied nations' fight against Hitler.

In the early 1970s, opposition to the Vietnam War in some quarters of Congress, coupled with the expansive use of presidential power by which Presidents Johnson and Nixon launched and widened that war, gave rise to a widespread assumption that Congress was inherently more likely to demonstrate prudence and restraint in such matters than the president. There is no valid historical proof for that thesis. Congress helped push Madison into the War of 1812 and McKinley into the Spanish-American War, in both cases reflecting an inflamed public opinion that was at odds with this country's long-range role in world affairs. President John Adams, in contrast, resisted heavy congressional pressures for a war in France that he was convinced our infant republic could not survive. President John F. Kennedy, in opting for a limited naval quarantine around Cuba at the time of the 1962 Missile Crisis, acted contrary to the advice of congressional leaders, who, after being briefed just prior to his telecast declaration of U.S. policy, warned him in no uncertain terms that only an air strike or invasion of Cuba would suffice.

Even on Vietnam, the early complaints from Congress criticized President Johnson, not for going too fast, but for going too slowly, for not bombing Hanoi and mining Haiphong and generally widening the war. Having already presented the president, by way of resolution after the Gulf of Tonkin incident, with a blank check to fill in as he wished, Congress continued to approve all requests for war funding and, until it was virtually over, to defeat all meaningful curbs on U.S. participation.

I do not maintain that all American presidents have surpassed their legislative colleagues in prudent international statesmanship. But it should at least be recognized that the congressional claim of being "closer to the people" through more frequent elections also means that its members are more subject to the short-term popular passions and prejudices, and to the local pressures and economic interests, that can lead foreign policy astray. In a representative democracy, public opinion is not always identical wih the public interest.

Nor is it clear that Congress in fact knows and represents the public on foreign affairs any better than the president. The legislative branch, particularly in the House of Representatives, is dominated by incumbents who are repeatedly reelected largely on the basis of the constituent services they provide and rarely on the basis of the foreign affairs position they take. As noted below, presidential campaigns are also not known for their careful attention to foreign policy issues; but surely no principle of democratic government requires a president to regard his mandate from the nation's voters on these issues as any weaker than that of Congress.

Finally, there is nothing wrong with a little disharmony between president and Congress, even in foreign affairs. That is what our system of checks and balances is intended to produce: "power as the rival of power," in Hamilton's words. The old "politics stops at the water's edge" adage has been largely invoked only when convenient by presidents and only when expedient by members of Congress. Foreign policy has rarely been above the strains and stresses of politics in this country, and in government by the consent of the governed, that is the way it should be.

In short, a supine presidency has no more to recommend it in the foreign affairs arena than an imperial presidency. The framers of the Constitution wanted the president's power to be shared, balanced, and held accountable. But they also knew, after brief experience with the Articles of Confederation, that decisive, unified initiative and implementation in foreign affairs were properly the prerogative of a single, nationally elected executive.

IV

He should not demur; he cannot dominate; he must, therefore, try to lead. "Leadership" becomes an overused and much-abused word around election time, rendered nearly meaningless by the spate of self-serving definitions that are offered. But leadership is in fact a legitimate issue in presidential elections. It is particularly important now that the rules have changed, and the process is more difficult to master, and the problems still cry out for attention, and neither domination nor submission will work.

Are there any tangible criteria for this term "leadership"? What are the sinews of presidential leadership in foreign policy? What are the means by which a president, unable to take it all over and unwilling to turn it all over, can fulfill the role intended by the framers? The answer, in my view, lies not so much in the presidential *powers* granted by Constitution and statute but in the *opportunities* afforded by his high office—broad, recurrent opportunities that are his to make the most of if he can and will. I would suggest three major types of opportunity.

First is the opportunity to persuade. A president, as I have written and illustrated elsewhere, can actually give commands to very few people. But in that "bully pulpit," as Theodore Roosevelt described the Oval office, he has an opportunity unequaled by anyone else in the country to convince and cajole, to arm-twist and argue, to preach and plead, to urge a course of action upon the Congress, to mobilize support wihin the country, to woo the press and win over the bureaucracy. The international problems faced by this country today do not lend themselves to easy solutions or even easily understood explanations. The president's task is to place those problems in a perspective that enables a majority to accept his position—to define those issues in terms that are weighted in his favor—to place boundaries on the debate that will enable his proposals to be considered strictly on their merits. He must sacrifice personal preference in order to make friends with political enemies, agree to bargains on moral issues, and listen even more than he talks. If he is uncomfortable in the role of pleader, trader, and persuader; if he eschews eloquence as old-fashioned or beyond his reach, if he is unaccustomed to building coalitions with unlikely partners or building bridges to inhospitable territory; if he tends too often merely to stake out positions and leave their adoption to others, then he is wasting one of his principal opportunities for leadership—and American foreign policy will suffer.

Second is the opportunity to take the initiative. The language of the Constitution contemplates the president reporting to the Congress, communicating with other countries, and giving directions to his appointees. Each of these functions provides him with an occasion to set forth, publicly, before anyone else can effectively do so, an agenda for the nation, his understanding of current problems and his intended solutions. He can keep the congressional plate full with his proposals. He can keep the press focused on his solutions. He can and should periodically present to the nation, as no one else can, his long-range concept of where he thinks the world is headed, where he thinks it should be headed, and what role the United States should play.

In the short run, immediate events around the world will more often than not fix the focus of discussion; but in a very real sense the president not only determines—or at least has the opportunity to determine—the subjects for debate on foreign affairs but also determines the terms of the propositions to be debated. No major accusation or threat by his detractors, either foreign or domestic, should long go unanswered. No major issue should long go unexplained.

Seizing the initiative, of course, it is not always the same as rushing into print or on the air. It means first carefully but rapidly ascertaining all facts and facets of a problem, weighing the advantages and consequences of each option, deciding on a course of action to be adopted, and then presenting that information forcefully to the public before events or other actors have irrevocably altered the situation to this country's detriment. If the president does not seize the initiative for whatever reason—indecision, inattention, inability, or individual style—if he remains silent in the face of dramatic developments or disputes; if he leaves a vacuum certain to be filled by misinformation, speculation, and exaggeration if not demogoguery; if he defers to others who must consider their political needs before his, then he has wasted this unique presidential opportunity to take and keep the initiative, and as a consequence his leadership in foreign affairs cannot be effectively maintained.

Third and finally is the opportunity to build and utilize his own foreign affairs team. Despite the ordeal to which public servants in this country are increasingly subjected—the long hours at comparatively low pay, the sacrifice of leisure time and privacy, the inquisition into their personal and financial affairs, the suspicion, criticism, and complaints that greet their every decision—nearly all the ablest men and women in the land are potentially available for service in positions of national security responsibility. In addition, the career services, at all levels, offer the president an unequaled if sometimes uneven fund of irreplaceable knowledge and experience. Despite the enormous growth of the past two decades in both the quality and the quantity of the staffs, information, and expert resources available to Congress in the foreign affairs area, it cannot field a team comparable in manpower, brainpower, or drawing power to that which a president can assemble.

But, like the other opportunities mentioned, this one is not automatically fulfilled. The president must know how to identify and select the best as distinguished from the best known—not always easy, for distinguished citizens rarely equal their reputations (some exceeding and many falling short). He must be able to attract them to his banner, enlist them in his service, and fit them into the right positions and relationships. He must be able to stimulate and encourage their thinking without either suppressing his own views or influencing theirs. He must be able to meld a diverse group of independent minds into a unified and relatively harmonious structure that speaks as with one voice to the press, the Congress, and the world. The members of his team must accept the fact that he was elected president and is accountable to the country and that they are there to advise him, not to dispute or resist the final decisions he has made public. If he permits his subordinates to represent political interests other than his own; if his exercise or allocation of responsibilities is insufficiently clear or logical to prevent a struggle for power; if his administration speaks with more than one point of view on sensitive international issues; if he cannot create the kind of atmosphere of loyalty, understanding, and support that dries up freewheeling "leaks" to the press and anonymous dissents from within the White House and national security agencies, if private backbiting and public potshots among rival members of his team become a focus of foreign speculation and comment, then the potential advantage of team leader becomes instead a burden to the president and to his effectiveness in foreign affairs.

Not every president who chooses the path of leadership over the path of submission will succeed in every respect. Failure may result not in congressional supremacy but simply in ineffective presidential leadership. That is what some of the people some of the time apparently prefer.

V

In theory, the American public has an opportunity every four years to determine the kind of leadership it wants in foreign as well as domestic affairs. But in practice, it rarely works out that way—and here we are all at fault.

We are all at fault because we pay comparatively little attention to foreign policy issues in a campaign, and those issues rarely determine the outcome of the election—not the League of Nations in 1920, not national defense in 1940, not the onset of the cold war in 1948, not Vietnam in 1964, not even Korea in 1952 or Vietnam in 1968.

Moreover, to the extent these foreign policy issues are debated at all in presidential campaigns we condone and sometimes encourage a smattering of foolish, irresponsible talk—such as the Republican candidate for vice president in 1972 terming the State Department "Dean Acheson's Cowardly College of Communist Containment," comprised of "whining, whimpering, groveling" diplomats; or the Republican candidate for president in 1964 suggesting that we "lob a nuclear bomb into the men's locker room at the Kremlin"; or the Democratic campaigner in 1968 who said that a victory for Eugene McCarthy in the New Hampshire primary would be "greeted with great cheers in Hanoi."

But, name-calling aside, even when there are true and distinct differences between the candidates on foreign policy, they rank in importance to the voter well behind party, pocketbook, and personality. Perhaps that is not all bad—for if these were the issues that mattered most, an exhausted challenger with an inexperienced speechwriter might be tempted more often to reach for the White House with a demagogic pledge to reverse some U.S. policy abroad that will haunt him if he ever gets there; and a beleaguered incumbent might be tempted more often to take actions, decisions, positions, or trips that appeal to particular voting blocs or to popular whim but that will make a whole lot less sense when he awakens in a more rational postelection world. For example, in 1916 Secretary of State Lansing had to advise the British privately that Woodrow Wilson's position on Ireland was merely an election-year gambit. In 1948 Harry Truman's recognition of Israel, correct as it may have proved to be, was nevertheless urged by his political advisers over the opposition of his foreign policy advisers (whose argument weakened when they could not name even a single Arab precinct captain). President Johnson's Gulf of Tonkin resolution in 1964, President Ford's declaration on a "free" Poland in 1976, and President Roosevelt's pledge of "no foreign wars" in 1940 were all influenced by the fact that those happened to be election years; and the candidate who sought the presidency in 1960 as the man who stood up to Khrushchev in the kitchen ran for reelection in 1972 as the man who sat down with Mao in the parlor.

This country's role in world affairs, and the quality and philosophy of our presidential leadership in foreign affairs, are too important to the future of every American to be downgraded as issues in a presidential campaign that focuses solely on the economy or treats foreign affairs with mere slogans and gimmicks. That is the responsibility of us all. Let us hope that the 1980 elections demonstrate a will to do better.

The determination of who speaks for the national interest, I have tried to make clear, and how each president can speak more effectively in the national interest, is largely not a matter of statutes, procedures, and machinery. It is a question instead of human attitudes and abilities. I do not demean the various structural reforms discussed in other contributions to this volume. But "Governments," as Woodrow Wilson said in his Columbia lectures on the presidency, "are what politicans make them. . . . Government is . . . not a machine but a living thing . . . not a body of blind forces [but] a body of men. . . . It is accountable . . . not to Newton [but] to Darwin."

2

Foreign Perspective:
With Whom Do You Deal?
Whom Can You Trust?

H. E. Ambassador Ivor Richard

As I UNDERSTAND the purpose of this book, it is to examine the workings of the U.S. system of government in the field of foreign relations against the background of a period of growing congressional ascendancy; and, as I understand my function, it is to provide some degree of foreign indiscretion.

What I do not propose to do is enter into the arguments over the precise powers accorded in the Constitution to the executive branch of government, or the nature and extent of the accountability Congress can or should impose. For a foreign government, these discussions are interesting but arcane and totally outside our competence. Our problems arise and have to arise from our dealings with the executive and not the legislative branch of government. It is not the assertion of congressional review powers or legal supremacy with which we are concerned; it is far more the unpredictability of congressional influence and its effect upon the only branch of government with which we are entitled to deal. To be brutally frank, a strong executive and a compliant Congress is the easiest U.S. government for us to have to handle, though I recognize that this is hardly what the founding fathers appear to have intended.

Harold Nicholson quoted Sir Edward Grey as saying that the

aim of diplomacy is to enlarge the area of confidence between governments. This is certainly true in a bilateral post, and was probably even more accurate when he wrote it at the height of the dominance of bilateral diplomacy. A country's foreign policy was determined and adjusted by a careful assessment of one's own influence compared with that of one's potential allies and adversaries. Position in the world was then much more related to economic and military power. To be clear, and to make sure that others knew precisely the policy of one's country, was more important when it was "clout" that mattered most. Power, or its threatened use, was often enough to impose one's will, and diplomacy frequently became a process of confrontation in which the most powerful succeeded.

This is no longer necessarily true. The world has moved into an era where multilateral relations dominate. Harlan Cleveland has recently estimated that over 70 percent of a U.S. ambassador's time in a bilateral post is devoted to multilateral affairs. How will the host country behave at the UN, in NATO, OECD, the Warsaw Pact, GATT, the IMF, OAU, OAS, EEC, and so on? The history of international relations in the last thirty years is the gradual abrogation of national sovereignties, sometimes gradual, sometimes idealistic, more often pragmatic, invariably late.

It follows from this, and from the fact that my diplomatic experience is limited to five and one-half years as the United Kingdom permanent representative to the UN, that my knowledge of U.S. foreign policy, and of the decision-making processes that underlie it, is necessarily concentrated on their multilateral performance, and particularly on U.S. policy as it surfaced at the UN. Since, however, that covered all the major political trouble areas of the world, save Central Europe, from the Middle East, Southeast Asia to Southern Africa, and it also covered the evolution of U.S. policy in the North/South dialogue, to say nothing of human rights and disarmament, it was perhaps not too fragile a platform from which to observe.

If enlarging the area of confidence was the purpose of bilateral diplomacy, multilateralism has a somewhat different aim. It is no longer enough for the United States merely to make its position clear in the Security Council or the General Assembly. It now has to win friends and influence people sufficiently to enable that position to carry. There is thus a forensic or quasi-parliamentary element to the conduct of foreign policy in multilateral institutions that is new, and a fresh element has therefore been added to the decision-making process. The question whether the United States has been able to make its views carry is now just as important as whether it has been able to make its views clear. Whereas it is a truism that nations hope to win the day for their own particular policies, I sometimes feel that this obligation to win the forensic battle was not always reflected in the ways in which U.S. policy was arrived at or presented.

There is of course a worst-case and a best-case experience. Senator Moynihan was probably the ambassador I had to deal wih who was least concerned with winning support for the U.S. position and most concerned with making his views heard, which he did with skill, enjoyment, and regularity. Ambassador Young, though occasionally eccentric in some of his views and pronouncements, yet had, particularly on African affairs, a strong awareness of the need to lobby for support and maintain his vote. Ambassadors Scranton and Scali were both somewhere in the middle. Each was conscious of the need for a strong U.S. voice, but each was anxious to consult his natural allies and to concert an approach with the other democracies. Each was mindful of the forensic element in his job, and neither believed that confrontation for its own sake helped to further his multilateral aims.

It is this capacity or otherwise to extend one's influence in multilateral diplomacy that, I believe, must be one of the criteria by which a nation's foreign policy has to be judged. The prophet crying in the wilderness is not likely to be of much benefit to his country, however loudly he cries, unless he can attract at least a few disciples.

In dealing with the U.S. administration in the multilateral field, there were three qualities one looked for: speed of decision making and consultation in the decision-making process, continuity of policy once the decision had been made, and concerted advocacy of that policy once it had been formulated. Unfortunately, in my experience none of these three was inevitable, and all three together were rare.

The speed of decision making was frankly eccentric, and decisions were often taken much too late. There was no concerted pace, even when there was no crisis.

Part of the problem seemed to me to be institutional, and part personal.

When Dr. Kissinger was secretary of state, the main difficulty was in insuring that the necessary papers got to him in time. If he was on one of his periodic shuttles, this could sometimes be a major problem. I well remember Ambassador Scali sitting in a phone booth outside the Security Council trying to get instructions from Dr. Kissinger, who at that moment was thirty thousand feet in the air over the Middle East. In the situation where the secretary of state insisted on personalizing the work of the State Department to the extent that Dr. Kissinger did, it was inevitable that decision making lacked smoothness. He was, frankly, much too busy, and to an outsider he seemed to delegate too little. One was, however, reasonably sure that once he had taken a decision it was unlikely to be altered. If it came late, it did at least usually stand up.

The nature of the American system of government seems to a foreigner such that executive decision making is overcentralized and that legislative overseeing is too rigorous. In dealing with the French bureaucracy, for example, there is a sense in which one can see policy decisions emerging over a period of time. The Quai d'Orsay faithfully reflects a concerted evolving view of an issue in which the officials seem to be conscious of the eventual opinion that the foreign minister or even the president is likely to hold. The desk officers or heads of department in Paris seem more aware of how French government policy is being formed and how it is going to come out. Perhaps it is merely that battles inside the bureaucracy remain more "inside" in France or Britain than they do here in the United States.

I fear, however, that there is an institutional gap in the U.S. system that is filled in other countries. We need to know what the "American" position is much earlier, and far too often it is unpredictable.

In Britain the Cabinet exists to take the final decisions on major foreign policy issues. No foreign secretary would or could seek to embark on a major new initiative without first consulting his Cabinet colleagues. If this informal sounding indicated a division of opinion, the issue would have to be "taken to Cabinet," where the decision would eventually be made collectively. Once taken, the decision becomes that of Her Majesty's Government, and unless he resigns a Cabinet minister is bound by it. Differences inside the Cabinet do not get aired in public, and journalistic speculation is usually precisely that—speculation. Her Majesty's Government by definition (and pride) always tries to speak with one voice.

There is, too, in Britain close interlocking within the bureaucracy itself. The permanent heads of the different departments of state, civil servants all, not only know one another but (save for the Treasury and the Foreign Office) may well have served, themselves, in other departments. Possibilities of misinterpretation or of potential differences of view between, say, the Foreign and Commonwealth Office and the Ministry of Defence tend to be identified early and resolved at a bureaucratic level if possible; at ministerial level if not; and, if they prove really major, then within the Cabinet itself. There is thus within the British system a highly sophisticated, if not overtly institutional, system of conflict resolution. It produces emulsification of a high order.

One reason, too, why the process seems to work in Britain is the nature of the bureaucracy itself. It is by and large permanent. Civil servants in Britain do not change with a change of Government. They may change direction as the new political heads change policy, but their right to security of tenure is almost unchallenged. This has both its advantages and its drawbacks. On the credit side, it produces a group of people at the highest levels in Government with an unrivaled experience of the Government machine. On the debit side, it can result in a bureaucracy tinged with inertia, over-anxious not to jeopardize the status quo. But in terms of continuity of approach and smoothness of running, it has distinct advantages.

Neither at the political nor the bureaucratic level is there such sophisticated machinery in the United States. How many people, save experts in the field, could name the top career government employees in HEW, the Department of Defense, even the State Department? The well-known names tend to be those of political appointees who serve in government for relatively short periods and have no roots in the departments' policies and bureaucracy.

Cabinet discussions in Washington cannot hope to have the same political content as they do in Britain because executive decisions here are so entirely divorced from the legislative function. Indeed, cabinet members in this country tend to be neither traditional career bureaucrats nor political heavyweights with their own following in the legislature and the country. Therefore, getting the cabinet in the United States to agree to something does little to create a political consensus. This is, of course, not an argument for changing your Constitution. It is merely pointing out that a rigid insistence on the separation of powers carries with it a certain uneasiness in the operation of the government machine. Jeffersonian purity does not make for easy bureaucratic functioning.

Not only is there this divorce between the cabinet and Congress; there is also the extent to which government appointments change with a change of administration. The fact that so many of the top jobs go to political appointments must have an effect on the quality of people entering permanent government service. As a politician out of Parliament at the moment, I can certainly see the attraction of a system in which the spoils of office go to the victors, but the lack of a more permanent bureaucracy does have an inhibiting effect on the continuity of U.S. policy, and it deprives the system of those additional measures of conflict resolution that we take so much for granted. Quite frankly, you sack too many, too far down the ladder; and in my view lose something by it.

Although this does not matter too much once an administration has been established and has worked itself in, in the early days it creates strains that other systems of government seem to be able to avoid. The changeover in 1976 did not only mean that we had to deal with new political masters in Washington. It also meant that, at my level, I had suddenly to adjust to a situation in which the ambassador and all four deputies, including the representatives to ECOSOC and the Human Rights Commission, changed as well. In almost all other countries (even those like my own who

regard the post of ambassador to the UN as one which should
sometimes be filled by a politician) these other posts are accepted
as being appropriate to be filled by permanent members of the
Foreign Office. The changeover meant in practice a period of difficult adjustment as the people concerned learned to know and
work with one another, a process that lasted probably three or four
months. Certainly in terms of my working naturally and easily
with Ambassador Young, it took about six months and a number
of minor irritations on both sides before the two of us were at ease.
During that period there were inevitably difficulties that more per-
manence in the U.S. mission might have been able to avoid. In
March 1976 Young was president of the Security Council for the
first time. He felt that the time was appropriate for a U.S. initiative
on Southern Africa, which would embrace the Africans, the West,
the Soviet Union, and the other members of the Council. The idea
was that we should negotiate a Declaration of Aims and Principles
to which all would subscribe and that would then become the text
for the future so far as Southern Africa was concerned. Understandably it failed. It was found impossible to reconcile the conflicting views of the liberation movements and their desire to move
to sanctions on the one hand, with the combined intention of the
West to avoid any economic measures against South Africa on the
other. The result was the tabling by the Africans of three resolutions in the Security Council; which in the event the West had to
veto some months later in a debate when no fewer than nine vetoes (three each by the United States, France and the United
Kingdom) were cast in as many minutes. What this upset revealed
was the inevitable unpreparedness of the new U.S. administration
and the inability of the rest of us to deal with it. It might be that
a more permanent bureaucracy could have avoided some of the
uncertainties which this diplomatic confusion revealed. I am not
complaining that we were not consulted. We were, in the sense
that we were told what was envisaged by the United States. What
we could not do was persuade the United States in advance that
this initiative just would not work. A coincidental fallout of this
exercise, however, was the establishment of the Western Contact
Group on Namibia, a diplomatic exercise which was unique in the

extent and scope of its coordination, and which still provides the best prospect of a peaceful transition in Namibia.

There is, moreover, one constitutional irritant in trying to deal with a new administration. The U.S. Constitution, for some extraordinary reason that quite baffles those of us living in other Western democracies, insists on a lengthy period between the date of the election of a new president and the day on which he actually assumes office. Nor is it any response to point out that this delay used to be much longer. It makes no sense at all to paralyze governmental activity for three and a half months, though this is undoubtedly better than when it was paralyzed for six. In Britain we elect a new government on Thursday and it takes office on Friday. The duck has no time to hobble, let alone get lame.

Dealing with a U.S. president or secretary of state during this transition is almost impossible on any save the most immediate problems. Long-term consultation or planning is obviously prohibited. The outgoing administration will not be there. The incoming government has not yet been formed, or if formed is unbriefed and unfunctioning, and to compound the difficulties further the gap occurs after a year in which the United States is understandably obsessed with its election campaigns. Nor is this merely an academic irritant. The problem is not merely one of constitutional eccentricity and arose for me in an acute form in 1976 over Southern Africa.

In August 1976, Dr. Kissinger went to Africa and, after a series of protracted and difficult negotiations, had apparently succeeded in persuading Mr. Ian Smith to accept majority rule. In a memorable broadcast on 24 September 1976, Mr. Smith said that he accepted the principle of majority rule within two years on certain conditions which he had agreed with Dr. Kissinger. Included in the conditions was the commitment that Britain, as the legal colonizing power, should call a conference to work out the terms of an interim Government which was to run Rhodesia during the period of transition. I was then asked to chair that conference, which took place in Geneva and began on 18 October 1976, some two weeks before the presidential election here.

I faced two immediate problems in Geneva. One was that no

African delegation was prepared to trust Mr. Smith, particularly over the issues of defense and law and order during the transition, which under the Kissinger proposals were to remain in White hands, and on the other side that Mr. Smith was not prepared to move away from a rigid adherence to the Kissinger proposals.

Once the African leaders refused to accept those proposals, claiming that whoever had a contract with the United States the four at Geneva did not, Mr. Smith's strict attachment to those terms provided him with a successful way of frustrating the whole negotiation.

At the exact moment when these issues emerged, the presidential election took place, resulting in change of administration. If the Republicans had won the election on 2 November, continuity of government would have been assured. If a new administration had taken over on 3 November, again within a week or so, the United States would have had a firm leadership. As it was, precisely at the moment when I needed it most, American clout was not available. Decisive intervention by the United States might have induced Mr. Smith to negotiate seriously, which I am bound to say he signally refrained from doing throughout the whole conference. To make a success of the process, we had to wean him away from his adhesion to the Kissinger proposals, and probably the only person who could have done that, namely Dr. Kissinger himself, was totally inhibited by the vagaries of the system of government in the United States, and particularly by this "handover" period which not only the United States but the rest of the world has to endure.

The relation of the administration to Congress, particularly in a time of congressional ascendancy, seems to me to be a qualified burden for the administration and a source of confusion for the rest of us.

By definition, we have to deal with governments not legislatures, and while in a parliamentary system parliament is the ultimate authority, the instances where on a foreign policy issue the government cannot get its own way are very few. Even over Suez, the Conservative government of the day was never seriously in danger of losing its freedom of action on account of domestic pressure.

Despite everything the Labour opposition could do, the determining pressures which finally persuaded the government to change
its mind in 1956 were external rather than domestic. Save as a
forum of public scrutiny, the House of Commons plays a relatively
minor role in a government's assessment of its foreign-policy options. The potential wrath of the electorate at the next day of reck-
oning is a much more potent inhibitor than the actual wrath of the
Opposition in the House.

The same is not true in the system in the United States, given
the nature and extent of the congressional role. It controls the
purse strings in a much more real way than does Parliament, and
provides a form of accountability which, because of the specific
tasks accorded to Congress in the Constitution, makes its role in
the decision-making process much more intrusive than is that of
Parliament.

This means in turn that there is always an element of uncertainty in dealing with the U.S. administration in the field of foreign
policy. One is never absolutely sure what Congress might or might
not choose to do, and perhaps more important, one is never absolutely sure of the extent to which Administration policy is geared
to warding off possible Congressional trouble. By definition, foreign countries are excluded from the horse-trading which has to
go on between the executive and the legislature. We can of course
speculate and we do, trying to assess the extent to which an "upp-
ity" Congress weighs in the presidential calculation, but we can
rarely be absolutely sure.

Nor can we gain much enlightenment by careful lobbying in
Washington, or in New York, and the U.S. public delegates to the
General Assembly do not help much either. I can recall no instance in my time at the UN when a public delegate either appeared to play a significant role in decision-making or when it
seemed worth our while diplomatically to cultivate him extensively. They were, and seemed intended to be, somewhat exotic
adjuncts to the permanent delegation. The only issue I can recall
on which public delegates seemed to play a major role was a decision by the General Assembly on a resolution proposed by the
United States to deny first-class air travel to members of the Sec-

retariat. When there is a serious difference between the State Department and the White House or between either and the Hill, the best we can hope to achieve is to avoid committing ourselves to any one line too early until it is clear which is the more likely to win.

Possible sanctions against South Africa was one such issue. The U.S. Mission in New York clearly felt that some economic measures against South Africa would be inevitable at some time, though there were no clear ideas as to what or when. Discussion on the issue took place within the Administration and various differing views were expressed, ranging from those totally opposed to any economic measures, on the one hand, to those, on the other hand, who were prepared to apply Chapter 7 of the Charter; mandatory sanctions of one sort or another. The British view was that we were extremely reluctant to accept any Chapter 7 determination, but that it was essential that on this issue the United States, France, and the United Kingdom, as the three Western veto powers, should remain united. Our assessment of congressional opinion was that in the event Congress would not accept economic measures against South Africa, but this assessment unfortunately only made our task more difficult. Under the U.S. Constitution, it would have been possible for the administration to have accepted a sanctions resolution in New York, secure in the belief that Congress would later roll it back. Their good intentions would have been shown towards Black Africa, and it would in the event cost them nothing. The same could not be said of a parliamentary system of government. If we had allowed a sanctions resolution to pass, there would have been no shelter for the government in the House of Commons as there is for a U.S. administration in Congress. The whips would see to it that it passed. Fortunately, the situation did not in the end arise. The president and the prime minister successfully resolved the issue to their mutual satisfaction (and my relief), and Western solidarity was preserved.

From time to time what would appear to be a logical and natural extension of a line of emerging national policy fails to be pursued for reasons quite extraneous to the policy and which are usually domestic. It is not that the "democratic" pressures on governments are less in Britain than in the United States. It is that they are less immediate.

In July of 1979, the president seemed to be in serious trouble, both with Congress and the electorate. Salt II was in the process of being bitterly contested in the Senate. The gasoline shortages and the apparent impotence of the administration to produce a coherent response, the cabinet shuffle, all had together produced an atmosphere of crisis. At that precise moment an opportunity for a major move forward in Middle East affairs presented itself. That month, I happened to be president of the Security Council, and among other Middle East issues to be debated was one on the "inalienable rights of the Palestinian people." Early in the month, the Arabs, including the PLO, had informed me that the PLO was now prepared to accept Security Council Resolution 242, which explicitly contains a paragraph recognizing the right of all states in the area to live in peace within secure and recognized boundaries. If carried through, this would have been a major step in the resolution of the Middle East problem, a step, moreover, which had been urged on the PLO by President Carter and other U.S. leaders. The quid pro quo for PLO recognition of Israel as a state was to have been an addendum to 242, which recognized the right of the Palestinian people (however subsequently defined) to self-determination (again however subsequently defined). The objective of the PLO was presumably to commence a dialogue with the United States by clearing out of the way what had been expressed to be the major United States objection to such a dialogue, namely the nonrecognition of Israel's right to exist.

Prima facie, the deal seemed promising, and beneficial, to all sides. Israel got acceptance by the PLO of its right to exist, the PLO got recognition of the political rights of the Palestinians to self-determination, and the United States got direct negotiations with the PLO.

It did not, of course, take place. The United States asked for time to consider the issue more thoroughly. By the time the debate actually took place, the momentum had been lost and an opportunity for progress towards peace allowed to pass. Not only that, but

Ambassador Young later resigned for having tried to gain the time which the U.S. government clearly wanted by talking directly to the PLO.

The importance of these incidents is not that the pressures on the administration were unreal. They clearly were not. It is that they were widely perceived as being domestic, and it is precisely this relationship between domestic pressures and foreign policy decision-making which creates problems. Decisions are frequently taken very late on in a negotiating process, whether this be the North/South dialogue, a vote in the Security Council, or even one so momentous in character as the neutron bomb. Congressional power is such that the later the decision can be taken, the more accurate is the White House assessment of whether or not Congress is likely to react adversely. It makes long- or even medium-term planning within the administration more complex, and it makes dealing with the U.S. government hazardous.

None of this is, or is intended to be, a criticism of the present administration. It is inevitable, given the separation of powers explicit in your system of government. Nor is it any argument for changing your system of government that a different system would make it easier for foreigners. I do believe, however, that it is important that the United States recognizes the price it has to pay in return for a system of government in which an ascendant Congress can never be absent from the minds of the decision makers. The possibility of congressional intervention seems now to be omnipresent, as Angola, Panama, and SALT all illustrate. The pressures on a president to balance his foreign policy preferences against his domestic problems are now considerable, and unless some mechanism can be devised for resolving those pressures they may well prove damaging. In foreign policy the system seems to work well, either when the administration and Congress agree, as in the immediate postwar years, when the decision makers are perceived by Congress to be less vulnerable, as in the Eisenhower or early Kissinger years, or when Congress and the American people are less interested in foreign affairs and the administration itself is concentrating on domestic policy. Otherwise, the strains are inevitable, and although I have no answer to the constitutional problems, it does seem to me to be important to emphasize the fact that there is a real problem here for foreign governments.

These problems are, moreover, likely to be intensified rather than diminished as the world moves increasingly into an era of multilateral diplomacy, which is by definition infinitely more complicated and less cozy. Lines of policy have to emerge early and stay relatively firm if multilateral diplomacy is to be successful. All too often I fear our experience with the United States was that they emerged late and fluctuated.

The United States is not a good coordinator, despite its manifest goodwill. There is usually such a disparity in the power relationships that good intentions tend to be submerged in the immediacy of the problems. Even when this disparity does not exist, as for example in the U.S./EEC participation in the North/South dialogue, the record of transatlantic coordination is not good. At the seventh special session of the General Assembly in 1975, the United States played a major role in trying to avoid a repetition of the bitter North/South confrontational politics of the 1974 sixth special session. It was an effective, even visionary approach. The EEC, by comparison, was much less dramatic, though one hopes equally forthcoming. The Nine, however, had hammered out an approach months ahead, and we had indeed sought to coordinate our position closely with that of the United States. The fruit of our endeavor, however, was one Sunday evening meeting at which I was shown a rough draft of part of the U.S. position forty-eight hours before it was delivered.

There is, of course, nothing at all wrong in the United States deciding that it wishes to maintain its independence from the rest of us. What it cannot do, however, is to seek to have it both ways: remain aloof and later complain that the West as a whole has not been supportive. Noncoordination does not make any sense at all in situations where the West as a whole has a clear common interest. In such fields as human rights, we ought to be able to arrive at a joint approach. In November 1975, while watching the "Today Show," I was startled to hear Ambassador Moynihan say to Barbara Walters that that very day the United States was taking a major initiative at the UN in the field of human rights, namely a proposal for amnesty for all political prisoners. It was the first I had heard of it. Predictably, it went wrong, with the United States later having to seek to withdraw its own proposal, which was ill prepared and vulnerable. What added salt to the wound, however, was to find ourselves later berated for failing to support the United States in this initiative.

Coordination with other countries, however, can only follow the decision-making process within one's own government, and it seems to me that it is here that the real problems lie.

As a foreign government, what one seeks is a sufficient degree of institutional smoothness so that at any stage of the evolutionary process America's allies can feel reasonably sure of the lines along which policy is going to evolve. We have to be able to "plug in" at a working level and be fairly sure that we are going to get a clear sense of direction, whether the approach is at first secretary level in London, Washington, or New York; at ambassadorial level in the Security Council, at foreign minister; or even at summit levels. It is paradoxical that difficulties in coordination with the French are usually because of a lack of political will to coordinate on their part and not because of an institutional problem that they have inside their system of government, whereas coordination with the United States is difficult for precisely the opposite reasons. There is no lack of good intention; the problem seems to be within the system.

Is it resolvable? I frankly do not know. As a non-American, one can perceive the gap but not perceive how it should be filled. There is no one body capable of pulling Congress and the executive together. How could there be, given the nature of the separate arms of government? And good personal relations between the president and the chairman of the Senate Foreign Relations Committee is no substitute for an institutional answer. Quiet chats in the White House do not necessarily produce agreement. Instead, sometimes they produce precisely the opposite. One way out might be some joint coordinating body through which Congress could be made to feel involved in the creation of U.S. foreign policy, not merely as at present in passing judgment on policy when it has been developed. In the nature of things, Congress is a reactive body, not an innovative or creative one. When relations between the White House and the Hill are strained, as they seem to be at present, or when the president seems vulnerable, then the tendency for Congress to be more critical inevitably increases. When that happens, congressional pressure becomes even more of a factor in presidential decision making, and the rest of us are left to watch the gladiatorial spectacle.

I am, moreover, not in the least persuaded that this spectacle produces better results for the United States itself. It may produce better sport and hotter copy for the commentators, but does it actually help to evolve and pursue a coherent foreign policy line? The Middle East is perhaps the most obvious example where it seems to have failed. There are certain things that have to be done by the United States if we are ever to move toward peace in that part of the world. The most important is a recognition that resolving the problem of the Palestinians is central to the process. Yet, as the resignation of Ambassador Young proved, no administration can do what it knows it has to for fear of congressional pressure and the power of the lobbies at home. Publicity can be (and often is) inhibiting on governments when it comes to their taking difficult and unpopular decisions. Here, publicity is built into the system itself.

But there is an even more fundamental point. If one can equate (and this is in any event a dubious proposition) congressional examination with public awareness, foreign policy is one of those areas where public opinion is notoriously fickle and where dramatic results are difficult to achieve. "Eyeballing" the Soviets may be attractive in a *macho* sort of way, but negotiation of a SALT treaty is infinitely more important and more delicate. The public has to have some trust in an administration, even after Vietnam or Watergate, and in any event the history of the Vietnam War was largely one of congressional impotence, not assertion. People now tend to forget the lonely battle Senator Fulbright had to wage in the Senate and the fact that Vietnam came to an end by stealth and secret diplomacy rather than by open decisions openly arrived at—messily, perhaps, but stealthily.

I suppose the situation was ever thus, though we in Britain cannot help but remember that in 1940, when my country was at its most vulnerable, it was the administration acting quietly that helped us the most, and the Congress acting loudly that tended to inhibit the president. The United States is a very great, powerful, and generous country, as are its people, and the criticism here is peripheral to American purpose and to the good relations between our countries. We recognize the immense problems of global leadership, but your leadership is sometimes inhibited by the strains implicit in your system of government. I also accept that there is no easy answer to the problem.

The point that I am making is not a peevish one of criticism of the doctrine of the separation of powers. I recognize that the U.S. Constitution is designed to create tension between the various branches of government and also that its delicate mechanism of checks and balances has in the past produced its own correctives. My sole point (and it is a fairly narrow one) is that, if left unresolved, the arguments at present taking place between Congress and the executive in the field of foreign policy are weakening America's voice abroad because of the additional uncertainties they create. In time the pendulum may well swing back, and perhaps the process is already under way, but it is an undeniable fact that at present an ascendant Congress makes it more difficult for those of us who have to deal with the United States in the field of foreign policy, and that the situation would further deteriorate if congressional assertion increases.

The answers to the grammatically precise questions in the title to this paper—With whom do you deal? Whom can we trust?—are then very simple.

We deal with the administration because we have to.

Whom can we trust? No one entirely.

Why not? Because your system of government enjoins us that we should not.

Can anything be done about it? I do not know, but I wish you would.

3
Historical Perspective: The Swings and Roundabouts of Presidential Power

Professor Louis W. Koenig

COMPARED TO THE chief executives of other political systems, the power and influence of the American president in foreign policymaking are fluctuating and uncertain. In the American system, more than in other systems, the chief executive is unable to stabilize his political influence. His competitor, Congress, is more powerful in foreign policymaking than any other legislative body in the world. In American society and culture, potent forces and traditions are in play that also cause swings and discontinuities in the president's role. An overview of American foreign policy experience discloses rises and falls, ebb and flow in the president's impact and performance. If this description has merit, it provides an alternative perception to the contention that there is an "imperial Presidency."[1]

Partly these characteristics spring from the circumstance that power is shared between the executive and Congress, but the precise patterns of sharing are tentative and unclear, and even after nearly two centuries of constitutional practice they remain largely unpredictable. Also contributing to the erratic swings of power are the shifts in public moods that proceed to a degree unmatched in any other major nation. The American mood swings widely between high ideals and willingness to sustain heavy burdens in foreign policy, to absorption in domestic affairs, and even to moods of disillusionment and resignation, induced when foreign policy fails to satisfy activist expectations, whereupon the country resorts to withdrawal and isolation. The swings between involvement and withdrawal, their breadth and recurrence, are distinctly an American phenomenon, and they are indulged in by all categories of public opinion, the general public, the attentive public, and elites.[2]

To be sure, the earlier presidents, from Washington to Monroe, faced imposing foreign policy problems and were engaged in diplomacy of the most involving kind. There was no other alternative; most of the problems could not be avoided. But from Jackson to the Civil War, the country was preoccupied with domestic problems, and its foreign policies seldom reached beyond relations with our immediate neighbors. In the Civil War, foreign policy was important although ancillary, and no president between Lincoln and Cleveland emerges as more than a modest presence in foreign affairs. The Spanish-American War, which first brought the United States to stage center in world affairs in modern times, was a congressional war, promoted by legislators and supported by public opinion inflamed by the yellow press, and reluctantly acquiesced in by a peace-minded president, William McKinley.

America was kept at stage center by the bellicosity and other hyperactivity of Theodore Roosevelt, the dollar diplomacy of Taft, and Wilson's messianic mission to make the world safe for democracy and peace.[3] A mood of isolationism and the modest talents of Coolidge and Harding prompted the presidential presence to recede. World War II, followed close on by the cold war, caused a soaring presidential activism for two and a half decades. Then as the nation tired of the long-dragging Indochina war and the Watergate scandals set in, a tainted presidency passed into a diminished role, accompanied by a mood, heavily tinged with neoisolationism, which makes the public and its officials wary of foreign commitments potentially involving the engagement of American combat forces.

Clearly each political branch, Congress and the executive, has enjoyed ascendancy at different intervals and in different fields of foreign policy. The performances of both branches are mixtures of successes and failures. Neither branch has a monopoly of error or virtue. Presidents have successfully waged wars, proclaimed creative and utilitarian long-range policies like the Monroe Doctrine, instituted imaginative programs like Eisenhower's Atoms for Peace and Kennedy's Peace Corps; and Nixon opened up relations with communist China. But the presidential box score declines when Wilson fails to win the Senate's approval of American membership in the League of Nations, when the Bay of Pigs invasion goes awry, when a succession of presidents becomes entrapped in the protracted war in Vietnam, including a secret war in Cambodia.

But Congress' performance is also mixed. The country's most senseless and least defensible conflicts, the wars of 1812 and 1898, were congressional wars. And it was the Senate or Congress that blocked our entry into the League of Nations, withheld full support for the World Court, that continuously reduces foreign aid, and that passes resolutions mixing in the affairs of other countries for political rather than diplomatic reasons. Congress served as a most sympathetic audience for Gen. Douglas MacArthur and his call for "total victory," and when Kennedy struggled to establish a prudent policy in the 1962 Cuban Missile Crisis, congressional leaders urged an immediate air attack on the island.

But Congress also has a sturdy credit side. It established, for example, the exchange-of-persons program and the use of agricultural surpluses in foreign aid. Ideas for a Peace Corps and to create an Arms Control and Disarmament Agency, and employing foreign policy to enhance human rights abroad began in Congress.

It is further evidence of the volatility of both the presidency and Congress and their functioning in the political and policymaking systems, that each in recent times has been looked to admiringly by both liberal and conservative opinion. In the 1930s and 1940s, the presidency was favored by liberals and dreaded by conservatives, who were driven to sponsor the Bricker amendment by which they confidently proposed to make a good Congress the watchdog of a bad presidency. In the 1960s and 1970s, liberals, distressed by the presidency's war involvements, looked to Congress to rein in the office.

This notion of fluctuation and uncertainty is affirmed if we consider foreign policymaking to be most frequently a continuum—that is, from an idea and plan, it passes through many stages of formation, adoption, implementation—and the degree of the president's personal or institutional control is normally quite different at each stage. It is one thing for Nixon, acting autonomously and with dramatic effect, to journey to China. Far less is his and his presidential successors' control over the countless detailed decisions to give actuality and substance to his important symbolic act. It is easy to be overimpressed with the importance of presidential policymaking, to undervalue the progression of concrete steps to implement his choices. The further down the road policies go toward implementation, the remoter they become to his control, the more dependent he becomes on the discretion and support of others. He can decide to escalate the war in Vietnam, but he depends on others to finance and wage it; he can encourage inventions to improve American technology and productivity and our international trade balances, but the brains of others must incubate the ideas and write the laws.

THE CONSTITUTIONAL FRAMEWORK

If the power and presence of the chief executive in foreign affairs are subject to fluctuation, it is because the framers intended that they be. In drafting the Constitution, they granted, after careful deliberation, substantial powers to both the legislative and executive branches. For the most part, the framers defined those powers vaguely and left the inevitable doubts and conflicts for struggle and resolution between the branches. The framers intended that no one branch should be lastingly ascendant in the struggle, nor that the conduct of foreign policy should wither and waste from prolonged interbranch deadlock. The policy machinery should keep turning but not swing too widely in erratic orbit.

With extraordinary economy of language, the framers vested the "executive power" in the president, and although this power was undefined, it is clear, as Louis Henkin notes, that the framers, who were conversant with Locke, Montesquieu, and Blackstone, intended that the terse language constitute a vast grant of power.[4] The Constitution's commander-in-chief clause provides another stout peg on which to hang wars and other violent engagements the president conducts with or without a declaration of war by Congress, and it enables the president to define the nation's stance in wars between other belligerents—George Washington's proclamation of neutrality in the Franco-British War, and Franklin Roosevelt's deviation from a legislated neutrality policy, prior to our belligerency in World War II, to assist countries fighting the Axis powers. The president's most explicit foreign affairs powers in the Constitution are the relatively modest ones to appoint ambassadors and ministers with the Senate's advice and consent, and to receive foreign diplomatic representatives. This has been expanded by presidents and courts to encompass the plenitude of diplomatic powers, indeed the conduct of all foreign intercourse.

To Congress, the Constitution assigns at least three major roles in foreign affairs: to legislate, to exercise control of the purse, and to review treaties and appointments—these latter by the Senate. The "legislative powers" given Congress in Article I, Section 8 include the commerce power, among others, whose scope might be sufficient to support any legislation relating to foreign affairs.[5] The power to legislate implies the power to investigate, and Congress' presence in foreign policy processes is sometimes felt most keenly in its conduct of investigations. Congress has the power to declare war, which in Madison's eyes clearly establishes its primacy in foreign affairs.

The obscurities of the Constitution's language and of the framers' precise intent give rise to the concept of "concurrent powers" of Congress and the president, a potent contributing force in fluctuations in his actual powers and efficacy. The concurrent powers throw up a zone of uncertainty, a gray area where Congress and the president each can reasonably claim a power to act, especially when the other has not acted. Prominent among the concurrent powers is the president's prerogative to make international executive agreements, by which he can avoid use of the treaty power with its sometimes onerous requirement of a two-thirds approving vote in the Senate. Executive agreements have been applied to an extraordinary variety of subjects, often against congressional objections, and sometimes to matters which the Senate has rejected in the treaty process. The annexations of Texas and Hawaii and Theodore Roosevelt's takeover of the Santo Domingo customs-houses are cases in point.

Concurrent powers include the president as commander in chief committing the armed forces to combat or deploying them abroad to sites where combat becomes likely, steps that distress congressional defenders of their body's war-declaring power.

In 1940 President Roosevelt dispatched forces to Greenland and Iceland, even though legislation seemed to forbid it. In a "Great Debate" in 1950–51 over the commitment of additional troops to Europe, Congress considered and the president opposed legislation limiting the number of troops the United States could station in allied countries in time of peace. Sponsors of this effort cited Congress' authority to raise armies and to spend for the common defense. In resisting, President Truman invoked his authority as commander in chief and other foreign affairs powers. Ultimately, the limitations were not imposed, and, as usually happens, the constitutional issue was not resolved.

In the interbranch struggles over the concurrent powers, advantage most often lies with the branch that outraces the other in taking the initiative; whoever "gets there first" prevails. Generally, the president has run faster than Congress and therefore usually occupies a far greater sector of the gray area. The president can act more quickly than 535 legislators arrayed in two houses and functioning by delay-prone procedures. The president has better information and stronger staff support, and it is directly to him and his associates in the executive branch that the multitudinous communications lines of foreign policy run. He enhances his gains by convenient techniques of constitutional and legal interpretation. When challenged, the president is apt to stand on all his powers and, rather than particularize their applicability to a given instance, cite them in the aggregate. And the course of the presidency has been one of depending on "precedents" commenced by past presidents and built upon and expanded by their successors. The little undeclared wars against the Barbary pirates become the big wars in Indochina; where early executive agreements dealt with consular matters and fishing rights, later ones relate to military bases and the limitations of strategic arms. In presidential hands, precedents in foreign policymaking and practice are as stretchable as taffy.

Nonetheless, although the outcomes of the interbranch struggle over foreign policy repeatedly favor the president, he has never achieved a place that is fixed and secure. His fortunes shift; his usable powers can be reduced. Indeed, it was the framers' intention that if presidential ascendance proceeded too far, redressing forces in the political system—the mechanisms of checks and balances—would automatically come into play.

But concurrent powers, by their nature, contribute to the instabilities of presidential power. Since the courts seldom intervene to provide authoritative definitions of foreign affairs powers, presidential power is susceptible to challenge and constraint by counterassertions of legislative fiat. The later stages of the Vietnam War illuminate the possibilities of new developments, new manifestations of power in the continuing struggle between the branches.

In 1970 President Nixon sent troops into Cambodia, and subsequently, when this new extension of the war became known, members of Congress, fearful of further extensions or wishing to end the long-lasting Indochina war, brandished the mighty sword of the appropriation power, forbidding various expenditures for its further conduct, and cutting off funds at a specified date. Between 1973 and 1975, Congress adopted seven statutory provisions expressly prohibiting the expenditure of funds for "combat activities" or for "military or para-military operations in, over, or off the shores of" the nations of Indochina.[6] To this grouping should also be added the War Powers Resolution of 1973, passed over Nixon's veto, which limits the president's power to engage in hostilities anywhere without congressional authorization.

Something of the uncertainties and quandaries for presidential power provoked by this extraordinary legislation became evident when President Ford ordered an evacuation of Phnom Penh, Cambodia, on April 12, 1975. Although the forces had been readied for combat, the president contended they were not involved in a situation contemplated by the War Powers resolution, and its duty of prior consultation with Congress or its sixty-day limitation on combat not authorized by the legislative branch. Similarly, Ford on April 30, without serious consultation with Congress, ordered the evacuation of Saigon. Nine hundred marines participated in the two-day operation. The president merely made brief subsequent reports to Congress with statements of constitutional justification for his position.[7]

Clearly, the president could not permit Americans to be taken prisoners by the oncoming North Vietnamese armies, and his only recourse was to mount a large rescue operation, regardless of the possible contravention of the War Powers resolution. As Richard Pious observes, the president had to act or face political suicide and the shattering of morale in the armed forces and their confidence in their commander in chief.[8]

Ford also ordered the forces into combat to rescue the *Mayaquez* from its Cambodian captors, and although he briefed beforehand a selected body of representatives and senators, he again provided no opportunity for consultation. A similar pattern developed when, as part of the *Mayaguez* rescue, Ford dispatched eight hundred troops to Thailand. After the combat terminated, Ford reported the event to Congress, citing his authority as commander in chief. His utilization of the forces ignored Congress' previous funding prohibitions on military actions in Cambodia and its adjacent areas. Legislators complained of the lack of even a semblance of the consultations required by the War Powers resolution, but public opinion rallied to the president—as it frequently does in a crisis.

In the legislative-executive chess game there is never a final move, only a next move. Critiques of the experience of the War Powers resolution argue the necessity of future amendments to toughen its consultation features by designating, for example, the congressional leaders with whom the president shall communicate, such as party leaders or the foreign affairs committees in each house. Thus far the Carter administration has taken a reserved stance toward the resolution, emphasizing "the constitutional responsibility of the Commander-in-Chief to act, expeditiously when necessary, to preserve the security of our Nation."[9]

Although the War Powers resolution is usually dismissed as a harmless curio, some surprises may lurk in its provisions which only experience can draw forth. For example, if the president embarks upon what presumably will be a limited war, he is constrained to report its progress and status to Congress every six months, creating an opportunity both for consultation and for the president and Congress to renew their agreement on the purposes and terms on which the war will continue to be waged. If the war becomes protracted, it is easily imagined that the president's task under the resolution will become increasingly onerous, with antiwar sentiment rising when conflict is not concluded quickly. Thus, the president will acquire a powerful incentive to finish a war promptly, and the employment of nuclear weapons could take on a new allure.[10]

THE PERSONAL AND POLITICAL FRAMEWORK

Uncertainty and fluctuation in the president's performance in foreign affairs, induced by the nature of his constitutional and other legal powers, are reinforced by the American system's institutional deficiencies. Institutionalization is a major component of political systemic stability; it tends to minimize variations in the system that would otherwise result from differences in the personal political effectiveness of a succession of incumbent officeholders. Although over time, the American system has developed a luxuriant growth of institutionalization in the presidency—the White House Office and the bureaucracy of the Executive Office of the President—the presidential system lacks two basic stabilizing institutions of Western parliamentary systems: first, political parties of strength and discipline; second, a cabinet, consisting of the party's factional leaders, founded on the principle of collective responsibility. If anything, American parties are disappearing before our eyes, and the historic impotence of the cabinet is suggested by the report that Lincoln, calling upon his assembled secretaries for a vote, heard a chorus of ayes. Hereupon Lincoln declared, "I say 'nay,' and the nays have it."

A strong party coupled with a collectively responsible cabinet helps compensate for a chief executive of lesser political talents. Cabinet and party hold the chief executive to established channels of behavior and processes of policymaking; and, as a kind of bargain or exchange, they extract support from a disciplined legislative majority. System deadlock and nondecision are minimized, and a deliberated positive policy response to a given public problem is most likely. The absence of the instrumentalities of a strong party and a strong cabinet in the American instance places enormous reliance and burden on the president's personal political talents. If his political gifts are of a high order, well and good. But if his talents are of lesser strength, no collective structure exists to assure decisions and policies of sufficient quality, backed by votes and other political support that the undertalented president alone cannot command.

That presidential personalities vary enormously is emphasized in studies like those of Hargrove and Barber.[11] As Hargrove and other political scientists contend, presidents and others who enter politics are apt to have certain personality needs that are better gratified in political endeavor than in private pursuits. Theodore Roosevelt, for instance, according to Hargrove, had an insatiable hunger for public attention and popularity, and a dread of rejection by the voters and of losing public office with its opportunities for self-display.

In Roosevelt's day, foreign affairs and policymaking provided a ready arena in which to indulge his penchant for flamboyant assertiveness. Further spurred by his virtually open-ended "stewardship theory" for conducting the presidency, Roosevelt made outrageous sorties in foreign affairs like his pyrotechnic drive to build a Panama Canal. Years after leaving the presidency he explained: "The Panama Canal I naturally take interest in because I started it. If I had acted strictly according to precedent, I should have turned the whole matter over to Congress; in which case Congress would be debating it at this moment [1911], and the canal would be fifty years in the future. Fortunately the crisis came at a period when I could act unhampered. Accordingly, I took the Isthmus, started the Canal, and then left Congress—not to debate the

Canal, but to debate me—the debate still goes on as to whether or not I acted properly in taking the Canal. But while the debate goes on the Canal does too."[12]

But a talented, activist president may also be driven into costly disaster in foreign policymaking. According to Barber, Woodrow Wilson and Lyndon Johnson were compulsive chief executives who wrecked their presidential careers, Wilson in his uncompromising stance in the League of Nations fight, and Johnson in excessive commitment to the Vietnam War, his concern not to become "the first President to lose a war." Strong presidents, yes, in policy initiatives; but weak, defeated presidents in the processes of policy implementation.

In their study, *Woodrow Wilson and Colonel House,*[13] Alexander and Juliette George explain the League of Nations fiasco in terms of Wilson's driven need to maintain his self-esteem by proving to himself periodically that he was an adequate and virtuous human being. These imperatives are traced back to a Calvinistic upbringing and an exacting, overbearing father. To do good works, Wilson needed to dominate others, especially those whom he perceived as wrong and evil. In the League of Nations fight, Henry Cabot Lodge was a tailor-made foe, ideal for Wilson's needs. Unfortunately, this became one more fight that Wilson, blind to political realities and the necessities of compromise, could not win. Instead, the result was a disaster for the nation and mankind.

In the Barber analytic scheme, some presidents are denoted by low activity or even passivity in discharging their presidential tasks. Taft and Eisenhower, among others, fall into this category, although this assessment of Eisenhower is challenged by recent scholarship. A mark of this general category is large-scale delegation of initiative in foreign affairs to the secretary of state. In effect, the president is yielding up large portions of foreign policymaking to a dominant subordinate, a recourse not uncommon in presidential history.

Secretary of State Philander Knox, a transplanted corporate lawyer, was far more the architect of dollar diplomacy than the cautious, reticent Taft. At times in the Eisenhower administration, Secretary of State John Foster Dulles exercised such sweeping responsibility as foreign policy formulator, negotiator, and spokesman that the Senate's own leading figure in that arena, J. W. Fulbright, protested that "Secretary Dulles seemed at times to be exercising those 'delicate, plenary, and exclusive powers' which are supposed to be vested in the President."[14]

Most presidents who delegate freely and fully to their secretaries of state are well removed from the image of the presidency as an office of awesome power. Taft was passive; and Harding, who had little gift or inclination for foreign affairs, left the field to his secretary of state, Charles Evans Hughes, whose abilities he revered and whose recommendations he automatically approved.

If the secretary of state becomes an administration's chief figure in foreign affairs, he—unlike the president—is subject to several constraints that tend to contribute to a greater sharing of power, as well as to instability and uncertainty in the handling of foreign policy. The secretary is subject to questioning by congressional committees; and he interacts, directly and significantly, with his peers, his fellow secretaries, and with the State Department and foreign service bureaucracies, the most professional of staffs. The president has no comparable interactions with these entities, which have their own power base as well as the resources and skill to question the secretary of state's policy choices.

Richard Neustadt, in his study, *Presidential Power,*[15] asserts that every chief executive has a choice between being a leader, in the sense of using the office' great store of power effectively, or being a clerk, who leaves power largely unused. The power of the president, Neustadt contends, is not the power to command but the power to persuade. The president may, by bargaining with his fellow actors, be they foreign leaders, members of Congress, or others, induce them to act as he prefers, convincing them that it is their interest to do so. This requires skill in managing the economy of presidential resources, of which repute is the most valuable. A well-tended reputation for political efficacy will help the president make his way in the community of president watchers—the press, fellow politicians, foreign diplomats, and leaders. But let him falter, his political reputation slip, and the going quickly becomes rough.

Again, in this crucial realm of presidential behavior unevenness, uncertainty, and instability reign because presidents vary widely in their persuasive skills. A Franklin Roosevelt brings a high order of excellence evident in the volume and quality of legislation passed and foreign policy initiatives boldly and successively undertaken. Critics of Jimmy Carter see him falling well short of Neustadt's prescriptions, a poor bargainer in Congress, often rebuffed, barely scraping through with the Panama Canal Treaties and the implementing legislation; and with SALT II, suffering serious delays, and, eventually being forced to withdraw rather than suffer defeat.

A potent contributing factor to the presidency's volatility is the dependence of the office and its policies on public opinion. The public speaks as an electorate, and its pulse is taken regularly by the polls. Foreign policy issues are recurrent in modern presidential elections, and an incumbent president's stewardship, particularly its flaws, or a rival's initiatives, preoccupy a campaign. In 1952 Eisenhower in effect promised to end the Truman-made Korean War; Kennedy pledged to overcome an alleged missile gap; to those weary of the Vietnam War, Nixon offered a "secret plan" to end it. The fact that the Senate is a hatching nest of modern presidential candidates is largely attributable to its involvements in foreign affairs and the readiness with which its candidates can manipulate that subject in presidential campaigns. In the first weeks of the 1980 campaign, the issue of the Russian brigade in Cuba was quickly transformed from a molehill into a mountain by enterprising senators who were also presidential candidates.

Clearly, public opinion is a potent force that can hobble or facilitate a president's purposes in foreign affairs. Congress, whose members make regular soundings of their districts' opinion, often set their course toward presidential foreign policy initiatives according to the polls' findings. Franklin Roosevelt was impeded by a divided public opinion in his efforts to help an imperiled Britain prior to Pearl Harbor. On the other hand, Polk's machinations to annex Texas were eased by the public's bellicose spirit, and Theodore Roosevelt gave the Monroe Doctrine, originally designed to prevent intervention by European powers, a new twist, by directing American intervention into the bankrupt Dominican Republic. Earlier the Senate refused to back his step, but Roosevelt went ahead anyway, spurred by widespread public approval of his venture.[16]

Presidential power has an impressive cast if our gaze concentrates on policy formation and promulgation, and if it is directed less at another phase of the policy process, less dramatic and visible, but nonetheless crucial, the stage of implementation. For most foreign policies, the president depends on the vast bureaucracy of the executive branch for implementation and sometimes for initiation as well. Seen by presidential eyes, the bureaucracy is self-protective, handcuffed by routinization, invariably playing a waiting game until the president, a temporary intruder, passes from the stage after a brief tenure.

The precise nature of the president's relation with the foreign affairs bureaucracy is left unclear by the Constitution, nor can it be readily inferred from many decades of operating experience. Presidents testify that it is not imperial or even regal. Truman said it well, contemplating the likely plight of the general become president, Dwight Eisenhower. "He'll sit here," Truman said, tapping his desk, "and he'll say, 'Do this! Do that!' And nothing will happen. Poor Ike—it won't be a bit like the Army. He'll find it very frustrating."[17] John Kennedy was not long in office when, impatient with the State Department's lagging responses to his need for foreign policy information and initiatives, snapped that he could do more work in the White House in a week than the Department could do in a month.

A not uncommon experience of presidents in the world of foreign policy is the habit of high-level associates to take matters into their own hands or engage in outright disobedience. As American diplomatic history makes clear, Andrew Young is by no means the inventor of high-level insubordination. To President James K. Polk, his peace negotiator with Mexico, Nicholas Trist, who continued to negotiate after he was recalled, was an "impudent and unqualified scoundrel."[18] Truman bridled at his secretary of state's,

James F. Byrnes, freewheeling style, and after one of the secretary's self-directed negotiations with the Soviets, Truman reacted, "Another outrage, if I ever saw one." [19]

PATTERNS OF FOREIGN POLICYMAKING

A historical review of American foreign policymaking discloses at least four common patterns of presidential role performance. In each the president as policymaker does not function as a solitary, self-willed official, but interacts with other members of the political system, and the relationships have important impacts in different stages of his foreign policy activity. The president shares power with others, especially Congress, is counseled by department heads and staffs, and faces criticisms by political opponents and review by public opinion. Let us examine these contentions in the context of the following common policymaking patterns.

Conflict. Foreign policymaking often proceeds in a milieu of conflict and doubtless provides the readiest support for our thesis that presidential power is largely shared power. The treaty process, requiring a supermajority, the two-thirds vote, is an invitation for minority opinion in the legislature to be asserted. The opposition party, the president's rivals in an upcoming election—senators who would rather be president—provide the seeds of conflict.

Jay's Treaty (1794) was a conflict-type episode of foreign policymaking, illustrative of the variety of external forces that impinge upon the president, question his judgment, challenge his decisions. As President Washington's special emissary, John Jay was assigned to clear up issues remaining under the Treaty of Paris of 1783 that ended the Revolution, and new issues stemming from the Franco-British War, such as British depredations on U.S. shipping, and cutting off our trade with the West Indies. [20]

Within the administration, the principal department secretaries, Jefferson (State) and Hamilton (Treasury), battled over the negotiations, and their embroilment caught up Washington and required his deliberation and decision. In Congress, the treaty was clearly a party issue, with Madison organizing the Republican opposition, and directing parliamentary maneuvers. In the Senate, to foil the Federalist majority and the required two-thirds treaty vote, Republicans strove to split off the southern federalists by moving to seek compensation for impressed blacks. The effort failed by 3 votes.

Ultimately, the Senate approved the treaty, by 20 votes to 10, whereupon the Republicans carried the fight to public opinion. Bonfire rallies were held in the cities, and letters, petitions, and newspaper editorials poured in on Washington opposing the treaty, driving the president to exclaim, "The affairs of the country cannot go amiss. There are so many watchful guardians of them, and such infallible guides, that one is at no loss for a direction at every turn."[21] Madison also extended the conflict to the state legislatures, seeking resolutions opposing the treaty, and the Virginia legislature, at his prodding, proposed an amendment to the federal Constitution to make treaties subject to a majority vote of the U.S. House of Representatives, center of Republican strength.

Finally, Jay's Treaty required not only Senate approval but implementing legislation, which enabled Madison and the Republicans again to flay the treaty. The legislation squeaked through the House by 51 to 48. Washington attributed his success in that close result to popular petitions the Federalists had accumulated to counter the Republican attack.[22]

Consensus. Occasionally consensus overtakes public affairs, and one of the stellar practitioners of that brand of politics was James Monroe, whose tenure coincided with "the era of good feeling." The Federalist party had now disappeared and the Democratic-Republicans flourished as the country's only party. Monroe's most memorable foreign policy is, of course, the Monroe Doctrine, ideally suited for consensus politics. According to Dexter Perkins, the leading scholar of the doctrine, its original power stemmed from the fact that it "expressed what many men, great and humble, had thought, were thinking then, and were to think in the future. The ideas which it set forth were in the air."[23]

But notwithstanding the unanimity at every side, the consensus politics of the Monroe Doctrine subjected presidential policymaking to the discipline of challenge, deliberation, and discussion. Monroe faced questions about facts and their assessment in the international environment and how to proceed with the doctrine's immediate implementation. In the cabinet, opinion divided over how serious the danger was of European intervention in the newly independent countries emerging from Spain's former Latin American countries.

According to Secretary of State John Quincy Adams, Monroe was "alarmed" and Secretary of War John Calhoun "moonstruck" by the danger that the Holy Alliance would intervene in South America. Adams coolly discounted this possibility. Attorney General William Wirt opposed the proclamation of the doctrine unless the country were willing to go to war to protect South American independence, but, he contended, public opinion would not tolerate that step. Adams and Calhoun argued against and prevailed over Wirt's position, and the development of the doctrine proceeded.[24]

Despite the high unanimity it engendered, the Monroe Doctrine encountered hard questions and serious opposition in Congress. Senator John Branch of North Carolina feared that it would "excite the angry passions and embroil us with foreign nations." James Buchanan led a maneuver of introducing amendments to eviscerate it.[25] Again the doctrine prevailed. Ironically, neither Monroe, his friends, nor his opponents, really grasped the large importance the doctrine was to have, its enduring vitality, its influence on future foreign policy.

Autonomy.   Not only are alternate paths of politics open to the president's choice. He also can sometimes choose between several methods of policymaking—whether to act autonomously or in collaboration with other members of the political system such as Congress. Franklin Roosevelt largely followed the autonomous path at a crucial interval of foreign policymaking in the months before Pearl Harbor and after the Axis conquest of France (June 1940–December 1941). During this interval Britain stood alone, threatened with invasion. Faced with congressional and public opinion closely divided between isolationism and intervention, Roosevelt chose to act on his own initiative and discretion, including, when necessary, the committing of warlike acts.

Among other things, Roosevelt handed over to beleaguered Britain fifty overage but still serviceable destroyers in return for grants of bases for American forces on British territories in the Western Hemisphere. After Germany overran Denmark, Roosevelt dispatched forces to occupy Iceland and Greenland, an overt act of participation in the European war.[26] To assure the delivery of American arms to Britain, Roosevelt provided naval convoys and ultimately ordered the shooting of Axis naval craft at sight, and several violent encounters took place.

In this extraordinarily difficult and critical wartime situation, Roosevelt clearly took into his own hands matters that in earlier and easier times either belonged to Congress or were handled by the branches jointly. In expiation of Roosevelt's seemingly imperious conduct, elements of the larger context in which he operated as well as several other of his methods are noteworthy. His autonomous actions cannot be judged in isolation.

First, Roosevelt was sensitive to public opinion, alert to assessing its reaction to his policies, and in undertaking the educative function of the presidency respecting which he was extremely diligent. Time and again in speeches, he pointed out to the public the deadly peril afoot in the world, the necessity for wider awareness of the danger, and the inevitability of citizen sacrifices.[27] Even with his best efforts prior to Pearl Harbor, public opinion remained mixed, even incoherent, although it provided a sufficient base for the president's initiatives.

Roosevelt regularly ran the gauntlet of Congress, where isolationist sentiment was strong. The foundation of large-scale aid to Britain and subsequently to other Allies was the Lend-Lease Act, appropriately called the "blank check" bill. An opponent, Senator Robert Taft, attacked the contrivance of "lend-lease," observing that "Lending war equipment is a good deal like lending chewing gum. You don't want it back." In effect, the act was a legislated abandonment of neutrality, an unofficial declaration of war on the Axis, and largely a ratification of Roosevelt's previous autonomous course. Roosevelt also had to renew the Selective Service Act, which squeaked through the House by 1 vote. And he had to traverse the presidential election process in 1940, on a Democratic platform mirroring the ambivalence of public opinion by pledging abstention from "foreign wars" while promising aid to countries resisting aggression.

Collaboration.   Both the Constitution and the practicalities it imposes on foreign policymaking require active cooperation between the legislative and executive branches, and the large volume of their combined actions and routine cooperation goes unnoticed. Some eras, such as the immediate post–World War II years, are marked by exceptional outputs of collaborative policymaking: approval of the U.N. Charter, aid to Greece and Turkey, point 4, the regional security treaties—Rio, NATO, SEATO—and the Marshall plan.[28]

Sometimes these collaborations are criticized as excessive, as speeding the ascendance of the presidency and lowering the impact of Congress. But a closer look at these policy ventures, the Marshall plan, for example, discloses that the distribution of influence between the branches was not really so one-sided.

The Marshall plan was enacted in 1948, a rare interval, when the Republican party controlled Congress. Through Truman, the Democrats controlled the White House. The dominant Republican motif was the necessity of cutting taxes, and the worst of sins was government's penchant for pouring money down a "rathole." Since the Marshall plan, at least in some eyes, threatened these imperatives, President Truman looked for help to the Republican chairman of the Senate Foreign Relations Committee, Arthur Vandenberg, a former isolationist recently converted to internationalism.

The evolution of the Marshall plan from a kernel of an idea in speeches of the State Department's leaders, George Marshall and Dean Acheson, to enacted legislation and a brilliantly implemented foreign policy is a saga of collaboration between the European powers, eager to recover from the ravages of World War II, and the United States, between government and the private sector, between the White House and the bureaucracy, between the executive branch and Congress. The last was by no means presidentially dominated.

Vandenberg, an imperious personality, with great capacity for instant indignation, wrested important concessions from the Truman administration. For example: Vandenberg insisted that a business executive run the program, and his handpicked candidate, Paul Hoffman of Studebaker, was appointed. The senator rebuffed the administration's plan to have the State Department run the program, and substituted a new separate agency of cabinet-level rank, the Economic Cooperation Administration. Other Vandenberg additions included pulling the administration away from a proposed but politically impractical four- or five-year authorization and substituting a generalized authorization and yearly cash appropriations.[29] Vandenberg inserted a watchdog committee into the legislation and provisions stipulating the obligations of the recipient countries. That the balance of Vandenberg's stewardship favored internationalism is suggested by the protests of isolationist legislative friends that he had sold them out, and Truman's gratitude for his indispensable help.[30]

THE PRESIDENCY TODAY

Since Watergate and Vietnam, the presidency has been sustaining a downward turn in its efficacy and impact. Partly this is the harvest of those events, of the flawed talents of recent incumbents, of changes in institutions of the political system which interact with the presidency, changes that, on the whole, are deleterious to the office and its policymaking effectiveness in both domestic and foreign affairs. Clinton Rossiter's observation that the presidency's responsibilities exceed its powers has special force today. The question is not whether there is an imperial presidency but whether there still is a presidency as that office has traditionally been known.

Recent changes in the political system, changes that are still transpiring, are debilitating to the presidency. Certain of these changes are the following:

1. A vital two-party system is a historic foundation stone of the strong, responsible presidency. But our major parties are declining, the body of independent voters continues to expand; the historic presidential selection system is superseded by a presidential primary system run amuck. Unfortunately, the latter can produce presidents and presidential entourages whose talents apply more to electoral campaigning than to governing.

2. Congress, too long a little changing institution, is now changing markedly and in ways detrimental to an effective presidency. Theodore Roosevelt once said that a strong presidency required a strong Congress. Unfortunately, current trends are leading to increasing dispersal of power in Congress. Committee chairmen have lost power, which has flowed to a multitude of subcommittees, largely secluded and dealing with public policy idiosyncratically. The power of the Speaker and other party leaders has faded; "Tip" O'Neill, however gifted, is not in the same power league as Sam Rayburn. The historical function of congressional party leaders to assemble votes to support the president's major foreign and domestic policy projects, after ample legislative review, is gravely impaired.

Increasingly, Congress is limiting the president's foreign policy options. By one recent count, Congress has used its appropriations power to impose more than seventy "constraints" on the president, such as insisting that no American foreign aid be spent on abortions, barring military assistance to Thailand unless authorized by Congress, and direct financing of any assistance to Angola. Subsequently, President Carter complained that because of congressional restraints the United States was unable to provide assistance to indigenous forces in Angola fighting the Cubans.[31]

Congress is also increasingly inserting its own veto provisions into legislation. The legislative veto allows Congress to negate a given presidential action without going through the process of enacting legislation requiring the president's signature. The legislative veto enables Congress to neutralize presidential power by circumventing the normal procedures of legislation. The veto can be cast by both chambers acting concurrently, by a single chamber, or by a legislative committee. In the past four years, provisions for forty-eight such vetoes have been inserted into laws. President Ford protested that the inclusion of a legislative veto in a pending foreign aid and arms sales bill "would forge impermissible shackles on the President's ability to carry out the law and conduct the foreign relations of the United States." Carter has said that his administration would not be bound by what it considers abuses of the legislative veto.[32]

The Senate is increasingly immersing itself in the negotiation, actually the renegotiation, of treaties made by the executive branch. Sometimes this heightened senatorial activity comes at the consent rather than at the advice stage. The further reaches of these possibilities became evident when Senate Majority Leader Robert C. Byrd and Minority Leader Howard H. Baker negotiated treaty changes in Panama City with Panama's chief of government.[33]

3. The presence of domestic interest groups in foreign policymaking is expanding. Important domestic groups are aroused over foreign policy issues; for example, Greek-Americans over the Cyprus dispute, American Jews over Israel, and black civil rights groups over African and Middle East issues.[34] Political Action Committees (PACs), predominantly business organizations, well financed, politically sophisticated, and often hard driving on one or several issues, will become increasingly assertive in foreign economic policymaking as that sector of foreign policy continues to expand.

4. Of all the historical forms of communications technology and organization, television, far more than the press and radio, is the most ambivalent in its impacts on the presidency. In some respects, television has clearly weakened the office.

Television has indeed enhanced the presidency's position as the supreme symbol of the political system. But the trouble is when events take a downturn—when Middle East oil prices soar, when inflation and unemployment worsen, when the Soviet-Cuban axis makes a new sortie—the president is the readiest symbol on which to affix blame, a national scapegoat, even though his powers for dealing with those eventualities are extremely limited. It is the president who is blamed for soaring oil prices, not the American motorist who insists on driving in his car alone, at high speed.

Since Watergate and Vietnam, television has sprouted with reporters who not only follow the historical journalistic priority for bad news over good news but who have a fillip of frequent moralizing over the policies and performance of presidents and their administrations. Since public policies seldom constitute clear-cut moral choices and their implementation is easily hobbled by unexpected, untoward events, and the frailties of the many human beings on whom their implementation depends, the president and his administration are easy prey for televized moralizing that reinforces the scapegoat function.

5. America's position in world affairs has changed from its ready predominance after World War II and through much of the 1960s to a position in the 1980s where its power is more easily challenged and rebuffed. During that interval, the Soviet Union rose from a state of clear military inferiority to a state of essential nuclear equivalence, attained in the 1970s, thanks to an extraordinary arms buildup, unequaled in history. The military superiority that strengthened Kennedy's hand in the 1962 Cuban Missile Crisis has disappeared. Events, it is clear, have their own fluctuations that effect swings in the president's powers.

As presidents struggled to extricate the United States from the futile Indochina war in the 1970s and to persuade the nation that not every foreign involvement could "lead to another Vietnam," Soviet-Cuban adventurism progressed on several fronts in Africa, and the American petroleum lifeline to the Middle East was jeopardized by war in Somalia, by the overthrow of the shah in Iran and his replacement by the hostile regime of the Ayatollah Khomeini, and by the Soviet takeover of Afghanistan. Like North Vietnam and Cuba, Khomeini's Iran demonstrated the capacity even of relatively weak countries to defy the United States. In the 1970s the presidency was constrained by the increasing inefficacy of its formidable military power to command results, and by the impact of new kinds of power, derived from the possession of oil and other energy resources by militarily less powerful countries, to whose manipulations the United States proved extremely vulnerable.

THE FUTURE

A major factor in the presidency's historical success in surviving the major swings and roundabouts in its usable powers is its remarkable capacity to adapt to the changing circumstances of the environment in which it functions.

The outline of its necessary adaptations in the 1980s is beginning to emerge. Most likely, the presidency will need to develop more of its foreign policy in collaboration with Congress, with the latter a genuine and active partner. Congress' foreign policymaking role will continue to expand, fostered by its practice of remaining almost continuously in session in contrast to the lengthy adjournments of the past; by its enlarged professional staffs; and by the likelihood that future foreign policy will be more substantially economic in character, embracing topics such as inflation, unemployment, and energy. In the economic realm, Congress enjoys broad constitutional powers that will give it ample leverage in future foreign policymaking. The successful president of the 1980s will need to be skilled in the politics of interbranch collaboration.

The greater sharing of power as a modus operandi must also be pursued by the presidency in its future relations with America's allies. The economic foreign policies of the 1980s will require the synchronized efforts of many national economies, and the role of the president will no longer be that of enforcing the will of a vastly dominant power but of building consensus among allies enjoying full status as partners.

If the presidency appears to be in a downswing both for the present and possibly in the immediate future, history counsels continued reliance on the framers' balancing mechanisms that ought soon to move the presidency into an upswing. History also counsels caution toward even well-motivated fundamental reforms of the system's messy architecture: whether in the form of constitutional amendments or institutional changes. They seldom work out the way we hope and anticipate. A better course is to rely upon the presidency's amply proven capacity to adjust to new circumstances and to regain and restore powers that have been diminished or weakened, and to find new uses for its powers for new problems.

NOTES

1. See Arthur M. Schlesinger, Jr., *The Imperial Presidency* (Boston: Houghton Mifflin, 1973).

2. These categories are like those of Gabriel Almond, *The American People and Foreign Policy* (New York: Praeger, 1960).

3. Harold Laski, *The American Presidency* (New York: Harper, 1940), pp. 175–76.

4. Louis Henkin, *Foreign Affairs and the Constitution* (Mineola, N.Y.: The Foundation Press, 1972), p. 42.

5. *Ibid.*, p. 69.

6. Richard M. Pious, *The American Presidency* (New York: Basic Books, 1979), p. 411.

7. For discussion of the War Powers resolution, see *Congressional Quarterly Almanac, 1973* (Washington: Congressional Quarterly, 1974): 905–7.

8. Pious, *op. cit.*, p. 411.

9. U.S. Congress, Senate, Hearings before the Committee on Foreign Relations, *War Powers Resolution*, 95th Cong., 1st sess. (Washington: Government Printing Office, 1977), p. 190.

10. Pious, *op. cit.*, p. 415.

11. Erwin Hargrove, *Presidential Leadership: Personality and Political Style* (New York: Macmillan, 1966); James David Barber, *The Presidential Character: Predicting Performance in the White House* (Englewood Cliffs, N.J.: Prentice-Hall, 1972).

12. From Malcolm Moos, "Theodore Roosevelt at Berkeley, Charter Day, March 23, 1911," in Benjamin V. Cohen et al., *The Prospect for Presidential-Congressional Government* (Berkeley: University of California, 1977), p. 3.

13. Alexander L. George and Juliette L. George, *Woodrow Wilson and Colonel House: A Personality Study* (New York: John Day, 1956).

14. In Sherman Adams, *First-Hand Report* (New York: Harper, 1961), pp. 89–90.

15. Richard E. Neustadt, *Presidential Power: The Politics of Leadership* (New York: Wiley, 1960).

16. Thomas A. Bailey, *A Diplomatic History of the American People* (New York: Appleton-Century-Crofts, 1950), pp. 271 and 559.

17. In Neustadt, *op. cit.*, p. 9.

18. Milo M. Quaife, ed., *The Diary of James K. Polk* (Chicago: University of Chicago Press, 1910), vol. 3, p. 301.

19. Robert J. Donovan, *Conflict and Crisis: The Presidency of Harry S. Truman* (New York: Norton, 1977), p. 158.

20. The classic study of this episode is Samuel Flagg Bemis, *Jay's Treaty* (New Haven: Yale University Press, 1962).

21. In Jerald A. Combs, *The Jay Treaty* (Berkeley: University of California Press, 1970), p. 163.

22. *Ibid.*, p. 187.

23. Dexter Perkins, *The Monroe Doctrine* (Cambridge, Mass.: Harvard University Press, 1932), p. 103.

24. *Ibid.*, pp. 75–81.

25. *Ibid.*, pp. 42 and 221.

26. William L. Langer and S. Everett Gleason, *The Undeclared War* (New York: Harper, 1953), p. 575.

27. *Ibid.*, p. 195.

28. Francis O. Wilcox, *Congress, the Executive, and Foreign Policy* (New York: Harper and Row, 1971), p. 8.

29. Arthur H. Vandenberg, Jr., ed., *The Private Papers of Senator Vandenberg* (Boston: Houghton Mifflin, 1952), p. 384.

30. Harry S. Truman, *Memoirs* (Garden City: Doubleday 1956), vol. 2, p. 119.

31. *New York Times*, May 24, 1979.

32. Dom Bonafede, "The Legislative Veto-Proof Congress," *National Journal* 10 (July 1, 1978): 1057, "Congress's Tools to Impose Its Will on the President's Foreign Policy Options," *National Journal* 10 (July 5, 1978): 1119–20.

33. Thomas M. Franck and Edward Weisband, "Advice and Consent," *New York Times*, February 28, 1978.

34. William J. Lanonette, "Who's Setting Foreign Policy—Carter or Congress?" *National Journal* 10 (July 15, 1978): 1118.

4

Institutional Perspective: Misunderstandings, Myths, and Misperceptions: How Congress and the State Department See Each Other

Honorable Patsy T. Mink

RELATIONS BETWEEN Congress and the State Department are unique and problematic. The alliances with Congress that shape the tactics and command the attention of other bureaucracies in the executive branch are absent from State. The premier department and Congress do not see each other in a symbiotic relationship. State does not have a pork barrel of distributive benefits and redistributive programs with which to nourish responsible congressional interest and reward cooperative behavior on the part of legislators. On the other hand, State is less beholden to Congress than are other departments for programs, bureaucratic structure, and authority to implement policy. By tradition, the foreign policy machinery has been allowed to operate relatively autonomously. As a result of this lack of symbiosis, relations between Congress and State have been characterized by frequent sparring in the post-Watergate, post-Vietnam era. Congress is not anxious to win a role in foreign policymaking, and the State Department seems determined to protect its autonomy.

Much of the conflict has to do with access to information. To the congressional rank and file, the State Department appears like a giant octopus, sucking up information and intelligence the world over, which it hoards for privileged, departmental use. Because State considers even the most ordinary bureaucratic chores to be "delicate missions," it fastidiously cultivates distance between itself and Congress. Its modus operandi is to distribute information selectively to Capitol Hill: when necessary, but not necessarily. And when State does deign to answer questions put to it by members of Congress, the reply issues from a central Liaison Office, so that it can be screened for policy consistency and "appropriateness." Except when a senior official is actually squirming under tenacious congressional cross-examination, it is usually assumed that a pro forma reply is all that is required.

To the Foreign Service personnel in State, Congress appears to be the bellwether of public opinion. This is not, however, regarded as a positive trait. Thus, Congress is believed to reflect an amateurish, uninterested, unschooled, and mildly xenophobic middle America, to hold in the lowest possible regard anything "foreign" and to believe that State regularly plots to give away what rightfully belongs to the American people. Individual members of Congress are seen to busy themselves full-time with the domestic agenda, generally taking foreign policy positions only to support their domestic priorities. "Intellectualizing" about foreign relations or challenging old foreign policy directions is perceived to elicit no audible applause from voters. Hence, midwestern "bread-basket" congresspersons cheer wheat sales to the Soviet Union as a great boon to their home state farmers, while eastern congresspersons— often more consumer oriented—express nervous alarm over their likely impact on domestic prices and commodity supplies. It is observed by the foreign policy bureaucracy that this parochial tendency to tailor foreign policy positions to fit domestic constituency priorities is periodically reinforced by the voters, as it was in 1978 when Iowans reportedly did not reelect Dick Clark to the U.S. Senate after his opponent had succeeded in portraying him as the "great Senator from Africa," an epithet earned by his studious attention to the problems of that continent.

As with most myths, this bleak perception of the members is not wholly false, but it is far from the whole truth. More important, this negative and persistent perception of Congress by the State Department is a self-fulfilling prophecy. It leads State to conclude that Congress should have no active role in foreign policy and that Congress cannot be trusted with highly sensitive information. Acting on this perception, the bureaucracy feels justified in withholding information that Congress needs to keep apace of international developments. Precisely because it is not adequately informed, Congress is impelled to "shoot from the hip," often with consequences more disastrous than any "leaks" or "meddling" that might have been seen to require secrecy in the first place.

State's overly parsimonious sharing of information is certainly at the root of its poor relations with the Hill. Until State undertakes to bridge the chasm between Foggy Bottom and the Hill, members must make their foreign policy decisions based on news articles and the reports of broadcast media. By failing to invite judicious assessment of international options by legislators, the Department guarantees congressional flag waving, hysteria, and the political exploitation of paranoia.

Furthermore, information deprivation engenders congressional skepticism about State's capacity to provide even itself with accurate intelligence about international political developments. Many members see secrecy as a strategy for hiding the secret that there is no secret, that State has little—or mainly false—information. This suspicion is reinforced by evidence that the State Department and CIA, for all their hoarded secrets, are often actually misinformed, as in their woeful misassessment of the power balance in Iran before the fall of the shah. Lack of confidence in reporting by the Foreign Service thus compounds State's difficulties with Congress, as members refuse any longer to defer to the self-proclaimed superior wisdom of those who guard the secrets.

The self-inflicted wound caused by unnecessary refusal to share information is aggravated by the outmoded tactics of Congress-handling still too often employed by State. This proceeds on two false assumptions: first, that most members of Congress are "the enemy"; second, that they can best be neutralized by the traditional congressional leadership. The majority of legislators are neither venal nor dedicated to the frustration of the Department's policies. But neither are they overawed by it, in view of its record in recent years. There is healthy skepticism and an open mind.

The latent distrust between Congress and the State Department is easily exploited by a very small group of members, either to embarrass the Department or to play to the galleries of homefolk. State has yet to learn how to respond to these forays, which frequently are the work of a small minority that can be successfully repulsed. Faced by many such small-band attacks, especially during the past seven years, State persists in believing that Congress is still run from the top. It caters to the leadership; it works the Hill from the foreign policy committee roster. It makes no special effort to play to the silent majority of members who would support its policies and vote in favor of its requests if given sufficient reason to do so and if made to feel part of the process. Instead, the Department still tends to ignore the rank and file, particularly when they make what they perceive to be friendly, constructive suggestions for new directions or put forward unexpected options.

This is unfortunate. In its "constituent services" to members, State's cupboard is bare of the sorts of goodies and favors that other executive departments can distribute to win members' support. The one "goody" State has at its disposal is information. Nevertheless, it still fails to exploit this opportunity for "outreach" to congressional offices. It publishes little in sufficient quantities and of broad enough public interest even to warrant members arranging a courtesy distribution to their districts. It eschews public information programs. It prefers to manage its own public relations rather than to reach the voters through the legislators.

Nor does State do much to encourage the growth of cooperative personal working relations between its policymakers and the legislators. Every reply to a member of Congress, for example—except for "star" mail to VIPs in the congressional leadership, which is personally signed by the secretary—is signed by the head of the Congressional Liaison Office rather than by the official responsible for administering the policy in question. This is, perhaps, the most counterproductive rule currently governing departmental behavior: it keeps members needlessly but deliberately at arm's-distance from those very persons with whom they ought to be on an informal network. And in a member's office, the staff is left either to accept the reply or to try to track down its real source within the Department so that further questions can be put to clarify the response.

There is little merit to a policy that prohibits presidentially appointed assistant secretaries and their immediate deputies—those with the real substantive power and responsibility—from signing their own bureau's correspondence with the Hill. If State wants a centralized censor to insure policy coordination and "appropriateness" of messages to Congress, the Liaison Office could be empowered to clear each draft communication. In any case, it is irrational to allow the highly structured internal regimentation that is so characteristic of the Foreign Service Corps to permeate and jeopardize bureaus' and desk officers' relations with Congress.

A dangerously common assumption in State is that Congress' questions about foreign policy constitute interference in the normal operations of the Department and in the conduct of foreign affairs. Questions are seldom regarded as helpful, even though they play the useful role of early warning signals indicating those issues that are likely to become politicized. Congress is simply not considered a partner in the foreign relations process. In part, this is because State does not perceive Congress to represent the whole of the American people, but only the sum of its constituency parts. Thus, State prefers to use the presidency as its exclusive pipeline to the people. Where legitimacy is at issue, State hangs its claim on the plebiscitary presidency. In this it errs gravely; for if it looked to Congress to reflect the sentiments of the people, it would understand the need to seek prior approval and engage in prior consultations before embarking on new or altered foreign policy directions.

If the bureaucracy sees little political reason to consult the people by consulting Congress, it likewise perceives no legal obligation to consult, despite language mandating consultation in various laws such as the War Powers resolution. As typified by the *Mayaguez* incident, State simply "notifies" Congress or briefs the leadership once a course of action has been chosen: prior consultation is presumed unthinkable. Foreign Service Officers, busy preparing option papers for their principals, cannot fathom opening that process to the chaos of congressional participation. Thus, "consultation" always seems to come after the choices have already been made.

In more recent Congresses, it appears that the foreign policy process sometimes incorporates feedback, at least from the committee and party leadership. Should this become institutionalized—by habit or by rule—it would be a healthy shift to a more open and more responsive foreign policy process. However, consultation solely with members of the foreign affairs committees and with the party leadership presents the risk of cooption. An exclusive relationship between State and a handful of members would simply replicate the collaborative committee-agency alliances that characterized Congress-bureaucracy relations during the first decade of the Vietnam War. When members perceive their leaders and key committee members as captives of the executive branch, they cease to pay much attention to them.

Admittedly, foreign policy cannot be made by 535 "secretaries of state" on the Hill. Most do not in the least covet the job. But most feel some responsibility to their voters, whose interest in foreign policy is much greater—and less parochial—than it used to be (or than State thinks it is). If this makes government less clubby, more complex, so be it. Any difficult foreign policy choice must reckon with public controversy and must be able to withstand public scrutiny.

What Congress wants is an enhanced ability to evaluate and question executive performance. Understandably, the tendency, currently, to sharpen its tools for review is not well received by the foreign policy bureaucracy: it would be irrational for a bureaucracy jealous of its own autonomy willingly to furnish its potential critics with information that could be used to challenge policy choices that have already been made after thorough review of the options by expert managers. But it is at least as improbable that Congress will any longer abandon its quest for information and consultation. This poses the dilemma and sharpens the adversary relationship. If the *tight-fisted management of the flow of information* from the State Department persists, there will be a serious lack of verified information from State in most congressional offices, and that, in turn, insures that some members will play to inflamed public reaction with informed equanimity. The days of unquestioned congressional docility are over, which means that State, like all other executive departments, must yield a little to the younger, better-educated, and more activist legislators. The only question is whether State will compromise or will be compromised.

So far, the Department seems to prefer being compromised, so they can have the satisfaction of railing against the venality of their tormentors. For example, since single-issue politics have come to command the national attention, more than seventy single-issue riders have been tacked onto bills affecting foreign policy. Congressional distrust of the State Department is at the heart of these efforts to constrain State's autonomy. Legislative riders have proven to be the only sure way that members with narrow views or particular concerns can have a voice in making foreign policy. In many instances, these particular concerns are not shared by a majority of the members, yet they succeed in roll call votes precisely because most members have some specific "pet" interest in a foreign policy matter, and most have come to the conclusion, on the basis of personal experience and group perception, that they do not get a fair hearing or serious consideration in Foggy Bottom. The result is that members express their personal frustration by supporting one another's hobbyhorses, even when they have doubts.

The State Department's management of the flow of information to Congress is self-serving. It is designed to cast an aura of privileged knowledge—thereby reserving for State the wisdom to make sound policy judgments. Hence, Congress must rely on its own synthesis of popular information to choose from among policy alternatives or to react to State Department actions. Often, Congress is easily persuaded to follow the lead of a few vocal members on a single topic. State's broad-gauge view not having been disseminated, often and frequently, its policies fall under the sharp attack of narrow interests.

When foreign policy matters directly affect constituency pocketbooks, they become highly spirited contests between arrogant policymakers and instrumental politicians. One example is the implementation of the two-hundred-mile fisheries conservation zone on March 1, 1977, which was my direct responsibility as assistant secretary of state for oceans, international environmental, and scientific affairs.

In this case, State was viewed as dragging its feet in enforcing a congressionally initiated law. State had fought its enactment, so it was natural that it would be suspected of deliberately frustrating its enforcement. As a result, each of our decisions not to seize certain foreign (mostly Soviet) vessels fishing illegally within the two-hundred-mile zone were loudly and vigorously denounced by members from the affected coastal states. I was summoned to appear before both houses to explain our reticence. Members with fishing constituencies—for example, Senators Magnuson, Kennedy, Pell, and Stevens—took turns to excoriate the Department for interfering in a police enforcement matter, which Congress had specifically delegated to the Department of Commerce. What annoyed them most was the belief that we were not only operating on the basis of a policy that ran against the intent of the legislation but that we were doing so on the basis of a secret order that Congress was not allowed to see. The House Merchant Marine and Fisheries Committee minced no words in condemning our reliance on secret orders giving the State Department—not Commerce—final authority over the seizure of foreign fishing vessels. Bombarded from all sides, we were fortunate enough to win a concession from within the bureaucracy: the orders were revised and, more important, were released to the public.

In another widespread misperception, State Department officials are frequently viewed by members of Congress as apologists for their foreign clientele. State is commonly expected to place the protection of foreign governments above the defense of American constituent interests. In part this misperception, too, is the result of executive secrecy. Congress will generally accept State's generosity to foreign governments so long as it satisfies a compelling national interest—such as military necessity, the balance of trade, energy supplies, or keeping democracy strong and its concomitant, fighting communism. When our national interest is served, Congress will advocate economic assistance and preferential treatment, even in the face of gross violations of human rights—as happened in Iran under the shah and as continues in those Third World nations to whom we sell chemicals banned in our own country as hazardous to human health. However, members must be satisfied that "parochial" (i.e., voters') interests have been balanced carefully against national and international concerns. If the decision to punish Russia for its invasion of Afghanistan by banning wheat sales is the result of a thorough examination of all other options, and if the grain farmers and their representatives are convinced that the cost to them has been taken sympathetically into account, then the nation and the Congress will rally to the cause despite their doubts and regardless of the burden imposed on some. But the process of considering other options and of weighing costs and benefits too often takes place behind the facade of executive secrecy, so that it is only the bare decision that makes its appearance on the public stage. When that happens, it is inevitable, and probably healthy, that Congress should perform the public function of assessing alternatives, costs, and benefits as part of the process of educating and legitimizing the final choice.

In this process, both sides should realize that there are few devils and even fewer saints: there are merely differences of perspective and function. Nor are there nearly so many frozen postures and fixed positions as each side appears to detect in the other. For example, the policy of stressing human rights as a vital component in U.S. foreign policy originated with Congress and is generally still stressed—sometimes it appears excessively stressed—by members. But occasionally the State Department speaks as the guardian of human rights in pitched battle against Congress. In the debate over hunting restrictions for the bowhead whale, for example, State and Congress sparred over the weight to be given to the Alaskan Eskimos' native rights. Although the bowhead whale has long been considered an endangered species, both the International Whaling Commission and the U.S. Marine Mammals Act have exempted it from limitations on hunting by Alaskan Eskimos. When the International Whaling Commission in 1977 voted to ban all bowhead killing because of the repeated failure of the U.S. government to regulate the hunt and to prevent reckless killing, members of Congress demanded that the State Department refrain from defending the Eskimos' native rights. Congress' argument with State—specifically with OES—was based on an environmentalist view that tolerated no exception. Ultimately, however, State's view prevailed—and a modest hunt continues today under U.S. regulation. In this case, the environmentalist lobby, with roots broadly implanted all over the country, moved Congress to fight for the life of the whale rather than for the cultural and human rights of the Eskimo people, whose constituency was limited to a part of one state. The State Department, on the other hand, was willing to try to persuade members that the livelihood of the Eskimos deserved special consideration, even at some cost in political support and in environmental quality. That State succeeded was due to its willingness to concede that there were no good guys or bad guys in this contest, only differing perspectives to be respected, examined thoughtfully, and, if possible, reconciled. The environmentalist concerns of legislators were not dismissed as venal toadying to parochial voter groups but as a proper and serious manifestation of the democratic process. By the Department's willingness to consult, to share both its information and its own ambivalences, it was able to achieve through cooperation and accommodation what might easily have been frustrated by a congressional rider.

Within the foreign policy establishment, the most compelling claim against Congress has been that parochial, electoral interests inhibit members from arriving at considered, prudential foreign policy decisions. This misperception has led the executive to embrace the idea that the best foreign policy is a nonpartisan or bipartisan one. Politics, it is argued, stops at the water's edge. Foreign policy should be played as a game of follow the leader—or, if the other party's top officials can be persuaded to join in, as a game of follow the leaders. This guiding principle is invalid and counterproductive. It pretends that democracy is not as applicable to foreign as to domestic affairs when it is increasingly obvious that the two are frequently sides of the same coin. It focuses on bipartisanship—alliance between party leaders in support of presidential policy—when the concept of "party," if not of "party leadership," has become almost meaningless in a Congress in which autonomous members owe their loyalty first to the voters they represent and, second, to loose bloc coalitions that usually cut across party lines. Worst of all, the notion of a nonpolitical or bipartisan foreign policy leads to a misperception of the tactics necessary to effective presidential leadership. Thus, in many instances, lack of consultation with the Hill results from the mistaken belief that foreign policy made by a president with the blessing of a few senior statesmen of both parties can withstand attack from those in Congress who are habitual obstructionists, self-seeking publicity hounds, and spineless creatures of the politically expedient. It is folly to believe, as many in the top echelons of State and White House staff sincerely do, that good foreign policy necessarily stands above the pressures of domestic politics and constituent interests. Politics is the art of reconciling and educating, not of avoiding, those interests.

So long as this view goes unchallenged within the State Department, Congress will continue to scramble anarchically for a voice in foreign policymaking. Foreign assistance bills will continue to be riddled with riders. Members will continue to exploit changes in policy and crisis situations for political mileage. Foreign policy, in the long run, will suffer: it will go undefended by responsible members who feel they don't know enough to come to its defense; it will tend to be challenged out of ignorance and uninformed passion; and it will continue to confront ineffectively the moral and economic constraints imposed by domestic priorities. The least democratic bureaucracy will continue to govern the most dangerous branch of American public policy.

Part II
The Struggle for Control of Foreign Policy

5

Congressional Veto in the Conduct of Foreign Policy

Professor Bernard Schwartz

I N THE NOW CLASSIC Steel Seizure Case,[1] Justice Jackson stressed the fact that the power at issue there touched the internal economy of the country. It was turned inward, not because of rebellion, but because of a lawful economic struggle between industry and labor. A different situation, said Jackson, is presented where governmental authority is turned against the outside world for the security of our society.[2] From the beginning of the republic, it has been recognized that federal power over external affairs is different, both in origin and in essential character, from that over internal affairs. As the Supreme Court has put it, "That there are differences between them, and that those differences are fundamental, may not be doubted."[3]

Do the differences referred to affect the power of Congress to control executive action? More specifically, is the exercise of congressional oversight authority through the so-called legislative veto (under which executive action may be annulled by resolution of one or both houses) limited to executive action that affects internal affairs, or may it also be exercised over action that affects foreign affairs?

These are the questions to which this paper is devoted. We shall first trace the development of the legislative veto, as well as its recent use in statutes dealing with the conduct of foreign policy.

There will then be a discussion of the constitutional issue, both
with regard to the legislative veto generally and its use to control
foreign policy matters. If increased use and burgeoning interest
are indicative, the legislative veto technique may be an idea whose
time has come. This chapter will seek to determine whether that
should be true for external as well as internal affairs.

DEVELOPMENT OF LEGISLATIVE VETO

As a starting point, it should be pointed out that it is unfortunate
that the term "veto" has come to be used to describe congressional
review of executive action by resolution. The term has acquired a
pejorative connotation, which implies infringement on presidential
veto power. Yet, as Justice White has indicated, the congressional
power to disapprove is not at all equivalent to legislation and hence
has nothing to do with the president's veto power.[4] Congressional
annulment power is a technique designed to meet Woodrow Wilson's criticism: "it is quite evident that the means which Congress
has of controlling the departments and exercising the searching
oversight at which it aims are limited and defective."[5] The increasing use of the legislative veto is a direct reflection of the growing
interest in more adequate legislative oversight.

Congressional use of the legislative veto begins with the executive reorganization provisions of the Legislative Appropriation Act
of 1932.[6] A recent article tracing the history of the device contains
the heading: "Blame It All on Hoover?"[7] That is hardly fair. Although the 1932 statute was passed at the request of President
Hoover, who sought authority to reorganize executive departments
and agencies, it was Congress that inserted the legislative veto
provision as a check on the broad powers granted.[8] The statute
provided that Congress could disapprove any presidential reorganization plan by resolution of either house.[9]

Since 1932 Congress has been willing to delegate reorganization
power to the president only on condition that the law contain a
legislative veto provision. The Reorganization Acts of 1939, 1945,
1949, and 1977[10] all provided that presidential reorganization

plans were not to become effective for a stated period during which they could be disapproved by Congress—under the Acts of 1939 and 1945 by concurrent resolution of the two houses[11] and under the Acts of 1949 and 1977, by a resolution passed by a majority of either house.[12]

Although employment of the legislative veto began in the reorganization field, Congress soon used it in other areas. According to a 1976 report of the House Committee on the Judiciary, legislative veto provisions "have been included in federal legislation at least 183 times in 126 different acts of Congress in the last 43 years."[13]

A 1976 list compiled by the Library of Congress shows how pervasive the legislative veto technique has become. According to it, legislative veto provisions are contained in federal statutes dealing with the following subjects:

Military Services and National Defense
Public Works and Buildings
Interior Affairs
Foreign Affairs
National Aeronautics and Space Administration
Executive Reorganization
Agricultural Matters
Atomic Energy
Immigration
National Science Foundation
Education
Transportation
Stockpile and Surplus Disposal
District of Columbia
Budget and Taxation
Labor Relations and Private Pensions
Economic Regulation
General Government and Miscellaneous[14]

The list reflects the widespread congressional use of the legislative veto. The statutes included in it cover virtually the whole range of executive and administrative action, from presidential employment of the armed forces abroad[15] or impoundment of funds[16] to plans for improvement of Pennsylvania Avenue between the White House and Capitol Hill.[17] Of particular significance is the growing use of the legislative veto technique by recent Congresses. Almost all the federal statutes containing legislative veto provisions were enacted during the past decade.

These statutes indicate how inaccurate it is to regard the legislative veto as an occasional congressional device, employed primarily in the reorganization field. On the contrary, Congress has been moving toward development of the veto as a major instrument of oversight. Its effort culminated in an attempt to establish a general system of congressional review of rules and regulations.

H.R. 12,048, the Administrative Rule Making Reform Act, was introduced in the Ninety-fourth Congress. It provided that any federal agency promulgating a rule must transmit copies to the secretary of the Senate and the clerk of the House. Rules would not become effective if disapproved by a concurrent resolution of both houses within ninety days or by a resolution of one house within sixty days that is not disapproved by the other house within thirty days thereafter. Either house could also require that an agency reconsider a rule.

The House Judiciary Committee approved the bill. Although the committee's report acknowledged that the complexity of modern society made broad delegations of rulemaking power necessary, it also insisted that "this very reality requires that Congress have a practical means to disapprove regulations or require their reconsideration in certain instances in a deliberate and reasonable manner. . . . In the judgment of the committee this supervision is the responsibility of elected representatives of the people. [The proposed bill] will provide the Congress with an effective means for supervision of rulemaking activity."[18] H.R. 12,048 was voted on in the House on September 21, 1976. The vote was 265 to 135 for the bill.[19] However, the bill failed to pass by 2 votes because it was brought to a vote under an expedited procedure requiring approval by two thirds of the voting members.

Bills similar to H.R. 12,048 have been introduced in more recent Congresses. Of particular importance is a bill providing for congressional review of rules and regulations introduced in the

Senate.[20] At a Senate hearing held for the first time on the matter, senators from both parties testified and spoke in support of the bill.[21]

CONGRESSIONAL VETO IN
FOREIGN AFFAIRS LAWS

Among the subjects enumerated in the Library of Congress list, to which reference has already been made, is that of foreign affairs. Indeed, in a later part of the Library of Congress study, where pre-1976 statutes providing for congressional review are catalogued according to primary subject matter, twenty-two statutes are listed that deal with foreign affairs.[22] Statutes providing for congressional review in only three other subject areas (military services and defense;[23] public works and buildings;[24] and interior affairs[25]) are more numerous.

The large number of statutes relating to foreign affairs that provide for congressional review indicates that the technique of direct legislative review of executive action has not been confined to internal affairs. On the contrary, the legislative veto has increasingly found its way into recent statutes relating to foreign policy.

It should, however, be borne in mind that statutes providing for direct congressional review of foreign policy are concentrated almost exclusively in the areas of foreign assistance and foreign trade. Of the twenty-two pre-1976 statutes whose primary subject matter is foreign affairs listed by the Library of Congress study, ten involve foreign assistance, seven foreign trade, and only one each deal with educational exchange, the Export-Import Bank, departmental personnel protection, civilian personnel in Sinai, and war powers.[26] Of these, only the last two may arguably be said to encroach on an area where the president possesses primary constitutional authority. In 1976, 1977, and 1978, fourteen statutes were enacted dealing with foreign affairs that provide for congressional review. Of these, ten involve foreign assistance or trade, and one each deal with regulations governing collisions at sea, the Export-Import Bank, foreign intelligence electronic surveillance, and expenditures for peacekeeping forces in the Middle East. Even the last of these, since it involves the power of the purse, deals with a matter over which Congress has direct constitutional responsibility.

In addition, it should be noted that, of the twenty-two pre-1976 laws listed by the Library of Congress study as providing for congressional review of executive action in the field of foreign policy, and the fourteen enacted in 1976–78, only half make use of the legislative veto technique—authorizing annulment of executive action by concurrent resolution[27] or resolution of either house.[28] All but one of the other statutes provide for lesser forms of congressional review, involving a requirement of reporting to Congress or congressional committees.[29]

At the same time, it cannot be denied that the provisions for congressional review in these statutes relating to foreign affairs do permit Congress to play a direct role in the formation and implementation of the nation's foreign policy. This is particularly true of the statutes that use the legislative veto technique. They authorize Congress to override foreign policy decisions, elevating the legislature to the virtual role of hierarchical superior of the secretary of state and the president so far as the matters covered by them are concerned.

Nor should it be assumed that the legislative veto under these statutes can be exercised over only inconsequential matters. The opposite is true; some of the executive acts subject to congressional veto may involve important foreign policy decisions. Thus, a presidential decision to employ the armed forces abroad (already severely limited in duration by the substantive provisions of the War Powers resolution) may be overridden by a concurrent resolution directing removal of such forces.[30] Similarly, despite a presidential determination that U.S. personnel are necessary to monitor an early warning system in the Sinai, their removal may be ordered by concurrent resolution.[31] Other legislative veto provisions empower Congress to overrule presidential decisions on military and other assistance abroad, particularly to countries that may grossly violate human rights.[32]

THE CONSTITUTIONAL ISSUE:
INTERNAL AFFAIRS

Attorney General Opinions. During the hearings on the 1977 Reorganization Act, Attorney General Bell stated that the proposed statute's legislative veto was constituional. The attorney general limited his opinion to the narrow context of the reorganization statute and did not approve "the constitutionality of the procedure of Congressional disapproval of executive action by resolution in other statutes."[33] Instead, the attorney general stated that "Congressional action outside the check of the Presidential veto should be constitutionally suspect as it carries the potential for shifting the balance of power to Congress and thus permitting the legislative branch to dominate the executive."[34]

Other critics of the legislative veto have not distinguished between its use in the Reorganization Acts and in other statutes. They assert that all applications of the technique of annulment of executive or administrative action by congressional resolution are unconstitutional. Their principal contention is that the legislative veto violates the veto clause of the Constitution,[35] which requires that "Every Order, Resolution, or Vote to which the Concurrence of the Senate and House of Representatives may be necessary," as well as every bill passed by Congress, be presented to the president for his veto before it can become law. They argue that when Congress disapproves executive action such as a reorganization plan or an agency regulation, it exercises legislative power in which the president must participate. As the argument was recently summarized by Attorney General Bell, "[i]f a statute authorizing control by Congress over executive action by later resolution has the effect of evading the constitutional safeguards of concurrence of both Houses and Presidential veto, then it violates article I, section 7 of the Constitution."[36] Can Congress, by use of the legislative veto, enact what amounts to veto-proof legislation?

Until recently, there had been no federal judicial answer to this question. The question had, however, been dealt with by two attorneys general, who reached opposite results.

In 1932, after delegating reorganization power to President Hoover subject to veto by resolution, Congress considered another bill making tax refunds of over $20,000 subject to prior disapproval by the Joint Committee on Internal Revenue Taxation.[37] In a 1933 opinion,[38] Attorney General Mitchell stated that the portion of the bill providing for committee veto of executive acts was unconstitutional. Mitchell referred disapprovingly to the congressional veto power over executive reorganization plans, asserting that "[t]he attempt to give to either House of Congress, by action which is not legislation, power to disapprove administrative acts, raises a grave question as to the validity of the entire provision in the Reorganization Act of June 30, 1932, for Executive reorganization of governmental functions."[39]

As a memorandum on the Reorganization Act of 1949 submitted to a Senate committee by Attorney General Tom C. Clark pointed out, Mitchell's statement on the 1932 reorganization statute "was obiter dictum."[40] Certainly, Mitchell's animadversions did not have practical effect, either upon the operation of the 1932 law or upon subsequent delegations of reorganization power. President Roosevelt signed the next important Reorganization Act[41] without questioning its congressional veto provisions. Moreover, later presidents have not questioned more recent reservations of veto power over executive reorganizations.

The Mitchell opinion was repudiated in the 1949 memorandum by Attorney General Clark, which approved the legislative veto provision of the bill that became the 1949 Reorganization Act.[42] Disavowing the conclusion of the Mitchell opinion, the Clark memorandum expressly approved statutory provisions for invalidation of reorganization plans by concurrent resolution: "[I]nsofar as it intimated the unconstitutionality of the reorganization provisions of the Act of June 30, 1932, [the Mitchell opinion] was based upon an unsound premise, namely, that the Congress in disapproving a reorganization plan is exercising a legislative function in a nonlegislative manner." The 1949 memorandum strongly affirmed the constitutionality of the legislative veto provision. The key portion of the memorandum stated: "There would appear to be no reason why the Executive may not be given express statutory authority to communicate to the Congress his intention to perform a given Executive function unless the Congress by some stated means indicates its disapproval. The Reorganization Acts of 1939 and 1945 gave recognition to this principle. The President, in asking Congress to pass the instant reorganization bill, is following the pattern established by those acts, namely by taking the position that if the Congress will delegate to him authority to reorganize the Government, he will undertake to submit all reorganization plans to the Congress and to put no such plan into effect if the Congress indicates its disapproval thereof. In this procedure there is no question involved of the Congress taking legislative action beyond its initial passage of the Reorganization Act. Nor is there any question involved of abdication by the Executive of his Executive functions to the Congress. It is merely a case where the Executive and the Congress act in cooperation for the benefit of the entire Government and the Nation." [43]

Election Act Cases. A 1976 report to the National Conference of State Legislatures on the constitutionality of the legislative veto states: "The [conference] has found no case law resolving this issue." [44] This statement that no case law existed may have been accurate in 1976. More recently, however, the legislative veto was challenged for the first time in the federal courts. *Buckley* v. *Valeo* [45] concerned the constitutionality of the Federal Election Campaign Act, as amended in 1974, [46] which established the Federal Election Commission (FEC) and gave it substantial rulemaking powers. It provided, however, that FEC regulations could be disapproved within thirty days by resolution of either house. The Supreme Court referred to this legislative veto provision as "but the most recent episode in a long tug of war between the Executive and Legislative Branches of the Federal Government respecting the permissible extent of legislative involvement in rulemaking." [47] But it did not reach the merits of the challenge to the legislative veto, holding that the manner of appointment of FEC members was unconstitutional and precluded the commission from exercising its rulemaking powers.

In a separate and highly significant opinion in *Buckley,* Justice White addressed the merits of the constitutional issue. His opinion is important enough to be quoted extensively: "I am also of the view that the otherwise valid regulatory power of a properly created independent agency is not rendered constitutionally infirm, as violative of the President's veto power, by a statutory provision subjecting agency regulations to disapproval by either House of Congress. For a bill to become law it must pass both Houses and be signed by the President or be passed over his veto. Also, 'Every Order, Resolution, or Vote to which the Concurrence of the Senate and House of Representatives may be necessary . . .' is likewise subject to the veto power. Under §438(c) the FEC's regulations are subject to disapproval; but for a regulation to become effective, neither House need approve it, pass it, or take any action at all with respect to it. The regulation becomes effective by nonaction. This no more invades the President's powers than does a regulation not required to be laid before Congress. Congressional influence over the substantive content of agency regulation may be enhanced, but I would not view the power of either House to disapprove as equivalent to legislation or to an order, resolution or vote requiring the concurrence of both Houses. . . . [I]n the light of history and modern reality, the provision for congressional disapproval of agency regulations does not appear to transgress the constitutional design, at least where the President has agreed to legislation establishing the disapproval procedure or the legislation has been passed over his veto. It would be considerably different if Congress itself purported to adopt and propound regulations by the action of both Houses. But here no action of either House is required for the agency rule to go into effect and the veto power of the President does not appear to be implicated."[48]

Justice White's reasoning appears sound. As he points out, if congressional action under the legislative veto technique is legislative in the sense the veto clause anticipates, the same is true of administrative action under the rulemaking power.

After *Buckley* v. *Valeo*, Congress amended the Federal Election Campaign Act to correct the constitutional defect in the appointment procedure,[49] but left the act's legislative veto provision unchanged. A subsequent suit challenging the validity of the veto provision was dismissed by the United States Court of Appeals for the District of Columbia Circuit on grounds of standing and ripeness.[50] The Supreme Court affirmed without opinion.[51] Neither tribunal reached the merits of the constitutional claim.

In the U.S. Court of Appeals, however, Judge MacKinnon, dissenting, urged the invalidity of the legislative veto provision. Judge MacKinnon stated that "the one-house veto . . . is a completely different method of accomplishing a legislative result by a congressional procedure *not* authorized by the Constitution; i.e., by one house instead of by two houses and the President." The one-house veto, in MacKinnon's view, "clearly violates the constitutional requirement that legislation should be passed by both houses and be signed by the President."[52]

Judge MacKinnon explicitly disagreed with Justice White's opinion in *Buckley*, asserting that White's approach "ignore[s] the actual situation created in Congress"[53] by the Election Act's veto provision. In Judge MacKinnon's view, Congress' failure to veto an FEC regulation was the legislative equivalent for each house of enacting legislation. To assume with Justice White that a regulation becomes effective without "any [legislative] action at all with respect to it"[54] is, according to Judge MacKinnon, to assume that Congress will act irresponsibly and fail to consider regulations submitted to it pursuant to a legislative veto statute.

The author respectfully believes that Judge MacKinnon misunderstands the actual operation of the legislative veto. Experience with provisions for legislative annulment of executive acts demonstrates that the full legislature will not consider every act laid before it. Instead, the house concerned directs attention only to executive acts questioned by committees or members when resolutions to disapprove are actually filed. Thus, Justice White correctly asserts that "no action of either House is required for the agency rule to go into effect."[55]

Salary Act Cases. Another line of legislative veto cases involves federal employee salaries. The Federal Salary Act of 1967[56] authorized the president to adjust federal employee compensation, subject to annulment by either house of Congress. This legislative veto provision was challenged in two cases after Congress disapproved by resolution salary increases recommended by the president. In *McCorkle* v. *United States,*[57] the district court dismissed the constitutional challenge, stating only, "I think as the single house veto has been provided for here, it is constitutional." The United States Court of Appeals for the Fourth Circuit affirmed without reaching the constitutional issue.[58]

In *Atkins* v. *United States,*[59] 140 federal judges challenged the constitutionality of the act's legislative veto provision. The majority of the Court of Claims held the provision constitutional. The majority opinion has been characterized as "well written and reasoned" by a recent critic of the legislative veto.[60] The court's reasoning resembles Justice White's view that congressional action pursuant to the legislative veto provision is not legislative action subject to the requirements of the veto clause: "We reach this decision by virtue of the simple fact that the single House, in voting by a majority to block the otherwise automatic effectiveness of the President's recommendations, is not doing anything for which the Constitution requires the concurrence of both Houses. The single House is certainly not making new law. Plaintiffs seem to think that the House, when it casts its 'veto,' is attempting to make law, which act they define as one that 'repeals, modifies, or amends the law.' However, even accepting that definition for the sake of argument, plaintiffs' view is erroneous, for the one-House veto does not alter the existing law in any fashion, but only preserves the legal *status quo.*"[61]

Moreover, the Court of Claims correctly recognized that the need for effective congressional oversight is relevant in determining the constitutionality of the legislative veto: "[W]hen Congress delegates authority of the kind we have here to a member of the executive branch, the delegation does not convert the authority granted into an irrevocable executive power, because in exercising the delegated functions, the executive officer merely acts as an agent of the legislative branch of the Government. . . . To plaintiffs' argument that Congress cannot meddle once it has delegated power, it may be observed that legislation is itself a form of supervision. Congress has two roles: initial formulation of policy and supervision. The only pertinent question is in what manner Congress can oversee. In this case, whether the answer is by full-fledged statute or by one-House veto, there would be neither a violation of the separation-of-powers principle nor an invalid intrusion on executive power."[62]

Though concurred in by three judges, the dissenting opinion in *Atkins* is weakly reasoned. Its quality can be judged from the following key portion of the opinion: "If it could be assumed *arguendo* that the one-House veto is not legislative in character, then it would have to be a judicial or executive power. Clearly, it is not judicial. If it is neither legislative nor judicial, it is then executive. But neither House nor both Houses nor officials thereof can exercise executive power or functions. . . . It is clear that if the one-House veto is the exercise of executive power or function, it violates the above article of the Constitution, and violates the principle of Separation of Powers of our government."[63]

The dissent's approach is reminiscent of the familiar parlor game: "It is not animal. It is not vegetable. Therefore it must be mineral." One wonders whether it is a proper way to deal with a difficult problem of separation of powers. When a power does not manifestly belong to one of the three branches, it should, in Justice Holmes's phrase, "fall into the indiscriminate residue of matters within legislative control."[64] This approach, which recognizes the existence of equivocal powers which need not be arbitrarily fitted into a procrustean trichotomy, permits the legislature to determine which branch shall exercise such powers.[65]

The overriding need for congressional control of executive power and increasing attempts to meet that need through provisions for legislative review lend support to the validity of the legislative veto. Experience with the legislative veto under the Reorganization Acts demonstrates its substantial contribution to the effectiveness of congressional oversight. The contention of critics who argue that the provision violates the veto clause is unsupported by authority. Indeed, the recent decisions suggest that the weight of authority, as well as experience, validates the legislative veto. The logic of the claim of unconstitutionality rests upon a perverted construction of the separation-of-powers doctrine. Such a construction is neither desirable nor justified at this late date of our administrative law, when we recognize, in the words of Justice Cardozo, that the separation of powers is not a "doctrinaire concept to be made use of with pedantic rigor."[66]

Moreover, consistent application of the view that the legislature cannot be empowered to disapprove executive action because disapproval is the exercise of a power to make laws would destroy the rulemaking powers of executive agencies themselves. Executive agencies are clearly empowered to make law through their rules. Otherwise, how can the legislature be enacting a change in the law through its disapproval power? If that is true, under the rigid separation-of-powers approach, are not delegations of such "lawmaking" powers to the agencies equally invalid? To invoke the separation-of-powers doctrine against the legislative veto is to return to a time when the maxim against the delegation of powers was inexorably applied.[67] There is no more reason today to invalidate delegation of the annulment power to the legislature on separation of powers grounds than to invalidate delegations of the rulemaking power to agencies on a similar basis.

As Justice White and the Court of Claims have noted, legislative disapproval of an executive act is not to be equated with enacting a law. Legislative approval by failure to pass a resolution of disapproval is merely a condition specified in the enabling statute by which the agency exercise of power is governed. It is now beyond dispute that the legislature, in delegating authority, can specify contingencies that must occur before delegated power may be exercised. This approach is applicable to the legislative veto: "The failure of Congress to pass such a concurrent resolution is the contingency upon which the reorganizations take effect. Their taking effect is not because the President orders them. That the taking effect of action legislative in character may be made dependent upon conditions or contingencies is well recognized."[68]

It would be most unfortunate if specious construction of a constitutional doctrine should bar the use of one of the most promising methods of control of executive action. Congress is in a unique position to supervise administrative authority,[69] and the legislative veto can be a valuable tool in this task.

THE CONSTITUTIONAL ISSUE: FOREIGN POLICY

What has just been said relates to the constitutionality of the legislative veto in statutes dealing with internal affairs. Do the same considerations apply to the constitutionality of the legislative veto in statutes dealing with foreign affairs?

An answer to this question should recognize the intent of the framers not to concentrate the power over foreign affairs in any one department. Though the principal theoretical writers of the day were united in the view that foreign affairs must be committed to the executive alone, the framers rejected it. However proper it might be, where the executive magistrate is a hereditary monarch, to commit to him the entire field of external affairs, they felt that it would be unsafe to entrust that field absolutely to an elective magistrate in a republic.[70]

The result is that, while the federal government has both exclusive and plenary power over the subject of foreign affairs, the subject itself is not confided to any one department alone. What the Constitution does, so far as it contains affirmative provisions on the matter, is to divide the field of external relations among the president, the House, and the Senate. As Corwin puts it,[71] the Constitution confers on the president certain powers capable of affecting our external relations, and certain other powers of the same general kind on the Senate, and still other such powers on the House. But it leaves open the question of which of these organs shall have the decisive voice in determining the foreign policy of the nation.

What has just been said, Corwin goes on, is the same thing as saying "that the Constitution, considered only for its affirmative grants of powers capable of affecting the issue, is an invitation to struggle for the privilege of directing American foreign policy."[72] It can hardly be denied that this assertion is true as far as it goes. Throughout the history of the republic, the field of external affairs has been a battleground between the executive and legislative departments. Under our less vigorous presidents, indeed, the primacy in foreign affairs has at times seemed to pass from the White House to the other end of Pennsylvania Avenue. Congressional committees and even individual legislators (particularly members of the upper house) exert an influence on American foreign policy that both amazes and dismays observers abroad.

Yet, although foreign affairs in this country has been a field of contention between the two political branches, few familiar with its history will doubt that the principal advantages in such struggle have been with the president. The president alone is equipped to perform an affirmative role in external affairs—to act as the organ of intercourse between the United States and other nations. His is inevitably the initiative in foreign relations—an initiative he possesses without any restriction whatsoever.[73] If the framers intended to divide the field of foreign affairs between the president and the Congress, the verdict of history has given by far the lion's share to the former.[74]

May we not go further and say that the concept of a constitutional division of power itself in the foreign affairs field is not entirely accurate? The Constitution contemplates a division between the executive and legislative departments—but it is not a division of power. What the organic document does in this field is to divide *power* and *responsibility*. The foreign affairs power is vested in the president; the responsibility to insure against overaudacious executive ventures abroad remains with Congress. The plan of the Constitution is thus to confide the power to conduct external relations to the executive department and, at the same time, to guard it from serious abuse by placing it under the ultimate superintendence of the legislative branch.[75]

If the conception just stated is correct, it supports the constitutionality of the legislative veto as a congressional check in statutes dealing with external affairs. It will, however, be objected that presidential prerogative over foreign policy may not thus constitutionally be restricted by legislative action. The objection was the basis of President Nixon's message vetoing the War Powers resolution of 1973. The veto message protested against the congressional "attempt to take away, by a mere legislative act, authorities which the President has properly exercised under the Constitution for almost 200 years."[76] In particular, Nixon objected to the provision requiring the president to withdraw American forces from hostilities abroad within sixty or ninety days unless Congress provides authorization and the provision for legislative veto, requiring immediate removal of forces if Congress so directs by concurrent resolution. "I believe," Nixon asserted, "that both these provisions are unconstitutional. The only way in which the constitutional powers of a branch of the Government can be altered is by amending the Constitution—and any attempt to make such alterations by legislation alone is clearly without force."[77]

The Nixon assertion overlooks the basic principle that presidential power is subject to statutory limitations. "A statute derogatory to the prerogative," declared one of the king's judges in the seventeenth-century Ship Money Case, "doth not bind the king."[78] The whole system of Anglo-American public law since the expulsion of the Stuarts has been based upon the repudiation of this theory. Even if the president possesses inherent power or prerogative in certain circumstances, when the Congress intervenes and provides by statute that such powers are to be exercised in a particular manner and subject to the limitations and provisions contained in the statute, they can only be so exercised. The supremacy of the statute in such a case is the only principle consistent with a Constitution that provides that all legislative powers have been vested in Congress.

Where Congress has provided a statutory procedure to cover the situation presented, whatever presidential prerogative might otherwise exist must give way. In such a case, there can be no justification for presidential reliance upon inherent power rather than upon the procedure the legislature has provided. When the chief executive acts upon his own in such circumstances, his actions are necessarily incompatible with the will expressed by the Congress. His power is then at its lowest ebb, for any power he might otherwise possess in the premises is countered by the constitutional power of Congress. Courts can sustain presidential power in such a case only by disabling Congress from acting upon the subject. When there is a statute on the subject, presidential power is rendered most vulnerable to attack and in the least favorable of possible constitutional postures.[79]

The president thus may not choose whether he will proceed under whatever prerogative power he may possess or under a statutory procedure enacted to meet the case. Any prerogative power that might otherwise exist must be deemed *pro tanto* suspended by enactment by the legislature of statutory provisions covering the same ground, even though (as in the Steel Seizure Case) they enact a different modus operandi for securing the desired result. Otherwise, what use would there be in imposing statutory limitations if the president could at his pleasure disregard them and fall back on his inherent powers? [80]

The subjection of presidential prerogative to the statute law of the land is the basic restriction upon prerogative in our system and one that insures that executive power in this country will not be absolute in the Stuart sense. As pointed out, the prerogative that his judges recognized in Charles I was not subject to any legislative restriction: "No Act of Parliament can bar a King of his regality." [81] Today, on the contrary, any prerogative the president may possess must yield before a law of Congress. Any presidential action is always subject to revision and disallowance by the legislature. This is a considerable check upon executive prerogative and one lacking in the law in Charles I's time. Whatever prerogative may be conceded in the president, it is wholly subject to the legislative power exercised, in our system, by the elected representatives of the people.

It will, however, be said that the principle of subjection of presidential power to statute must be limited to internal affairs. Yet it is one thing to say that the president has authority, even in the absence of legislative authorization, to conduct the nation's foreign policy. It is quite another to maintain that, in exercising such authority, he may override the provisions of a duly enacted act of Congress. The Constitution, in imposing upon the chief executive the duty to attend to the faithful execution of the laws, does not make an exception for laws relating to foreign affairs. Here, as in other areas of our constitutional law, the authority of the president is one that (to paraphrase Holmes) does not go beyond the laws or permit him to achieve more than Congress sees fit to leave within his power. [82]

There is, of course, very little law on the matter. But there is *some* legal authority which supports the view just advocated. Strictly speaking, it relates to the president's power to direct the armed forces abroad. But if that power is subject to control by statute, the same must be true of the president's foreign affairs power.

That even the president's power as commander in chief abroad is subject to statute was the view taken by Chief Justice Marshall in one of the Supreme Court's first pronouncements upon the powers of the president under the Constitution.[83] In *Little* v. *Barreme*,[84] the Court was confronted with the power of the president to order the seizure on the high seas in 1799 of the *Flying Fish,* a vessel bound from a French port. Marshall's opinion starts by assuming that, in the state of relations then existing between the United States and France,[85] the president might, on his own authority, both as chief executive and as commander in chief, order the seizure of vessels engaged in commerce with France. In this case, however, there was an act of Congress—the so-called Nonintercourse Law of 1799—which dealt with such seizures. "But when it is observed," states Marshall, "that [the act of Congress] gives a special authority to seize on the high seas, and limits that authority to the seizure of vessels bound or sailing *to* a French port, the legislature seems to have prescribed that the manner in which this law shall be carried into execution, was to exclude a seizure of any vessel not bound *to* a French port."[86]

It had been argued that a literal application to only ships sailing to France would defeat much of the purpose of the law and that this justified an executive construction better calculated to give it effect. This argument was rejected. According to Marshall, the president could not vary the unambiguous wording of the statute. The presidential instructions to the naval forces could not "legalize an act which, without those instructions, would have been a plain trespass."[87] As the Court has recently explained it, "Although there was probable cause to believe that the ship was engaged in traffic with the French, the seizure at issue was not among that class of seizures that the Executive had been authorized by statute to effect."[88]

What is of special interest, for the purposes of the present discussion, is that Marshall himself expressly acknowledged that his first inclination in the case had been in favor of drawing a distinction "between acts of civil and those of military officers; and between proceedings within the body of the country and those on the high seas."[89] In his actual decision, as Marshall tells us, he receded from this "first bias of my mind"[90] and held, as we saw, that the president's order was illegal. In other words, the basic principle of subordination of presidential power to a law of the land is followed even though the particular case concerns military, not civil, action, which is taken, not within the body of the country, but beyond its borders.

In referring to *Little* v. *Barreme,* Justice Clark declared, in his concurring opinion in the Steel Seizure Case: "I know of no subsequent holding of this Court to the contrary."[91] Marshall's holding, then, remains a fundamental limitation upon the executive power to protect American rights and interests abroad. In the absence of congressional action, the president may have independent power to use the armed forces beyond our borders. But where the Congress, as in *Little* v. *Barreme,* prescribes specific procedures to deal with a threat to American interests, the president must follow those procedures in meeting such threat.[92] According to Elihu Root, indeed, "Doubtless Congress could by law forbid . . . troops' being sent out of the country."[93] If we carry *Little* v. *Barreme* to its logical conclusion, even in such a case, presidential authority as head of the armed forces should give way to a duly enacted law of the land.

CONSTITUTIONALITY VERSUS DESIRABILITY

The foregoing discussion indicates that the legislative veto is constitutional, even in statutes relating to foreign affairs. If, as *Little* v. *Barreme* suggests, the legislative veto provision in the War Powers resolution is constitutional, it is difficult to see why the same is not true of the other provisions for congressional veto in statutes that affect foreign policy. There is, however, a vital difference between constitutionality and desirability. A law may not violate the

Constitution but still be undesirable as a matter of policy. That the legislative veto is valid as a matter of constitutional law does not necessarily mean that its use as a broadside instrument of foreign policy control is advisable.

In certain areas relating to foreign affairs, the legislative veto technique would clearly be inappropriate. This is true, for example, of the conduct of diplomatic intercourse. It is true that Congress has at times asserted authority in the conduct of diplomacy independent of the executive. Indeed, it has even gone so far as to assert independent recognition authority.[94] Constitutionally speaking, such a congressional attempt must be considered a nullity, in view of the president's legal position as the sole organ of the nation in diplomatic intercourse.[95] Practically speaking, assertion of legislative authority over matters of diplomacy, such as questions of recognition, could lead to disastrous results. A government recognized by Congress, but not by the executive, might be able to recover property in this country, which might directly contravene the president's foreign policy in relation to the country concerned. In the words of the Supreme Court, "No well regulated government has ever sanctioned a principle so unwise and so destructive of national character."[96]

Thus far, Congress has not sought to extend the legislative veto into foreign policy areas, where it would be plainly unsuitable, such as diplomatic intercourse. As already seen, almost all the congressional review provisions in federal statutes that deal with foreign policy involve foreign assistance and foreign trade. These are areas in which Congress can play a legitimate role, both constitutionally and practically. They touch directly upon the power of the purse—the basic legislative birthright in the Anglo-American system. That is true also of congressional review of expenditures for Middle East peacekeeping.[97] Congressional review in statutes relating to educational exchange,[98] the Export-Import Bank,[99] State Department personnel protection,[100] regulations on collisions at sea,[101] and even foreign intelligence surveillance without a court order[102] also fall within areas of legitimate legislative intervention.

The debatable legislative veto provisions in the field of foreign policy, so far as their appropriateness is concerned, are those in the War Powers resolution[103] and the Sinai Early Warning System Agreement resolution.[104] Yet we have learned enough about abuses of the presidential war power to be more tolerant of congressional efforts to assert direct control even here. After all, before the War Powers resolution, the presidential power to wage war had become so far-reaching that it threatened to alter the very constitutional balance. The dominant constitutional fact during the second half of this century has been the commitment of the nation to two major wars on the authority of the president alone.

We can thus conclude that, until now at least, congressional review power over the conduct of foreign policy—even when exercised through legislative veto provisions—has not been abused. In the main, the power has been asserted over the areas of foreign assistance and trade, which fall directly within the congressional constitutional sphere. Where the legislative veto has been used to curb the presidential war power, a strong case can be made that Congress acted in response to executive abuses that, if unchecked, would have fundamentally shifted the constitutional center of gravity. There is, it is true, always a danger that the legislative veto may be extended to areas such as the conduct of diplomacy, where congressional direction would be inappropriate. Thus far, however, the danger in question is more potential than actual.

NOTES

1. *Youngstown Sheet & Tube Co. v. Sawyer*, 343 U.S. 579 (1952).
2. *Id.* at 645.
3. *United States v. Curtiss-Wright Export Corp.*, 299 U.S. 304, 315 (1936).
4. *Buckley v. Valeo*, 424 U.S. 1, 284–6 (1976).
5. Wilson, *Congressional Government* 270 (10th ed., 1894).
6. Act of June 30, 1932, ch. 314, §407, 47 Stat. 414.
7. Keeffe, *The Legislative Veto: Now You See It, Now You Don't* (I), 63 *A.B.A.J.* 1296 (1977).
8. See H.R. Rep. No.1036, 72d Cong., 1st sess.5–6 (1932).
9. Act of June 30, 1932, ch. 314, §407, 47 Stat. 414.
10. Reorganization Act of 1977, 5 U.S.C.A. §§901–912 (West Supp. 1977); Reorganization Act of 1949, ch. 266, 63 Stat. 203; Reorganization

Act of 1945, ch. 582, 59 Stat. 613; Reorganization Act of 1939, ch. 36, 53 Stat. 561.

11. Reorganization Act of 1945, ch. 882, §6, 59 Stat. 616; Reorganization Act of 1939, ch. 36, §5, 53 Stat. 562–63.

12. Reorganization Act of 1977, 5 U.S.C,A. §906 (West Supp. 1977); Reorganization Act of 1949, ch. 226, §6, 63 Stat. 203.

13. H.R. Rep. No. 1014, 94th Cong., 2d sess. 14 (1976).

14. Norton, *Congressional Review, Deferral and Disapproval of Executive Actions: A Summary and an Inventory of Statutory Authority*, Table of Contents (1976).

15. War Powers Resolution, 87 Stat. 555 (1973).

16. Congressional Budget and Impoundment Act, 88 Stat. 297 (1974).

17. Pennsylvania Avenue Development Corporation Act of 1972, 40 U.S.C. §874(d).

18. H.R. Rep. No. 1014, 94th Cong., 2d sess. 7 (1976).

19. 122 *Cong. Rec.* H10, 690 (daily ed., Sept. 21, 1976).

20. S. 104, 96th Cong., 1st sess. For a similar House bill, see H.R. 1776, 96th Cong., 1st sess.

21. The hearing was held by a subcommittee of the Senate Judiciary Committee on July 18, 1979. The proceedings have not yet been published.

22. Norton, *supra*, note 14 at 11.

23. *Ibid.*, listing 28 statutes.

24. *Ibid.*, listing 27 statutes.

25. *Ibid.*, listing 24 statutes dealing with the Department of the Interior and Energy.

26. *Ibid.*

27. Assistance to Greece and Turkey Act, 61 Stat. 103 (1947); Trade Agreement Extension Act, 72 Stat. 673 (1958); Foreign Assistance Act 75 Stat. 444 (1961); War Powers Resolution, 87 Stat. 555 (1973); Amendments to the Mineral Leasing Act of 1920, 87 Stat. 582 (1973); Department of Defense Authorizations, 88 Stat. 399 (1974); Foreign Assistance Act, 88 Stat. 1795 (1974); International Broadcasting Board Authorization, 89 Stat. 509 (1975); Sinai Early Warning System Agreement Resolution, 89 Stat. 572 (1975); International Security Assistance and Arms Export Control Act, P.L. 94-329 (1976); Export Administration Amendments, P.L. 95-52 (1977); International Navigational Rules Act, P.L. 95-75 (1977); International Security Assistance Act, P.L. 95-92 (1977); Nuclear Non-Proliferation Act, 95 Stat. 120 (1978); Outer Continental Shelf Lands Act Amendments, 92 Stat. 629 (1978); International Security Assistance Act, 92 Stat. 730 (1978).

28. International Development and Food Assistance Act, 89 Stat. 857 (1975); International Development and Food Assistance Act, 92 Stat. 937 (1978).

29. Reporting to Congress: Mutual Education and Cultural Exchange Act, 75 Stat. 527 (1961); Foreign Assistance Appropriations Act, 84 Stat. 5 (1970); Foreign Assistance Act, 86 Stat. 20 (1972); Export-Import Bank Act Amendments, P.L. 95-143 (1977).

Reporting to committees: Foreign Aid Appropriations, 76 Stat. 1163 (1962); Foreign Assistance Act, 87 Stat. 714 (1973); Foreign Assistance Appropriations, 97 Stat. 1049 (1974); Trade Act, 88 Stat. 1978 (1975); Foreign Assistance Appropriations, 89 Stat. 17 (1975); Foreign Relations Authorization, 89 Stat. 770 (1975); International Development and Food Assistance Act, P.L. 95-88 (1977); Foreign Assistance and Related Programs Appropriations Act, P.L. 95-148 (1977); Agricultural Trade Act, 92 Stat. 1685 (1978); Foreign Intelligence Surveillance Act, 92 Stat. 1783 (1978).

See also Foreign Assistance and Related Programs Appropriations, P.L. 94-330 (1976) (prior approval of appropriations committees of both houses required).

30. War Powers Resolutions, 87 Stat. 555 (1973).

31. Sinai Early Warning Agreement Resolution, 89 Stat. 572 (1975).

32. E.g., International Development and Food Assistance Act, 89 Stat. 857 (1975); International Security Assistance and Arms Export Control Act, P.L. 94-329 (1976).

33. *Extension of Reorganization Authority of the President.* Hearings on H.R. 5045 Before the Subcomm. on Legislation and National Security of the House Comm. on Government Operations, 95th Cong., 1st sess. 40 (1977).

34. H.R. Rep. No. 105, 95 Cong., 1st sess. 10, reprinted in [1977] *U.S. Code Cong. & Ad. News* 491, 500.

35. U.S Const. Art. I, §7.

36. H.R. Rep. No.105, 95th Cong., 1st sess. 10, reprinted in [1977] *U.S. Code Cong. & Ad. News* 491, 500.

37. H.R. 13,975, 72d Cong., 2d sess. (1933).

38. 37 Op. Att'y Gen. 56 (1933).

39. *Id.* at 63–64.

40. S. Rep. No. 232, 81st Cong., 1st sess. 19 (1949).

41. Reorganization Act of 1939, ch. 36, 53 Stat. 561.

42. See S. Rep. No. 232, 81st Cong., 1st sess. 19 (1949).

43. *Id.* at 20.

44. *Legislative Review of Administrative Regulations, A Preliminary Report of the Legislative Improvement and Modernization Committee to the National Conference of State Legislatures Business Meeting* 2 (Sept. 3, 1976).

45. 424 U.S. 1 (1976).

46. 2 U.S.C. §§431–56 (Supp. V. 1975).

47. 424 U.S. at 140 n. 176.

48. *Id.* at 284–6.

49. The new statute provides for presidential appointment of all FEC members. 2 U.S.C.A. §437c(a)(1) (West Cum. Supp. 1977).

50. *Clark v. Valeo,* 559 F.2d 642 (D.C. Cir.1977).

51. *Clark v. Kimmitt,* 431 U.S. 950 (1977).

52. 559 F.2d 681 n. 4, 683–184.

53. *Id.* at 685.

54. *Buckley v. Valeo,* 424 U.S. at 284.

55. *Id.* at 286.

56. 2 U.S.C. §359 (1970).

57. No. 75-317-A (E.D. Va. Mar. 16, 1976). There was no written opinion by Judge Bryan.

58. *McCorkle v. United States,* 559 F.2d 1258, 1262–63 (4th Cir. 1977).

59. *Atkins v. United States,* 556 F.2d 1028 (Ct. Cl. 1977).

60. Keeffe, *The Legislative Veto: Now You See It, Now You Don't* (II), 63 *A.B.A.J.* 1474, 1475 (1977).

61. 556 F.2d at 1063.

62. *Id.* at 1068.

63. *Id.* at 1081.

64. *Springer v. Philippine Islands,* 277 U.S. 189, 212 (1928).

65. See *Wayman v. Southard,* (10 Wheat.) 1, 42 (U.S. 1825), in which Chief Justice Marshall recognized this more than 150 years ago.

66. *Panama Refining Co. v. Ryan,* 293 U.S. 388, 440 (1935).

67. See Schwartz, *Administrative Law* 33 (1976).

68. H.R. Rep. No. 120, 76th Cong., 1st sess. 6 (1939).

69. H.R. Rep. No. 1014, 94th Cong., 2d sess. 8 (1976).

70. *The Federalist* No. 75.

71. Corwin, *The President: Office and Powers* 171 (4th ed., 1957).

72. *Ibid.*

73. Wilson, *Constitutional Government in the United States* 77 (1917 ed.).

74. Compare Corwin, *loc. cit., supra,* note 71.

75. Story, *Commentaries on the Constitution of the United States* §1507 (1833).

76. *Public Papers of the Presidents: Richard Nixon* 1973, 893 (1975).

77. *Ibid.*

78. *Rex v. Hampden,* 3 Howell's *State Trials* 826, 1125 (1637).

79. Jackson, J., concurring, in *Youngstown Sheet & Tube Co. v. Sawyer,* 343 U.S. 579, 637–40 (1952).

80. Paraphrasing *Attorney-General v. De Keyser's Royal Hotel,* [1920] A.C. 508, 538.

81. *Rex v. Hampden,* 3 Howell's *State Trials* 826, 1235 (1637).

82. *Myers v. United States,* 272 U.S. 52, 177 (1926).

83. So characterized by Clark, J., concurring, in *Youngstown Sheet & Tube Co. v. Sawyer*, 343 U.S. 579, 660 (1952).

84. 2 Cranch 170 (U.S. 1804).

85. Characterized as "limited war" in *Bas. v. Tingy*, 4 Dall. 37, 43 (U.S. 1800).

86. 2 Cranch at 177–78.

87. *Id.* at 178.

88. *Butz v. Economou*, 438 U.S. 478, 490 (1978).

89. 2 Cranch at 179.

90. *Ibid.*

91. *Youngstown Sheet & Tube Co. v. Sawyer*, 343 U.S. 579, 661 (1952).

92. Compare *id.* at 662.

93. Root, *Military and Colonial Policy of the United States* 157 (1916).

94. See 30 Stat. 738 (1898) (joint resolution recognizing Cuba). Congress has also passed other resolutions of recognition. 1 Moore, *A Digest of International Law* 245 (1906) (Texas); 1 Hackworth, *Digest of International Law* 162 (1943) (Chinese Republic).

95. President Cleveland expressed such a view in 1896 with regard to a congressional resolution recognizing Cuba. See Warren, *Presidential Declarations of Independence*, 10 Boston U.L. Rev. 1, 31 (1930). A similar opinion was expressed in 1897 by the Senate Foreign Relations Committee. See Corwin, *The President's Control of Foreign Relations* 80 (1917).

96. *Williams v. Suffolk Ins. Co.*, 13 Pet. 415, 420 (U.S. 1839). Compare *Baker v. Carr*, 369 U.S. 186, 219 (1962).

97. International Security Assistance Act, 92 Stat. 730 (1978).

98. Mutual Education and Cultural Exchange Act, 75 Stat. 527 (1961).

99. Export-Import Bank Amendments of 1974, 88 Stat. 2333 (1975); Export-Import Bank Amendments, P.L. 95-143 (1977).

100. Foreign Relations Authorization, 89 Stat. 770 (1975).

101. International Navigational Rules Act, P.L. 95-75 (1977).

102. Foreign Intelligence Surveillance Act, 92 Stat. 1783 (1978).

103. *Supra,* note 30.

104. *Supra,* note 31.

6

The Treaty Power: The International Legal Effect of Changes in Obligations Initiated by the Congress

Professor Theodor Meron *

The object of this chapter is to discuss some recent cases in which the Congress has initiated changes in the scope of obligations involved in international agreements submitted to it by the president. Although such practice of the Senate is not new, its impact and importance appears to have grown.

SINAI II AGREEMENTS

On September 1, 1975, representatives of Egypt and of Israel initialed the text of the Sinai II [disengagement] Agreement, which was formally signed on September 4.[1]

Article IV of the agreement provided for the future deployment of the forces of Egypt and of Israel and for early warning and surveillance arrangements. Article 2 of the Annex to the agreement provided that in a buffer zone there will be established, under Article IV of the agreement, an early warning system entrusted to United States civilian personnel, "as detailed in a separate proposal, which is a part of this Agreement." The U.S. "Proposal"

---

* The author is grateful to his research assistant Anna M. Pappas for her help with the United Kingdom Double Taxation treaty case.

opened with the statement that it was made "[i]n connection with the early warning system referred to in Article IV of the Agreement between Egypt and Israel concluded on this date and as an integral part of that Agreement." In order to encourage Israel and Egypt to conclude the Sinai II Agreement, the United States on its part entered into certain bilateral agreements with Israel and with Egypt, respectively.[2] The U.S. government asked for congressional approval of its proposal for the stationing of up to two hundred American technicians in the Sinai, a proposal that required certain appropriations. In addition to the text of the U.S. proposal, it transmitted to certain congressional committees as classified documents, the text of the bilateral agreements entered into by the United States and Israel on the one hand and the United States and Egypt on the other.[3]

The involvement of the Congress of the United States in these various agreements gave rise to a number of important legal questions, which were discussed in an exchange of memoranda between the Office of the Senate Legislative Counsel and the Legal Adviser's Office of the Department of State, including questions pertaining to the allegedly *ultra vires* character of the agreements. According to the Senate legislative counsel, the agreements should have been concluded in the form of treaties rather than as executive agreements.[4]

The U.S. proposal provided, in paragraph 8, that the United States may withdraw its personnel only if it concludes that their safety is jeopardized or that continuation of their role is no longer necessary. Obviously, according to this language, as traditionally understood, the decision to withdraw could have been made by the executive branch of the U.S. government, not by the legislative branch. Nevertheless, by the joint resolution of October 13, 1975, that authorized, under certain conditions, the implementation of the U.S. proposal, the Congress decided that the U.S. technicians would be removed immediately in the event of an outbreak of hostilities between Israel and Egypt (thus introducing a material change in the conditions for a withdrawal), or if the Congress, by concurrent resolution determined that the safety of such personnel would be jeopardized or that continuation of their role would no longer be necessary. Thus, the technicians might have to be removed from Sinai regardless of the view of the executive branch.[5] A concurrent resolution of the Congress, it may be observed in passing, is not subject to a presidential veto.[6] Congress has thus modified one of the more important undertakings given by Secretary Kissinger to Israel and to Egypt.

Although the executive branch accepted the above language of the joint resolution, and this change was presumably acceptable, *faute de mieux,* to Israel and to Egypt, the congressional language clearly modified the earlier instrument both as regards substance and procedure and raised questions regarding mutuality of obligations between the contracting parties.[7] In this case, Egypt and Israel presumably had no choice but to accept the changes made by Congress in Secretary Kissinger's commitments. It is entirely conceivable, however, that other states, operating in a situation of a lesser dependence on the United States, would have rejected the changes and, as a result, the agreement in toto.

TREATY OF FRIENDSHIP AND COOPERATION WITH SPAIN

Debate on the nature of American relations with Spain has been going on since the early 1950s. Central to this debate has been the dependence of the United States on military facilities in Spain, American efforts to compensate Spain for the absence of clear security commitments to come to the defense of Spain, and the question of democratization of Spain.

In 1975 the administration decided to accelerate negotiations with Spain and to submit the text agreed upon to the Senate as a treaty of friendship and cooperation.[8] In the letter transmitting the treaty to the Senate, in February 1976, President Gerald Ford stressed the important contribution made by Spain in providing the United States with facilities and related military rights on Spanish territory.[9] In the Committee on Foreign Relations, a number of declaratory statements were proposed as a part of the resolution of ratification expressing certain concerns of senators. Thus, Senators Clark and Eagleton proposed statements supporting the concept of democratization of Spain and Spain's participation in

Western European and NATO structures. These became paragraphs 1 and 2 of the declaration. At the suggestion of Senator Pell, the third paragraph of the declaration urged Spanish adherence to the Non-Proliferation Treaty and the placing of its nuclear facilities under IAEA safeguards.

Paragraph 4 of the declaration related to the fact that the treaty provided that it may be extended for an additional five years if the parties so agreed. Since the treaty was not specific, however, as to how such an extension would be accomplished, the committee added to the consent resolution a declaration of the Senate's expectation that the executive branch would seek Senate advice and consent prior to entering into any extension agreement. The committee emphasized that this stipulation was directed solely at the process of U.S. government decision making.

The fifth and final paragraph of the declaration was related to the fact that the treaty constituted a commitment by the United States to carry out undertakings with regard to financial assistance to Spain. In view of the established procedures for appropriating security assistance funds only pursuant to statutory authorization, the committee decided that the treaty could not be a substitute for authorizing legislation. To emphasize this intent, the committee added to the consent resolution appropriate language to make it clear that funds would be made available to carry out the treaty from year to year through the normal appropriations process, including prior authorization procedures.[10]

On June 21, 1976, the Senate adopted a resolution of ratification to the treaty, subject to the above declaration. The contents of the declaration were communicated by letter by the U.S. embassy in Madrid to the Spanish Foreign Ministry.[11]

The Spanish government was offended by the first two paragraphs of the declaration, which referred to the democratization of Spain, and regarded them as interference in its internal affairs. It was unwilling to accept that declaration as part and parcel of the U.S. instrument of ratification. Although a number of senators and the legislative counsel of the Senate insisted that the declaration be made part of the instrument of ratification, the Department of State argued that whereas, as a matter of custom and practice, the president normally placed the senate's reservations or interpretations in the instrument of ratification, there was no legal requirement that he do so, as long as he informed the other party to the treaty of the Senate action. In support of this position, Article 23(1) of the Vienna Convention on the Law of Treaties was invoked. The legal adviser of the Department of State emphasized that none of the Senate declarations had, or were intended to have, international legal effect. Whereas the first three declarations were statements of hope or expressions of opinion, having no bearing on the treaty, declarations 4 and 5 related to the U.S. method of implementation of the treaty and, as statements of U.S. domestic processes, had no application to Spain.[12]

After what amounted in effect to attempts at mediation by the Department of State between the Senate and Spain, the declaration was annexed to the instrument of ratification of the United States, of September 4, 1976, without having been reproduced in the instrument itself. The instrument, as signed by President Gerald Ford, mentioned, however, that the declaration was annexed to it. The Spanish instrument of ratification, signed on September 18, 1976, by King Juan Carlos, studiously avoided any mention of the Senate declaration. Neither the declaration nor the difference between the instruments of ratification was mentioned in the Protocol of Exchange of Instruments of Ratification, of September 21, 1976. This procedure, which enabled Spain to ignore the declaration, as not being part and parcel of the process of ratification of the treaty by the United States, caused considerable resentment in the Senate, which had its revenge in 1978, in the context of the Panama Canal Treaties. The Committee on Foreign Relations included in its Report on the Panama Canal Treaties an explicit request that

> The President shall include all amendments, reservations, understandings, declarations and other statements incorporated by the Senate in its resolution of ratification respecting this Treaty in the instrument of ratification exchanged with the Government of the Republic of Panama.

In its statement of intent, the committee indicated that it intended that any material included by the Senate in its resolution of ratification for each treaty be included in the instrument of ratification for that treaty given to the government of the Republic of Panama. The committee elaborated as follows:

> This understanding has its origins in assertions made by representatives of the Department of State, following Senate approval in 1976 of the resolution of ratification respecting the Treaty of Friendship and Cooperation between the United States and Spain, that the President possessed the authority to exclude from the instrument of ratification respecting that treaty the five-part declaration attached by the Senate to that resolution of ratification. (Members of this Committee advised that, in their judgment, no such discretion existed, the declaration was incorporated by reference in the instrument of ratification, although its text was set forth in an annex to the instrument.)
>
> It remains the position of the Committee that the President is without such authority. Although the Treaty Clause of the Constitution does not expressly address this question, neither does it expressly authorize the Senate to condition its advice and consent to treaties. Traditional United States practice has nevertheless been that the Senate may grant its approval conditionally, just as traditional United States practice has been that, when conditions are attached, those conditions are transmitted as an integral part of the instrument certifying Senate and Presidential approval. That such conditions must be so included is as much a part of customary constitutional law in this country as the right of the Senate to grant conditional consent.[13]

Despite explicit assurances given by the Department of State, the committee believed that "these understandings should be added to the resolutions of ratification respecting both treaties as a firm demonstration that the Senate will not countenance any interference with its constitutional prerogative of advice and consent and will take steps to counteract such interference on the part of any future Administration."[14]

In view of the position taken by the Senate in the Panama Canal case, it is most unlikely that the wishes of the Senate with regard to the inclusion in instruments of ratification of its declarations, interpretations, statements, amendments, or reservations would not be respected in the future.

THE SALT I EXTENSION CASE

SALT I (The Interim Agreement between the United States and the Soviet Union on Certain Measures with respect to the Limitation of Strategic Offensive Arms with Protocol)[15] was about to expire on October 3, 1977. The Soviet Union was interested in extending SALT I until SALT II would be ready.[16] The Arms Control and Disarmament Act, as amended,[17] provided, however, that any new agreement should be made pursuant to the treatymaking power or by further affirmative legislation. To overcome this difficulty, the administration decided to seek the extension of SALT I by Parallel Unilateral Policy Declarations (PUPD). On September 23, 1977, the United States issued a statement reading as follows:

> In order to maintain the status quo while SALT II negotiations are being completed, the United States declares its intention not to take any action inconsistent with the provisions of the Interim Agreement on Certain Measures with Respect to the Limitations of Strategic Offensive Arms which expires October 3, 1977, and with the goals of these ongoing negotiations provided that the Soviet Union exercises similar restraint.[18]

On September 24, 1977, the Soviet Union issued the following statement:

> . . . In accordance with the readiness expressed by both sides to complete within the near future the work on a new agreement limiting strategic offensive arms and in the interests of maintaining the status quo while the talks on the new agreement are being concluded, the Soviet Union expresses its intention to keep from any actions incompatible with the provisions of the interim agreement on some measures pertaining to the limitation of strategic offensive arms which expires on October 3, 1977, and with the goals of the talks that are being conducted, provided that the United States of America shows the same restraint.[19]

The continuation of the SALT I moratorium through the above unilateral declarations has been criticized as a means of evading congressional approval.[20] The administration defended its action by the arguments, made by the secretary of state, Cyrus Vance, that the policy declarations did not amount to an agreement and that, after October 3, 1977, and pending the conclusion of a new

SALT agreement, there would be no agreement limiting strategic offensive arms in force between the United States and the Soviet Union. The secretary pointed out that the possibility of a joint U.S.-Soviet statement, which might have raised the question of whether an international agreement was intended, was rejected.[21] Similarly, Paul C. Warnke, director of the U.S. Arms Control and Disarmament Agency, stated that "[b]ecause our non-binding statement is not part of an international agreement and does not impose any obligation on the U.S., we have not requested congressional approval for it."[22]

Herbert J. Hansell, legal adviser to the Department of State, stated that essential elements of a binding agreement were lacking: "there is no intent by either party to be bound; each may at any time cease to do what it has said it presently intends to do; and there would be no legal consequences if either changed its stated policy."[23] It is of particular interest that the legal counsel of the Senate Committee on Foreign Relations agreed with the views of the administration that the PUPD was not an international agreement and that since no international agreement existed, the question of whether a congressional approval was required was not even reached. The PUPD would not violate the Arms Control and Disarmament Act, since it was a nonbinding, unilateral policy declaration, that fell within the clear constitutional prerogatives of the president.[24]

Despite its strong case regarding the nonbinding character of the PUPD, the administration was nevertheless willing to support a congressional resolution of approval of the PUPD. Concurrent Resolution 56, which was designed to achieve this purpose, did not, however, emerge from the labyrinths of congressional procedures, for reasons for which the administration cannot be blamed.[25]

In the SALT I extension case, Congress did not initiate changes in any agreement. This case has, nevertheless, been included in this chapter because the PUPD technique reflected an attempt by the administration to evade congressional opposition to, and eventual congressional modifications of, an international agreement extending SALT I.

PANAMA CANAL TREATIES

A. CARTER-TORRIJOS STATEMENT

Article 274 of the Constitution of Panama of 1972 provides that "[t]reaties which may be signed by the Executive Organ with respect to the Panama Canal, its adjacent zone, and the protection of the said Canal, and for the construction of a new Canal at sea level or of a third set of locks, shall be submitted to a national plebiscite."[26]

On September 7, 1977, the governments of the United States and Panama signed treaties pertaining to the Panama Canal together with a number of accompanying instruments, exchanges of notes, letters, and related agreements.[27] These documents encountered fierce opposition in the Senate.

On October 14, 1977, following a meeting between President Carter and General Torrijos (Chief of Government of Panama), a Joint Statement of Understanding concerning the Neutrality Treaty was issued,[28] with the object of gaining greater sympathy in the Senate for consent to the ratification of the treaties.

On October 23, 1977, a plebiscite was held in Panama on the text of the treaties and related documents signed on September 7.[29]

The Carter-Torrijos statement was not included on the ballot but was read by General Torrijos on national television three days before the plebiscite,[30] and a number of Panamanian newspapers printed its text prior to the holding of the plebiscite.[31]

The Senate Foreign Relations Committee had recommended that the text of the Carter-Torrijos statement of October 14, 1977, be made an integral part of the Neutrality treaty, to have the same force and effect as the treaty provisions of September 7 submitted to the Senate for its advice and consent. Originally, the committee voted to include the joint statement in a single amendment that would have added a new article (IX) to the treaty, but after being advised by the Department of State that this could require a new Panamanian plebiscite, which would vastly complicate the ratification process, the committee decided on a "cosmetic" change and voted instead to recommend the addition of the same material in two parts to Articles IV and VI of the treaty. The committee was informed by the Department of State that no new plebiscite would be required for the approval of these two amendments, which together comprise the verbatim text of the joint statement, because it "is clear that the Panamanian people were fully apprised of the Joint Statement prior to the plebiscite, and were accorded a full opportunity to consider its provisions before approving the treaties."[32]

The Department of State regards the Carter-Torrijos statement as a correct interpretation of the Neutrality treaty and considers that, since the substance of that statement was placed before the Panamanian people before the plebiscite, there was no need for a second plebiscite. In this connection, a letter addressed to this author reads, in part, as follows:

> As you know, under Article 46 of the Vienna Convention on the Law of Treaties, a State's consent to be bound by a treaty may be insufficient if that consent has been given in manifest violation of an internal law of fundamental importance regarding competence to conclude treaties. Article 46 also stipulates that a violation is "manifest" if it would be "objectively evident to any State conducting itself in the matter in accordance with normal practice and in good faith."
>
> The Carter-Torrijos statement of October 14, 1977 (published in full in Panama on October 18) was issued by the United States and Panama as a correct interpretation of the Neutrality Treaty. The Government of Panama has informed the United States that the joint statement was placed before the Panamanian people prior to the October 23 plebiscite as the correct interpretation of the Neutrality Treaty, and that the plebiscite was carried out with the full understanding that the meaning to be given to the Treaty was set out in the joint statement. (Our Embassy confirmed that the statement was widely publicized in the Panamanian media prior to the plebiscite and was accurately represented as a correct and authoritative interpretation of the Treaty.) In the view of the Government of Panama, the substance of the joint statement was in effect approved by the Panamanian people by the October 23 plebiscite and there was therefore no need for a second plebiscite.
>
> While this question is, of course, a matter of Panamanian constitutional law, certainly Panama's opinion appears to us a reasonable interpretation of its constitutional requirements, and we believe that

it would appear as reasonable to most observers. If there has been any violation of the Panamanian Constitution (and we do not believe this to be the case), it is not "objectively evident" and is therefore not "manifest" within the meaning of Article 46 of the Vienna Convention.[33]

In this connection, the understanding of the Senate Foreign Relations Committee of the amendments is of interest. That committee stated that the first amendment allows the United States to introduce its armed forces into Panama whenever and however the Canal is threatened, and whether such a threat is internal or external, military or nonmilitary. When and what steps are necessary to defend the Canal is for the United States to determine on its own in accordance with its constitutional processes. As regards the second paragraph of the amendment, it does not prohibit the United States from doing anything that is not already prohibited under the United Nations Charter. If a conflict would somehow arise between the two paragraphs, "there is no question that the first would prevail. The rights conferred therein are stated in absolute terms and must therefore be construed as controlling."[34]

As regards the amendment to Article VI of the treaty, it confers upon U.S. warships and auxiliary vessels the right to go to the head of the line in an emergency. "What constitutes an emergency, and when one exists, is for the United States . . . alone to determine."[35]

It is certainly conceivable that an international lawyer would not construe these amendments as limited to an interpretation of the text of Articles IV and VI.

A number of senators argued that the treaty as amended by the text of the Carter-Torrijos statement should be submitted to another plebiscite in Panama. Thus, Senator Griffin argued that, under international law, an amended treaty is a rejected treaty. Once amended by one party, it must then be "reratified" as a new treaty by the other party. It was obvious, argued the senator, that if the Senate amended the treaty only by incorporating the text of the Carter-Torrijos statement, instruments of ratification would be exchanged without first submitting the new treaty to a vote of the people of Panama in a new plebiscite, as required by Article 274 of the Constitution of Panama. Yet, without such amendments, the Senate would not consent to ratification. If the revised treaty were submitted to another plebiscite in Panama, there was a possibility that it might be rejected. Invoking Article 46 of the Vienna Convention on the Law of Treaties, the senator argued that no one could seriously contend that the requirement of approval by plebiscite in the Constitution of Panama was not a rule "of fundamental importance"[36] and that a failure to follow the rule would be "manifest."[37]

"Charges of misdeeds on the part of Roosevelt and Bunau Varilla will be dwarfed by denouncements of the Carter-Torrijos maneuver in future history."[38] The Senate should not consent to the ratification but rather advise the president to renegotiate the treaties. Otherwise, "the foundation would be laid for future Panamanian claims that the treaties are invalid because in their final form they were not properly ratified in accordance with Panama's Constitution."[39]

Similarly, Senator Bartlett argued that nonsubmission of the treaty, as amended, to a new plebiscite would cause the treaty to be found wanting under international law or under the law of Panama. Although international law tends to avoid consideration of the internal affairs of states with respect to certain issues such as ratification of treaties, international law does not divorce itself completely from considerations of domestic law. Invoking Article 46 of the Vienna Convention on the Law of Treaties, the senator suggested that the requirement of a plebiscite was stated clearly in the fundamental law of Panama, that is, Article 274 of the Constitution, and that a failure to have a second plebiscite to consider changes involving the treaties would constitute a manifest violation. The senator proposed a reservation to the resolution of ratification that would direct the president to determine, before the date of the exchange of the instruments of ratification, that the Republic of Panama has ratified the treaty, as amended, in accordance with its constitutional processes, including the process required by the provisions of Article 274 of the Constitution of the Republic of Panama.[40]

This reservation, "which makes explicit the recognition that a

new plebiscite is required in Panama," was necessary, claimed
Senator Bartlett, inter alia, in order to guarantee that U.S. and
Panamanian rights under the treaty comply with international law,
and thus reduce the likelihood of misunderstandings with Panama
and the chances that subsequent Panamanian regimes would re-
fute the treaty, and comply with the Panamanian Constitution to
insure that the Supreme Court of Panama would not void the
agreement.[41]

Senator Church, in opposing the adoption of the Bartlett reservation, argued as follows:

> . . . this reservation would require that the President of the United
> States certify to the U.S. Senate that the Government of Panama has
> complied with the laws of Panama.
>
> I have little doubt how we would react if a similar reservation was
> adopted by Panama and directed toward the United States. We would
> regard it as the height of presumption.
>
> Furthermore, there is no way that the President of the United
> States can positively certify that Panama has compiled with Panama-
> nian laws.
>
> This is a matter that can be authoritatively determined only by the
> Government of Panama, and, furthermore, is the business of Panama.
>
> Now Article II of the treaty provides as follows:
>
> "This treaty shall be subject to ratification in accordance with the
> Constitutional procedures of the two parties."
>
> I submit . . . that this language is all the guarantee we need. In
> the normal court of comity between nations, Panama would certify
> that its own constitutional processes, its own laws, had been complied
> with, as we in turn would certify that our laws had been complied
> with.
>
> I do not think that it is within the competence of the Presidency or
> of the Senate to construe or to interpret Panamanian law for the Pan-
> amanians.
>
> It has been argued that since the Senate has adopted certain reser-
> vations to these treaties it is necessary to hold a second plebiscite
> under Panamanian law . . . that is for the Panamanians to deter-
> mine.[42]

The government of Panama itself claimed, in a communiqué issued by the Foreign Ministry on April 25, 1978,[43] following the
adoption by the U.S. Senate on April 18, 1978 of the resolution of
ratification of the Panama Canal treaty,[44] that the Panamanian

people approved the statement of understanding of October 14, 1977, agreed upon by Torrijos and Carter and that was "personally explained to the citizenry by General Torrijos before 23 October 1977. In other words, the people who supported the Torrijos-Carter treaties in the plebiscite approved the true interpretation given to those instruments by their signatories." The statement went on to point out that the two amendments to the Neutrality treaty corresponded exactly with the statement of understanding and contained an authentic interpretation of that treaty. The reading given by the government of Panama to the two amendments appears to be different from the reading given to it by the Committee on Foreign Relations of the U.S. Senate.

B. OTHER CONDITIONS, RESERVATIONS, AND UNDERSTANDINGS

In addition to the "leadership" amendments, that is, the two amendments based on the Carter-Torrijos statement, the Senate adopted a large number of conditions, reservations, and understandings to the two treaties.[45] These conditions, reservations, and understandings, whatever their precise title, were of differing scope and significance. Some of them were far-reaching in nature. Thus, the famous DeConcini proposal provided that, notwithstanding other provisions of the Neutrality treaty, the United States have the right—if the Canal were closed or its operations interfered with—to take such steps as it deemed necessary, in accordance with its constitutional processes, including the use of military force in Panama, to reopen the Canal or restore the operations of the Canal, as the case might be.[46] This reservation was somewhat neutralized by the reservation to the Panama Canal treaty providing that pursuant to the principle of nonintervention, "any action taken by the United States of America in the exercise of its rights to assure that the Panama Canal shall remain open, neutral, secure and accessible, pursuant to the provisions of this Treaty and the Neutrality Treaty and the resolutions of advice and consent thereto, shall be only for the purpose of assuring that the Canal shall remain open, neutral, secure and accessible, and shall not have as its purpose or be interpreted as a right of intervention in the internal affairs of the Republic of Panama or interference with its political independence or sovereign integrity."[47]

Resolutions of ratification of both treaties provided that the president of the United States should include in the instrument of ratification exchanged with the government of Panama all conditions, reservations, understandings, and so on incorporated by the Senate in the resolutions of ratification.

These developments give rise to two principal questions: What is the scope of obligations mutually agreed to by the two parties? How do the various reservations, conditions, and understandings—which no doubt affect the treaties—relate to the constitutional duty of the government of Panama to submit to a plebiscite all treaties pertaining to the status of the Panama Canal?

First one may ask oneself, however, whether the various conditions, reservations, and understandings made by the Senate in the resolutions of ratification can be regarded as mere interpretations of the two treaties or as substantive changes requiring renegotiation.[48]

Professor Louis Henkin observed that "[w]hether the Senate insists on a modification in the terms of a treaty, or on a particular interpretation of it, or on some limitation of its consequences, reservation usually requires renegotiation, to the dismay of Presidents and the impatience of other governments, but all now accept this additional obstacle in the American treaty process. The constitutional authority of the Senate to impose reservations has not been seriously questioned.[49]

Professor Henkin further suggested that when the Senate could be persuaded to clarify or even modify a treaty provision without entering a reservation, by expressing instead its understanding of a treaty provision, and if that understanding was communicated to the other party and was accepted or acquiesced in, the treaty need not be reopened. He pointed out, however, that failure of communication could engender doubt and controversy as to whether the parties agreed to the same terms.[50]

It is obvious that whether Panama has agreed to the same terms of the treaties as the United States depends on the meeting of the minds of the two parties, and particularly on the consent of Panama to the conditions, reservations, and understandings introduced by the U.S. Senate. Indeed, in a memorandum of law submitted by the legal adviser of the Department of State, it was suggested, correctly in the opinion of this writer, that there is no reason why an interpretation of the Neutrality treaty expressed in a reservation or understanding in the Senate resolution of ratification should not be binding *when concurred in* by Panama. "If both parties to a bilateral treaty agree in a separate instrument to an appropriate interpretation of that treaty, there is no legal reason why the special instrument should not be fully effective in accordance with its terms."[51]

Although the resolutions of ratification of the Panama Canal treaties contain provisions that go beyond mere interpretative statements, what is of importance is that the government of Panama accepted all of the Senate declarations.[52]

Indeed, the Protocol of Exchange of Instruments of Ratification, exchanged on June 16, 1978, in the wholly ceremonial exchange of instruments of ratification that took place in Panama between Carter and Torrijos, includes an explicit Panamanian acceptance of the amendments, conditions, reservations, and understandings adopted by the U.S. Senate since the treaties were signed on September 7, 1977, and after the treaties had been approved by the Panamanian plebiscite. The protocol states that:

> Said amendments, conditions, reservations and understandings have been communicated by the Government of the United States of America to the Government of the Republic of Panama. Both Governments agree that the Treaties, upon entry into force in accordance with their provisions, will be applied in accordance with the above-mentioned amendments, conditions, reservations and understandings.[53]

Moreover, the Spanish (Panamanian) text of the instruments of ratification reproduces the above amendments, conditions, reservations, and understandings. This largely resolves the difficulty with regard to the identity of the obligations accepted by the two parties. Largely, but not entirely, since the statement of the Panamanian Foreign Ministry of April 25 gives the various Senate declarations a minimal, low-key reading, suggesting that they offer reasonable interpretations of the treaty provisions rather than major modifications thereof. The conclusion reached in the statement was that the objectives of the treaties had not been changed or distorted by the Senate resolutions. Legal difficulties may yet arise in light of differences between the Panamanian and American interpretations of the scope and meaning of the conditions, reservations, and understandings included in the Senate resolutions.[54]

A more difficult question is, however, that of the status of the Senate conditions, reservations, and understandings in relation to Article 274 of the Panamanian Constitution.

This question was raised in the Senate by opponents of the ratification of the treaties. Thus, Senator Griffin, in considering "what will be the legal implications of the adoption by the Senate of reservations and understandings,"[55] invoked Article 46 of the Vienna Convention on the Law of Treaties and argued that the plebiscite requirement in Panama's Constitution is a rule of fundamental importance and that a failure to follow that rule would be manifest. He concluded that under international law,

> any condition applied to these treaties by the Senate—whether we call it an amendment, a reservation, or by some other term—must be accepted by Panama in accordance with its constitutional procedures. Its constitution requires approval by a vote of the people.
>
> If we permit President Carter and General Torrijos to exchange instruments of ratification without the required new plebiscite, we will invite a future Panamanian leader to denounce the treaty as null and void under international law.[56]

The opposite view was expressed by the Department of State. In the letter already mentioned, this writer was advised that:

> With respect to other [i.e., other than the two amendments arising from the Carter-Torrijos joint statement] Senate reservations and understandings, I have enclosed a copy of a communiqué from the Government of Panama [of April 25, 1978] which explains why, in their view, Panamanian law did not require a second plebiscite. Once again, we believe that the Panamanian interpretation of its own law appears to be reasonable. We do not perceive any violation of Panamanian law, and certainly no "manifest" violations within the meaning of Article 46.[57]

As already pointed out, the government of Panama chose to accept the Senate conditions, reservations, and understandings and viewed them as mere interpretative statements of the treaties. It will be recalled that the Vienna Convention on the Law of Treaties defined a reservation as a unilateral statement, however phrased or named, made by a state, when signing, ratifying, accepting, approving, or acceding to a treaty, whereby it purports to exclude or to modify the legal effect of certain provisions of the treaty.[58] When a reservation is accepted by the other state, it modifies the provisions of a treaty to which the reservation relates, in the relations between the reserving state and the state accepting the reservation.[59]

If the Senate conditions, reservations, and understandings are regarded as going beyond mere interpretations and as modifying the provisions of the treaty, serious difficulties may yet arise in relation to Article 274 of the Panamanian Constitution, despite the position taken by the Torrijos government. Probably as a safeguard against the possibility that a future Panamanian government may invoke Article 46 of the Vienna Convention on the Law of Treaties and argue that a manifest breach had occurred of Article 274 of its Constitution, the Panamanian texts of the instruments of ratification contain the following specific references to that article:

> Por cuanto la República de Panamá, mediante el plebiscito que ordena el articulo 274 de su Constitución Politica, ratificó el Tratado de Neutralidad [el Tratado del Canal de Panama] antes expresado.

> Considering that the Republic of Panama through the plebiscite provided for in Article 274 of its Political Constitution ratified the above-mentioned . . . Treaty. (author's translation)

In the Panama Canal case, the increasingly important phenomenon of objections as to the validity of certain agreements being raised in the Senate of the United States and the resultant parliamentary debates with their attendant notoriety served to put the negotiators on notice as to the allegedly *ultra vires* nature of certain agreements. Such notoriety may well force future negotiators to consider carefully the claims that have been made and decide on their strategy in light of the consideration that should an actual dispute arise in the future between the two contracting parties as to the possibly *ultra vires* character of the agreements, it would be difficult, indeed, to pretend that they had not been aware of the problem. But the fact that a claim of violation has gained notoriety does not mean that the violation—if any—is necessarily a manifest one.

While disclaiming any expertise in Panamanian constitutional law, this writer has not been persuaded by the arguments advanced by the government of Panama to the effect that all the amendments, conditions, reservations, and understandings introduced by the Senate subsequent to the signing of the treaties on September 7 were mere interpretative statements rather than substantial modifications of the treaties. Whatever the strength of the Panamanian claim that the amendments to Articles IV and VI of the Neutrality treaty were based on the Carter-Torrijos statement that was "presented" to the Panamanian people prior to the plebiscite, and thus taken by the people into account in the plebiscite, may be, it does not help the Panamanian argument with regard to other conditions, reservations, and understandings. To this writer, it appears that these conditions, reservations, and understandings amounted to reservations (or, given the bilateral nature of the agreements, counteroffers) modifying the treaties signed on September 7, 1977, and approved by the plebiscite of October 23, 1977. Although the explicit acceptance by Panama of those reservations disposes of some of the queries as to the scope and mutuality of the obligations assumed by the two parties, it does not dispose of the question of compliance with Article 274 of the Panamanian Constitution. However, despite doubts regarding the soundness of the Panamanian position on this point, it may well be that the international legal standing of the treaties has not been adversely affected. Since the U.S. government was clearly and publicly advised by the government of Panama that another plebiscite was not required, there was no need, and possibly no justification, for the United States to question the Panamanian position.

The careful drafting of the Protocol of Exchange of Instruments of Ratification, which acknowledges Panamanian acceptance of the amendments, conditions, reservations, and understandings;

the fact that the Panamanian texts of the instruments of ratification reproduce the above amendments, conditions, reservations,
and understandings; and the explicit reference in those instruments of ratification to Article 274 of the Panamanian Constitution
provide important safeguards for the United States against future
Panamanian claims that a manifest breach of Article 274 had occurred. Should a future ruler of Panama attempt to claim that Panama's consent to be bound by the Panama Canal treaties has been
expressed in violation of a provision of its internal law regarding
competence to conclude treaties, thus invalidating its consent, the
United States could invoke the official position of the Panamanian
government as establishing that even if there was a violation, it
could not have been manifest. The likelihood that such a U.S. position might be upheld by an international tribunal does not dispose of the danger that the way in which this particular question
was handled may encourage a future Panamanian ruler to attack
the legal foundations of the treaties. This is not to say that easy
alternatives were available. Without the amendments, conditions,
reservations, and understandings the Senate would not have given
its consent to the treaties. Had the amendments, conditions, reservations, and understandings been presented to the Panamanian
people in the form of another plebiscite, it is entirely possible that
they would have been rejected. Legal caution pressed to its logical
conclusion would probably mean that there would be no Panama
Canal treaties, proving the saying that *le mieux est l'ennemi du
bien*. For there is little doubt that the Panama Canal treaties make
a considerable contribution to the normalization and progress in
American-Panamanian relations and in the international scene at
large.

Finally, another lesson that can be learned from both the Sinai
II Agreements and the Panama Canal treaty cases is that other
countries negotiating with the United States—which nowadays
means increasingly negotiating with the Senate as well—sometimes have no choice but to accept changes in the text of international agreements unilaterally introduced by the Senate if they are
to have the agreements that they desire. Of course, they can re-

gard such Senate changes as counteroffers and ask for the reopening of negotiations, but this is not always a practical option.

UNITED KINGDOM DOUBLE TAXATION TREATY CASE

A Convention between the United States and the United Kingdom for the Avoidance of Double Taxation and Prevention of Fiscal Evasion with Respect to Taxes on Income was signed at London on December 31, 1975, and an exchange of notes containing minor modifications of certain provisions of the convention took place in London on April 13, 1976. The convention and the exchange of notes were transmitted by President Gerald Ford to the Senate of the United States on June 24, 1976, for advice and consent to ratification,[60] and were, of course, referred by the Senate to its Committee on Foreign Relations.[61]

The convention as originally drafted contained certain innovative provisions in comparison with other U.S. tax treaties, as will be mentioned presently, but otherwise substantially conformed to U.S. tax treaty patterns and to the model tax treaty of the Organization for Economic Cooperation and Development (OECD).[62]

The principal novel provision of the convention, in the U.S. plus column, was contained in its Article 10, extending to U.S. shareholders of British corporations the benefit of refundable credit for Advance Corporation Taxes (ACT) paid at the corporate level upon distribution of dividends under the system of partial integration of corporate and individual income taxes adopted by the United Kingdom in 1973 (United Kingdom law makes allowance for such credit in the case of shareholders who are United Kingdom residents.)[63] The United States was hoping to utilize this clause as a precedent to strengthen its bargaining position in its tax treaty negotiations with other nations that employ the integrated tax system, such as France, West Germany, and Canada, among others; furthermore, it was felt that a return of such a substantial sum of funds to the United States would have a beneficial impact on the

U.S. balance of payments and help boost the value of the dollar in foreign currency markets.[64]

The most controversial aspect of the convention proved to be the U.S. concession[65] contained in Article 9(4), pursuant to which, states of the United States (and local taxing authorities), in addition to the federal government, would be precluded from utilizing the combined reporting method under the unitary apportionments system in assessing the income tax liability of British corporations doing business in a particular state, or of any subsidiaries (domestic or foreign) doing business within that taxing state and controlled by a British corporation.[66]

Only three states of the United States utilize the combined reporting system consistently (California, Oregon, and Alaska), though several other states make use of it intermittently, particularly on audit.[67]

The federal government of the United States employs, instead, the so-called arm's-length method to guard against improper shifting of income by multijurisdictional corporations, as do many foreign governments, and was thus not affected by the prohibition of Article 9(4) of the convention.[68]

Opposition to Article 9(4) of the Convention was not related only to the issue of states' rights within the U.S. federal system. It also rallied supporters of increased regulation and taxation of profits of multinational corporations, particularly foreign-controlled ones.[69]

Furthermore, it was argued that, particularly with Article 9(4) included in it, the convention would produce more loss than gains for the United States in terms of tax revenue (especially if the precedent were to be followed in subsequent tax treaties), the benefits, such as there might be, inuring to corporations, at that, and not to the American people as a whole. The counterargument that Article 9(4) would generate future increased tax revenues by serving as an impetus to foreign investment in the United States was discounted.[70]

The issue of infringement of states' rights and usurpation of legislative prerogatives by the executive was used, in the end, however, to buttress all the other objections, and vice versa. It was argued that Article 9(4) represented an unprecedented use of the treaty power by the executive to impose substantive limitations on states' rights and to formulate legislative policy, bypassing Congress as a whole.[71] Allegedly at stake was the acknowledged sovereign right of the several states in the federal Union to regulate their local affairs, such as the levy of state taxes, in the absence of preemptive legislation by Congress as a whole in the areas within its specific competence, and, generally, in the absence of interference with the execution of the powers of the federal government.[72]

Following its referral to the Senate Foreign Relations Committee, the convention was further modified in minor respects by a first protocol,[73] and, then, by a second protocol,[74] and the Senate Committee on Foreign Relations held hearings on it, as amended by the exchange of notes and two protocols, on July 19 and 20, 1977.[75] The committee considered it on March 15, 1978, and ordered it favorably reported, recommending that the Senate give its advice and consent to ratification of the convention,[76] which by then had been "approved" by the British Parliament.[77] Prior to the vote in the Senate Foreign Relations Committee, Senator Frank Church of Idaho proposed that a reservation be attached to the resolution of ratification providing for the elimination of the application of Article 9(4) of the convention to any political subdivision or local authority of the United States. The proposed reservation was defeated in the committee by a vote of 10 to 5.[78]

The Senate considered the convention, as amended by the exchange of notes and two protocols, on June 22, 1978.[79] On that date, Senator Church proposed his aforementioned reservation relating to Article 9(4) on the Senate floor[80] and was opposed by the administration.[81] Following resumption of the Senate debate on June 23, 1978,[82] the Church reservation was rejected by the Senate by a vote of 44 to 34.[83] Thereupon a vote on the resolution of ratification was held, and it failed to secure the requisite concurrence of two thirds of the senators present, the vote being 49 in favor to 32 against.[84]

Just hours after the voting, Senator Jacob Javits of New York, the leading supporter of the treaty, and Senator Church, the leading antagonist as to Article 9(4), announced on the Senate floor that in conversations just then held with Secretary of the Treasury

W. Michael Blumenthal they were advised that the administration was now willing to accept the convention subject to the Church reservation. Senator Robert C. Byrd, the Senate majority leader, then moved to reconsider the respective votes by which the convention and the Church reservation were defeated.[85]

Following a reconsideration of the voting and brief debate on parliamentary issues,[86] it was agreed, by unanimous consent, that a vote should be held on June 27, 1978, on the resolution of ratification subject to the Church reservation.[87] The vote took place as scheduled, and the resolution of ratification as amended by the Church reservation was consented to by a vote of 82 to 5.[88]

Thus, the opponents of Article 9(4) were able to muster a minority sufficient to defeat the convention (though they were unable to secure the simple majority of the vote required to have the Church reservation adopted by the Senate) and, in the end, succeeded in imposing that reservation on the administration and the majority of the Senate.

Faced with the Church reservation, the United Kingdom had three options: (1) to accept the convention as amended by the Church reservation and seek the approval of the British Parliament; (2) to seek further concessions from the United States so as to compensate for the Church reservation; or (3) to renegotiate the entire convention *ad novo*. Of these, the second option was adopted, and a third protocol to the convention was signed in London on March 15, 1979; it was submitted by President Carter to the Senate for advice and consent of ratification on April 12, 1979; and it was referred to the Senate Committee on Foreign Relations on April 23, 1979.[89] The committee held hearings on such third protocol on June 6, 1979.[90]

The purpose of the third protocol was to conform the language of the convention to the Church reservation and to set forth the one concession secured by the United Kingdom as the quid pro quo for that reservation, in addition to making one further substantive change (it limits the amount of United Kingdom Petroleum Revenue Tax allowable as a credit against U.S. tax liability) and some technical corrections and clarifications. The concession in question[91] primarily affects American companies involved in

United Kingdom offshore oil and gas exploratory activities, which will now become liable to United Kingdom taxation, as if they had permanent bases there, in the event they carry on such activities for more than thirty days in a twelve-month period.[92]

The United Kingdom announced that it "acquiesced to the Senate reservation . . . with the greatest reluctance"; that the third protocol "produce[d] a fair and balanced agreement"; and that it would submit it to the House of Commons following positive action by the U.S. Senate.[93]

The Senate Committee on Foreign Relations considered the third protocol on June 12, 1979, and ordered it favorably reported by a vote of 13 to 0, recommending that the Senate give its advice and consent to ratification.[94] The Senate considered the third protocol on July 9, 1979,[95] and gave its consent to its ratification by a vote of 98 to 0.[96]

The British House of Commons is due to consider the third protocol, as well as the entire convention, as amended, so that instruments of ratification could be exchanged, and the documents in question enter into force.[97]

It should be noted that considerable discontent persists in the United Kingdom with the elimination of Article 9(4).[98] Legislative action by the Congress to address the issue of the use by the states of the unitary system was urged by several senators and recommended by the Senate Committee on Foreign Relations, and it was hoped that movement in that direction would be taken into account by the House of Commons when considering the third protocol.[99]

In summary, the administration submitted to the Senate a tax treaty based on a balance of mutual concessions and considered by the executive branches of both signatory nations to be of international and national importance. The major concession on the part of the United States was met with opposition in the U.S. Senate on the issue of the division of power within the federal system, and on other grounds, and its elimination from the convention by means of a reservation to the Senate resolution of ratification was proposed. The administration objected to such a proposal, hoping to secure the necessary majority of votes in the Senate for consent to ratification of the convention "as is." However, its commitment to the integrity of the convention was quickly abandoned upon its rejection by the Senate by a small margin of votes, and it endorsed the reservation to the Senate resolution of ratification as it had been originally proposed. Thereupon the Senate promptly proceeded to adopt the resolution of ratification subject to that reservation. Inasmuch as the reservation in question effected a substantive modification of the convention, it necessitated the resumption of international negotiations. The United Kingdom then sought and obtained a substitute concession from the United States to redress the imbalance of obligations presented by the altered convention. Though encountering some opposition, the protocol to the convention embodying such a concession received the consent of the U.S. Senate to its ratification and, considerably later, of the British House of Commons.[100]

This case study provides an interesting example of senatorial assertion of an active and vigorous role in treatymaking, in defense of the prerogatives of the states of the Union.

CONCLUDING OBSERVATIONS

The involvement of Congress in the process of treatymaking has not been limited to the Senate's role under the Constitution to give advice and consent to treaties submitted to it by the president. In cases such as Sinai II [executive] Agreements, where appropriations were required, both houses of Congress were involved.

In numerous cases, the Senate has given its consent with reservations, conditions, understandings, declarations, and the like. Since the Senate can give or withhold consent, it is generally agreed that it can also give its consent on condition that changes be made.[101] Recent cases, such as the Panama Canal and SALT II, have focused attention on changes of international obligations initiated by the Senate. The legal significance of a "statement" of the Senate—to use a neutral term—depends upon its substance, not upon its designation. As has been observed, a "statement that modifies, limits or changes the treaty text or meaning is a true reservation; a statement that clarifies or explains, or deals with an incidental matter, does not change the treaty and is therefore not a reservation."[102] When the Senate initiates some such statements, the first question is whether they are acceptable to the executive branch. It is, of course, up to the president to make or not to make the treaty,[103] in light of the statements accompanying the consent of the Senate. He may return a treaty to the Senate for further consideration or else put it on the shelf instead of proceeding to its execution and the exchange of instruments of ratification. The second question is what the reaction of the other state is. Whatever the designation of a statement made by the Senate, the other state may reject any statement that, according to its understanding, changes or interprets the treaty relationship in an unacceptable way.[104] Renegotiation of a treaty may be required. Insofar as the other state is concerned, it is obvious that the acceptability of a treaty as "modified" by statements made by the Senate depends not only on their "legal" merits but also on the political factors involved. The frequent difficulty of distinguishing clearly between a reservation or amendment of a treaty on the one hand, and a "mere" "understanding" or declaratory statement may facilitate the task of the U.S. executive branch and its foreign counterpart in devising techniques that may be vital for the survival of the treaty (or other international agreements).

The preceding case study illustrates the modalities of the different responses and attitudes of governments.

In the Sinai II case, Israel and Egypt had no choice but meekly to accept the congressional position regarding the conditions under which American technicians may be withdrawn from Sinai, once that position had been accepted by the executive branch. In the Spanish bases case, the executive branch cooperated with Spain in a technique that enabled Spain to disregard the political declarations made by the Senate. Although the position of the administration may have been necessary in order to save the treaty, this type of approach may lessen the Senate's confidence in the administration and, in some cases, increase doubts about the meeting of the minds of the parties and about the mutuality of obligations undertaken by each state. In the SALT I extension case, the administration resorted to the PUPD technique in order to avoid altogether congressional involvement. The other state, the Soviet Union, extended to the administration full cooperation. Although the PUPDs do not constitute a binding international agreement, they nevertheless have a considerable moral and political significance and would not lightly be breached. In the Panama Canal treaties, far-reaching changes initiated by Congress were eventually accepted by the administration. In order to complete the process of ratification, the leaders of the United States and Panama have cooperated in downplaying the full significance of certain Senate statements. There is a possibility that despite legal precautions taken by the American side, a future Panamanian regime might claim that the treaties are *ultra vires* the Constitution of Panama. In the United Kingdom Double Taxation Treaty case, the Church reservation was, at first, rejected by the administration. Upon the rejection of the treaty as a whole by the Senate, the administration changed its mind and accepted the treaty as modified by the Church amendment. The Church reservation required the renegotiation of the treaty and the making of further concessions by the United States to the United Kingdom.

It is natural that the Senate will want to have a say about the scope of international obligations assumed by the United States. Senate statements will often be caused by internal political motivations. This is, of course, inevitable. What is, however, necessary is to find a way of strengthening the cooperation between the Congress and the administration so that each would be more aware of the international significance of the statements initiated by Congress, of the pitfalls, as regards the specific agreements themselves and of the potential danger to the international credibility of the United States. The administration, on its part, should make sure that the foreign state involved is apprised of the full significance of the statements made by the Senate. More important, it should avoid using techniques that may in the future give rise to controversies as to the scope and the mutuality of obligations undertaken by the parties.

NOTES

1. For the text of the agreements see *Report of the Secretary-General,* S/11818/Add. I. For the text of the protocol to the agreement see S/11818/ Add. 5, reproduced in 14 *ILM* at 1458 (1975).

2. Statement by Secretary Kissinger in *Early Warning System in Sinai, Hearings before the Committee on Foreign Relations, United States Senate,* 94th Cong., 1st sess. (hereafter *Sinai Hearings*) at 214–15.

3. For the text of the agreements see *Sinai Hearings, supra,* note 2 at 249–53; 14 *ILM* 1468 (1975); *TIAS* Nos. 8155–56.

4. See Meron, "Article 46 of the Vienna Convention on the Law of Treaties (*Ultra Vires* Treaties): Some Recent Cases," 48 *Brit. Y.B. Int'l L.* 175–82 (1978). The text of the various memoranda is contained in 121 *Cong. Rec.* S. 20102–15 (daily ed., Nov. 14, 1975); 14 *ILM* 1585–96 (1975); 15 *ibid.,* 187–98 (1976); The Senate legislative counsel (Michael J. Glennon) argued that at least one of the agreements, the Memorandum of Agreement between the Governments of Israel and the United States (Agreement E) (for the text of this agreement see *Sinai Hearings, supra,* note 2 at 249), contained far-reaching commitments, the exact scope of which it was difficult to determine. 121 *Cong. Rec.* S. 20108 (daily ed., Nov. 14, 1975).

Glennon's memoranda pointed out that Agreement E dealt with the following matters: Israel's defense requirements, long-term supply needs of Israel, oil arrangements and supplies for Israel, effect of Egyptian violation of Egypt-Israel Agreement, voting in the Security Council, U.S. position with regard to proposals detrimental to Israel, threats to Israel's security, emergency military supply operations, validity and duration of Egypt-Israel Agreement, negotiations with Jordan, freedom of navigation and overflights.

For the answer of the legal adviser of the Department of State, see *ibid.* at S. 20102; for the second memorandum of the Office of the Legislative Counsel see *ibid.* at S. 20105. For the reply of the Department of State see 15 *ILM* 198 (1976).

See, in general, Rovine, "Separation of Powers and International Executive Agreements," 52 *Indiana Law Journal* at 397 (1977); Franck, "After the Fall: The New Procedural Framework for Congressional Control Over the War Power," 71 *AJIL* at 605 (1977).

Secretary Kissinger warned that while statements of U.S. intentions served as a lubricant in the negotiations, they must be seen in perspective and in the light of historical practice and that Congress should take care not to create inadvertently commitments that were not intended (*Sinai Hearings, supra,* note 2 at 210). See, in general, Schachter, "The Twilight

Existence of Nonbinding International Agreements," 71 *AJIL* 296 at 303, n. 26 (1977).

5. P.L. 94–110, 89 Stat. 572. See *Report No. 94–532 of the House Committee on International Relations to Implement the United States Proposal for the Early-Warning System in Sinai* at 3, 94th Cong. 1st sess. (1975).

6. See, in general, *Sutherland, Statutes and Statutory Construction,* vol. IA at 335 (4th ed., 1973, by C. Dallas Sands).

7. See Secretary Kissinger in *Sinai Hearings, supra,* note 2 at 217. On the role of Congress in treatymaking and in treaty negotiation, see Franck and Weisband, "Advice and Consent," *New York Times,* Feb. 28, 1978, §C p. 33, col. 2. See, in general, T. Franck and E. Weisband, *Foreign Policy by Congress* 142–43 (1979). See 121 *Cong. Rec.* S. 20108 (daily ed., Nov. 14, 1975). The agreement as published in *TIAS* Nos. 8155–56 does not allude to the change introduced by the Congress.

8. S. Exec. Rep. No. 94–25 at 2, 94th Cong., 2d sess. (1976). The text of the treaty was transmitted to the Senate in February (1976). For the background, see Department of State Publication No. 8805 *Digest of United States Practice in International Law 1975* at 323–24 (1976).

On December 9, 1975, the assistant secretary of state for congressional relations advised Senator John Sparkman that "[w]hile the President has and must retain the authority to conclude important international agreements on the basis of his constitutional powers alone, the power to proceed on that basis is not proposed to be exercised in this case. Instead, affirmative action by both legislative and executive branches, either by treaty or joint resolution, is proposed." *Ibid.* at 324.

9. S. Exec. E., 94th Cong., 2d sess.

10. S. Exec. Rep. No. 94-25 at 5–8, 94th Cong., 2d sess. (1976).

11. Department of State Publication No. 8908, *Digest of United States Practice in International Law 1976* at 215 (1977). For the text of the resolution of ratification, see 122 *Cong. Rec.* S. 19390 (daily ed., June 21, 1976).

12. *Ibid.* at 215–16.

13. S. Exec. Rep. No. 95–12 at 10–11, 95th Cong., 2d sess. (1978).

14. *Ibid.*

15. *TIAS* 7504; 23 U.S.T. 3462.

16. T. Franck and E. Weisband, *Foreign Policy by Congress* 152 (1979).

17. P.L. 87–297, 75 Stat. 631, sec. 33, 22 U.S.C. 2573.

18. 123 *Cong. Rec.* S. 16133 (Daily ed., Oct. 3, 1977); Department of State Publication No. 8960, *United States Practice in International Law 1977* at 426 (1979).

19. *Ibid.* at 432.

20. See T. Franck and E. Weisband, *op. cit., supra,* note 16 at 152.

21. Department of State Publication No. 8960, *Digest of United States Practice in International Law 1977* at 426–27 (1979).

22. *Ibid.* at 430.

23. *Ibid.* at 431.

24. *Ibid.* at 429–30. Regarding circumstances where a unilateral policy statement may be legally binding, see Nuclear Test Cases, *Australia v. France* and *New Zealand v. France, ICJ Rep.* 1974 at 253, 457. See also Franck, "Word Made Law: The Decision of the ICJ in the Nuclear Test Cases," 69 *AJIL* 612 (1975).

25. See T. Franck and E. Weisband, *op. cit., supra*, note 16 at 152–54. For an eloquent opposition to a resolution of approval, see the supplemental views of Senators Clark and McGovern: "In response to an international agreement that does not exist, it purports to authorize what does not need authorization, in a form that cannot constitute authorization. While we are not unimpressed by the conceptual breakthroughs the resolution achieves, any merit it may have beyond novelty is imperceptible to us." Senate Rep. No. 95-499 at 13, 95th Cong., 1st sess. (1977).

26. *Constitution of Panama, 1972, General Secretariat Organization of American States* at 44 (1974).

27. Panama Canal Treaty, Agreed Minute to the Panama Canal Treaty, Treaty concerning the Permanent Neutrality and Operation of the Panama Canal, Protocol to the Treaty concerning the Permanent Neutrality and Operation of the Panama Canal, Agreement in Implementation of Article III of the Panama Canal Treaty, Agreement in Implementation of Article IV of the Panama Canal Treaty. For the text of these treaties and other instruments see Senate Executive Rep. No. 95-12, The Committee on Foreign Relations,95th Cong., 2d sess. (1978 (hereinafter *Panama Canal Report*) at 201–90; 71 *AJIL* 635–43 (1978).

28. For the text of the joint (unsigned) statement see *Panama Canal Report* at 291; 13 *Weekly Compilation of Presidential Documents* at 1547 (Oct. 17, 1977).

29. See 124 *Cong. Rec.* S. 3516–19 (daily ed., Mar. 13, 1978). See generally *ibid.* at S. 2944–62 (daily ed., Mar. 6, 1978).

30. *Panama Canal Report* at 8.

31. *Panama Canal Treaties.* Hearings Before the Senate Committee on Foreign Relations, 95th Cong., 1st sess., Part 1 (hereinafter Panama Canal Hearings), at 478–80.

32. See *Panama Canal Report, supra* at 8, Appendix I. See also 36 *Congressional Quarterly, Weekly Reporter* No. 16 at 1003–4 (Apr. 22, 1978); *Panama Canal Report* at 218.

33. Letter to the author, dated May 31, 1978, from Arthur W. Rovine, assistant legal adviser for treaties.

34. *Panama Canal Report* at 6–7.

35. *Ibid.* at 7.

36. 124 *Cong. Rec.* S. 3516–17 (daily ed., Mar. 13, 1978).

37. *Ibid.* at S. 3787–88 (Mar. 15, 1978).

38. Statement of Sen. Griffin. 124 *Cong. Rec.* S. 3518 (daily ed., Mar. 13, 1978).

39. *Panama Canal Report* at 200.

40. 124 *Cong. Rec.* S. 5743 (daily ed., Apr. 18, 1978). See also *ibid.* at S. 5741–45.

41. *Ibid.* at S. 5743.

42. *Ibid.* at S. 5744. The Bartlett reservation was not adopted. See *ibid.* at S. 5745.

43. Source: Incoming unclassified Department of State telegram of Apr. 26, 1978, on file in the Office of the Assistant Legal Adviser for Treaties.

44. The text of the resolution of ratification is in 124 *Cong. Rec.* S. 5796–97 (daily ed., Apr. 18, 1978). The text of the resolution of ratification of the treaty concerning the permanent neutrality and operation of the Panama Canal treaty can be found in ibid. at S. 3857-8 (daily ed., Mar. 16, 1978).

45. For the text see the two resolutions of ratification, *supra*, note 44.

46. The first "condition," resolution of ratification of the Neutrality Treaty, *supra*, note 45.

47. 124 *Cong. Rec.* S. 5796–97 (daily ed. Apr. 18, 1978).

48. The legal adviser of the Department of State stated that "substantive amendments and reservations to the Panama Canal Treaties put forth by Panama that would affect United States rights or obligations under the Treaties cannot be accepted by the United States unless approved by the President and the Senate." 124 *Cong. Rec.* S. 5735 (Apr. 18, 1978).

49. L. Henkin, *Foreign Affairs and the Constitution* 133–134 (1972).

50. *Ibid.* at 136.

51. 124 *Cong. Rec.* S. 5780 (daily ed., Apr. 18, 1978).

52. Statement of the Foreign Ministry of Panama of Apr. 25, 1978, *supra*, note 43.

53. The text of the protocol was supplied to this author by the assistant legal adviser for treaties in the Department of State.

54. *New York Times,* June 17, 1978, A 1, col. 6. The ceremonial nature of the exchange of instruments of ratification is made clear by the Senate reservation to the Panama Canal treaty whereby the exchange of the instruments of ratification shall not be effective earlier than March 31, 1979, and the treaties shall not enter into force prior to October 1, 1979, unless legislation necessary to implement the provisions of the Panama Canal treaty shall have been enacted by the Congress of the United States before March 31, 1979.

55. 124 *Cong. Rec.* S. 3787 (daily ed., Mar. 15, 1978).

56. *Ibid.*

57. See *supra,* note 33.

58. Article 2(1) (d).

59. Article 21.

60. S. Exec. Doc. K, 94th Cong., 2d sess. (1976). The agreement constituted by the exchange of notes was to enter into force on the same date as the convention (after the expiration of thirty days following the date of exchange of instruments of ratification, according to Article 28 of the convention).

61. 122 *Cong. Rec.* S. 20347 (daily ed., June 24, 1976).

62. Senate Comm. on Foreign Relations, 95th Cong., 2d sess., *Report on Tax Convention with the United Kingdom of Great Britain and Northern Ireland,* Exec. Rep. No. 95-18 (Apr. 25, 1978) at 2.

63. Under this provision, U.S. direct investors in United Kingdom corporations (i.e., U.S. corporations owning 10 percent or more of the United Kingdom dividend-paying corporation) are allowed an unprecedented refund of one half of the ACT paid (under Article 23 they are allowed a U.S. foreign tax credit for the one half of the ACT not refunded), and all other U.S. shareholders of United Kingdom corporations (portfolio investors) are granted the benefit of full refund of the ACT. Though U.S. investors would, under the convention, now be subjected to withholding taxes on dividends and on the ACT refund (at the rate of 5 percent for direct investors and 15 percent for portfolio investors), their overall United Kingdom tax burden would be substantially reduced prospectively, the total savings estimated at about $85 million annually, and, in addition, they would stand to receive a total of approximately $375 million in retroactive refunds of ACT for the period 1973–78. U.S. Department of State, Letter of Submittal, *supra,* note 60 at v; Senate Comm. on Foreign Relations Rep., *supra,* note 62 at 4, reprinted in 124 *Cong. Rec.* S. 9416 (June 22, 1978), and Appendix at 89–92 (prepared Statement of Assistant Secretary of the Treasury Laurence N. Woodworth); Proposed U.S.-U.K. Income Tax Treaty: U.S. Benefits and Concessions, printed in *Cong. Rec., ibid.* at S. 9441 (table submitted by Senator Pell); *Tax Treaties with the United Kingdom, the Republic of Korea, and the Republic of the Philippines.* Hearings on Exec. K, 94th Cong. 2d sess. Before the Senate Comm. on Foreign Relations, 95th Cong., 1st sess. (July 19–20, 1977) at 49–50 (Prepared Statement of Paul Oosterhuis, Legislative Counsel, and David Brockway, Legislation Attorney, Staff of the Joint Commission on Taxation).

64. *Cong. Rec., supra,* note 63 at S. 9431 (Letter of Secretary of the Treasury W. Michael Blumenthal).

65. The United States would continue to tax both corporate earnings and dividend distribution so that the U.S. tax burden of United Kingdom investors would be higher than vice versa (though lowered substantially by the terms of this treaty). Obviously, the United States had to offer other

concessions to the United Kingdom. Hearings Before the Senate Comm. on Foreign Relations, *supra*, note 63 at 50.

66. U.S. Department of State, Letter of Submittal, *supra*, note 63 at vi; Senate Comm. on Foreign Relations Rep., *supra*, note 62 at 4, at 19–21, Appendix at 92–96 (Prepared Statement of Assistant Secretary of the Treasury Laurence N. Woodworth). The unitary approach involves a determination of what activities of a corporation, wherever conducted, constitute a functional unit and what the total net income of that entity is. Thereupon, a computation of the share of that income attributable to the particular taxing jurisdiction is arrived at, according to a standard three-factor apportionment formula based on the ratio of sales, payroll, and property values of the corporation within the taxing State to the overall sales, payroll, and property values of the unitary entity in question. *Ibid.*, Hearings Before the Senate Comm. on Foreign Relations, *supra*, note 63 at 51–52.

The combined reporting method is required when the application of the unitary system of income allocation is extended to the income of affiliated or related corporations, which are not doing any business within the state in question, if it is determined that they are so interdependent functionally with a particular corporation that is doing business in that state that they constitute a unitary enterprise. Article 9(4) was intended to proscribe the use of the combined reporting method vis-à-vis foreign affiliates of British corporations or foreign affiliates of British subsidiaries, which affiliates are not doing business within the jurisdiction of a particular taxing authority. It was thus intended to enjoin the taking into account on a consolidated basis of the operations (income, sales, payroll, etc.) of such foreign affiliates in fixing the tax liability of British corporations or British subsidiaries doing business within a given jurisdiction. *Ibid.*

67. *Ibid.*

68. The arm's-length method entails review of transactions between related entities and testing them as against comparable transactions between unrelated parties to check whether they were made at genuine arm's-length prices. The convention does not disturb this method, and the U.S. Treasury Department was contemplating its adoption by all the states in lieu of the unitary system. *Ibid.; supra*, note 64.

The issue raised by this aspect of the convention is undoubtedly very complex. It involves controversy regarding the respective merits of the unitary system versus the arm's-length approach, both on substantive grounds and as regards the onus of administration and compliance on the taxing authorities and the multijurisdictional corporations, respectively. *Cong. Rec.*, *supra*, note 63 at S. 9430 (remarks of Sen. Church); *ibid.* at S. 9434–35 (remarks of Sen. Kennedy); *ibid.* at S. 9439 (remarks of Sen. Stevens); 124 *Cong. Rec.* S. 9547 (daily ed., June 23, 1978) (remarks of Sen. Hayakawa); *ibid.* at S. 9553–56 (California Franchise Board Response to U.S. Dept. of Commerce Paper); *ibid.* at S. 9560 (remarks of Sen. Church); *ibid.* at S. 9563 (remarks of Sen. Glenn).

69. The opposition to Article 9(4) was broad based and included labor and consumer groups. *Cong. Rec., supra,* note 63 at S. 9429 (remarks of Sen. Church); *ibid.* at S. 9434–35 (remarks of Sen. Kennedy); *ibid.* at S. 9439 (remarks of Sen. Stevens); 124 *Cong. Rec., supra,* note 68 (daily ed., June 23, 1978) at S. 9549 and S. 9552 (remarks of Sen. Stevens).

70. *Cong. Rec., supra,* note 63 at S. 9441 (table submitted by Sen. Pell); *ibid.* at S. 9429 and S. 9433 (remarks of Sen. Church); *ibid.* at S. 9439 (remarks of Sen. Stevens); *Cong. Rec., supra,* note 68 (daily ed., June 23, 1978) at S. 9546–47 (remarks of Sen. Hayakawa); *ibid.* at S. 9552 (remarks of Sen. Stevens and Letter of the Congressional Budget Office) and at S. 9553 (remarks of Sen. Stevens).

71. 124 *Cong. Rec.* S. 8867 (June 8, 1978) (remarks of Sen. Church); *Cong. Rec., supra,* note 63 at S. 9428–30 and S. 9433 (remarks of Sen. Church); *ibid.* at S. 9435 (remarks of Sen. Kennedy); *ibid.* at S. 9435 (remarks of Sen. Clark); *ibid.* at S. 9439 (remarks of Sen. Stevens).

72. *Ibid.* It was objected that action by the Senate alone in the context of the treaty power amounted to circumvention of the House of Representatives in the exercise of the powers of Congress to define internal tax policy, to regulate interstate and foreign commerce, and to resolve conflicts within the federal system.

Opponents of Article 9(4) did not, however, acknowledge any conflict between the use by some states of the unitary tax system on a worldwide combined-reporting basis and relevant powers of Congress (nor did most of them concede the desirability of congressional legislation in the matter). Those holding the contrary view seized upon a recent opinion of the Supreme Court and cited it as indicative of a growing inclination by the Court to declare such practices unconstitutional on the ground that they infringe upon the federal power to regulate foreign commerce in a uniform and efficacious manner. *International Tax Treaties.* Hearings Before the Senate Comm. on Foreign Relations on Six International Tax Treaties and Protocols, 96th Cong., 1ST SESS. (JUNE 6, 1979) at 22 (statement of former Sen. Cook) and at 23 (reprinted Supreme Court Opinion, *Japan Line, Ltd. v. County of Los Angeles,* No. 77-1378, Decided April 30, 1979), 47 U.S.L.W. (Sup. Ct.) 4477; 125 *Cong. Rec.* S. 8807–8 (daily ed., July 9, 1979) (Letter of California Franchise Tax Board).

73. The first protocol to the convention was signed in London on August 26, 1976, containing some technical modifications principally relating to the application of the convention to dual resident corporations. It was transmitted by President Gerald Ford to the Senate on September 22, 1976, for advice and consent to ratification. S. *Exec. Doc. Q,* 94th Cong., 2d sess. (1976). See U.S. Department of State, Letter of Submittal, *ibid.* at 3.

74. The second protocol was signed in London on March 31, 1977, and was transmitted to the Senate on June 6, 1977, by President Jimmy Carter. The provisions of the second protocol were aimed mainly at correcting an aspect of the convention adversely affecting some U.S. female citizens married to United Kingdom domiciliaries. S. *Exec. Doc. J.,* 95th Cong., 1st sess. (1977). See U.S. Department of State, Letter of Submittal, *ibid.* at v.

75. Hearings Before the Senate Comm. on Foreign Relations, *supra,* note 63.; 123 *Cong., Rec.* D. 1093 (July 20, 1977); Senate Comm. on Foreign Relations Rep., *supra,* note 62 at 7 (reprinted in Cong. Rec., *supra,* note 63 at S. 9416).

76. Senate Comm. on Foreign Relations Rep., *supra,* note 62 at 2, 9; 124 *Cong. Rec.* D. 346 (Mar. 15, 1978).

77. Hearings Before the Senate Comm. on Foreign Relations, *supra,* note 63 at 16, 22 (remarks of Laurence N. Woodworth, assistant secretary of the treasury); *Cong. Rec., supra,* note 63 at S. 9414 (remarks of Sen. Sparkman); 124 *Cong. Rec.* S. 9842 (daily ed., June 27, 1978) (remarks of Sen. Morgan); *Cong. Rec., supra,* note 72 (daily ed., July 9, 1979) at S. 8811–12 (Reprinted Statement of Michael Gryllis, M.P.).

In the United Kingdom, legislative approval of treaties that are subject to ratification is deemed secured under the practice, known as "the Ponsonby rule," of "lay[ing] on the Table of both Houses of Parliament" every such treaty "for a period of twenty-one days, after which the Treaty will be ratified and published and circulated in the Treaty Series." Quoted in L. Wildhaber, *Treaty-Making Power and the Constitution* at 29 (1971); A. McNair, *Law of Treaties* at 99, 190 (1961).

78. Senate Comm. on Foreign Relations Rep. *supra,* note 62 at 9; Senate Comm. on Foreign Relations, 96th Cong., 1st sess., *Report on Third Protocol to the 1975 Income Tax Convention with the United Kingdom of Great Britain and Northern Ireland as Amended,* Exec. Rep. No. 96-5 (June 15, 1979) at 2.

79. *Cong. Rec., supra,* note 63 (daily ed., June 22, 1978) at S. 9412–42.

80. The reservation added to the resolution of ratification the following wording: "Subject to the reservation that the provisions of paragraph (4) of Article 9, as amended by the Notes relating to the Convention which were exchanged on April 13, 1976, shall not apply to any political subdivision or local authority of the United States." *Ibid.* at S. 9414 and S. 9428 and at D. 912.

81. *Ibid.* at S. 9430–31 (Letter of Secretary of the Treasury W. Michael Blumenthal to Sen. Javits, dated May 2, 1978, introduced on the record by Sen. Javits).

82. *Cong. Rec., supra,* note 68 (daily ed., June 23, 1978) at S. 9546–64.

83. *Ibid.* at S. 9564–65.

84. *Ibid.* at S. 9565.

85. *Ibid.* at S. 9604–5, S. 9607.

86. *Ibid.* at S. 9605–7.

87. *Ibid.* at S. 9607, D. 920.

88. *Cong. Rec., supra,* note 77 (daily ed., June 27, 1978) at S. 9840–41.

89. S. *Exec. Doc. Q.,* 96th Cong., 1st sess. (1979).

90. Hearings Before the Senate Comm. on Foreign Relations, *supra* note 72 (June 6, 1979).

91. Article VI of the protocol adding a new Article 27A to the convention. *Supra,* note 89 at 3–4.

92. Hearings Before the Senate Comm. on Foreign Relations, *supra,* note 72 at 78–81 (Statement by Assistant Secretary of the Treasury Donald C. Lubick); *supra,* note 89 at v (Department of State, Letter of Submittal); Senate Comm. on Foreign Relations. *Rep. on Third Protocol, supra,* note 78 (June 15, 1979) at 3, 5–6, 12–13.

93. *Inland Review* Press Release, Mar. 15, 1979.

94. Senate Comm. on Foreign Relations Rep., *supra,* notes 36, 78, 92 at 4.

95. *Cong. Rec., supra,* note 72 at S. 8807–14 (daily ed., July 9, 1979).

96. *Ibid.* at S. 8814.

97. Source: Conversation with Mordecai Feinberg, associate director of the Office of International Tax Affairs of the U.S. Treasury Department; Hearings Before the Senate Comm. on Foreign Relations, *supra,* notes 72, 92 at 78.

98. The confederation of British industry has gone on record urging rejection of the convention in its present form, and an Early Day Motion was filed in the House of Commons on June 11, 1979 (originally sponsored by 59 members and later reported to have been endorsed by more than 100) urging the British Government to insure that the situation be rectified so as to avoid a harmful international precedent. Hearings Before the Senate Comm. on Foreign Relations, *supra,* note 72 at 17 (Statement of Michael Gryllis, M.P.) and at 18 (Text of Early Day Motion), both reprinted in *Cong. Rec., supra,* note 72 at S. 8811–12 (daily ed., July 9, 1979).

99. A proposed bill on the matter was introduced by Senator Charles McC. Mathias of Maryland and is pending in appropriate congressional committees. Hearings Before the Senate Comm. on Foreign Relations (June 6, 1979), *supra,* note 72 at 2. (Statement of Sen. Mathias); *Senate Comm. on Foreign Relations Rep. on Third Protocol, supra,* note 78 at 6, reprinted in *Cong. Rec., supra,* note 72 at S. 8812 (daily ed., July 9, 1979); *Cong. Rec., ibid.* at S. 8808 (remarks of Sen. Javits), at S. 8812 (remarks of Sen. Mathias and Sen. Glenn), and at S. 8813 (remarks of Sen. Percy).

100. *New York Times,* Feb. 20, 1980, at D 17, col. 6.

101. L. Henkin, *supra*, note 49 at 133–34.

102. Department of State Publication No. 8960, *Digest of United States Practice in International Law 1977*, 376 (1979).

103. L. Henkin, *supra*, note 49 at 136.

104. *Digest, supra*, note 102.

7

Investigating Intelligence Activities: The Process of Getting Information for Congress

Michael J. Glennon

IT HAS BECOME de rigueur, in any discussion of the subject of intelligence activities, to begin with a reference to a passage from the Gospel of St. John that appears on the wall of the lobby of the CIA headquarters in Langley, Virginia. It reminds us that "the truth shall make you free." While this edifying shibboleth is not particularly relevant to my topic because it serves as a yardstick by which to measure the accuracy of CIA reporting, another very big topic, there happens to be another passage from John's Gospel that is eminently relevant. It is unfortunately not inscribed at the CIA, either in stone or in spirit: "Ask and ye shall receive."

I have been asked to discuss the process by which a congressional committee goes about getting information from the intelligence community concerning a matter within that committee's jurisdiction. If the truth does, indeed, make us free, then I must give you the unvarnished bad tidings: the truth is that the process of prying comprehensive and meaningful intelligence-related information from the government can involve far more than simply asking. This is so even when the request comes from a congressional committee with clear jurisdiction.

Before discussing the process of pursuing information, the difficulties for the congressional investigators and the ramifications for effective oversight, let me describe generally the kind of information we sought during a recent inquiry in which I participated, and why it was important that we obtain that information.

Following numerous allegations of improper and illegal activities in the United States by various foreign intelligence agencies, the Subcommittee on International Operations, in April 1977, commenced an inquiry into the operations of six of those services. The agencies of Chile, Iran, the Philippines, Taiwan, the Soviet Union, and Yugoslavia were studied to determine whether and how they were harassing, intimidating, or monitoring U.S. residents. The subcommittee also sought to examine the response of the executive branch: the priority assigned to gathering information on such foreign agencies' operation in this country, the action taken by executive agencies in response to that information, and the types of relationships existing between our intelligence community and these foreign services.

In language of which the intelligence community is fond, our subcommittee had a legitimate "need to know" that information, for several reasons.

First, several statutes are relevant to such activities. The Foreign Relations Committee, of which we are a subcommittee, has jurisdiction, including oversight responsibility, for the operation of the Foreign Agents Registration Act as well as several other statutes requiring registration of persons carrying out these kinds of activities on behalf of a foreign government. If those statutes are not adequately enforced, or if the protection they afford is insufficient, then the committee, and, ultimately, the Congress needs to know.

Second, various civil rights statutes have the effect of limiting the assistance the United States can provide foreign intelligence services conducting these kinds of operations in the United States. Similarly, an executive order prohibits any agency of our intelligence community from encouraging, directly or indirectly, any organization to undertake activities forbidden by that order or by applicable law. If the U.S. law enforcement or intelligence community were violating the civil rights acts or an applicable executive order by providing prohibited kinds of assistance to a foreign intelligence service, then the Congress needs to know.

Third, the protection of human rights has been, in President Carter's words, the "cornerstone" of our foreign policy. Our government has been concerned about the way various foreign governments treat their citizens. Mostly, we can do little about it. But when those governments persecute their citizens and former citizens in this country, then we *can* do something, and, again, the Congress needs to know so it can act.

Fourth, and most important, every resident of the United States, irrespective of citizenship, is constitutionally accorded the rights of free speech, free association, and free assembly. If these rights are abridged through the harassment of a foreign secret police force, it is not simply the individual "target" who is the victim but the entire American body politic. For that body politic needs to be free to hear what each person has to say. The targets of these agencies are generally dissident émigrés or visiting students with important messages on the terror of authoritarianism. We need to be reminded that tyranny is all about. And if the forces of tyranny, over here, are preventing them from telling their story, then the Congress needs to know.

These reasons why Congress needed to know also suggest the kind of information the subcommittee sought. Let me review next *how* the information was sought, in the belief that our experience may provide a "case study" of some utility for officials of the executive branch responsible for dealing with future, similar inquiries, for persons on the Hill doing the inquiring, and for those concerned about insuring adequate oversight of the intelligence community.

If one central lesson emerges from the experience of our inquiry, it is that the tools the textbooks tell us are available to the two branches—the subpoena power, the appointment power, the power over the purse, executive privilege, and the rest—are, in practice, largely irrelevant to the daily give and take of congressional intelligence oversight, and that the real battles are fought in a practical arena in which the executive agencies maintain a significant advantage.

It would normally take a bureaucrat of impoverished imagination, for example, to recommend a claim of executive privilege in response to a congressional request for information. Readily available is a plethora of means for accomplishing the same result, without a messy public confrontation. Here are some of the most effective tools at the executive's disposal.

Delay. Committees and subcommittees come and go, as do their chairmen and staff members, but the executive bureaucracy goes on forever. Accordingly, their first principle in dealing with an unwanted congressional investigation is *delay, delay, delay again.* How is it done? Let me count only some of the ways: vacations, work overload, personnel transfers, meetings, sickness, marriage, divorce—the list of excuses is endless, but the consequence is always the same: the clock ticks ever closer to the inevitable date on which the subcommittee is abolished, a new chairman takes over, or the chief counsel returns to his law firm. Delays of months are not uncommon in the case of many document requests; certain documents requested of the Department of State were not furnished until over a year later. If Congress' power of the purse is the ultimate constitutional weapon, delay is the great equalizer, because many of our minor triumphs, in the end, were pyrrhic victories when weighed against the amount of time they cost us.

The "MOU." Before any executive agency agrees to give any comprehensive information to a congressional committee investigating an intelligence matter, it has become customary to require the committee to enter into a memorandum of understanding, or MOU, setting forth the conditions under which classified information will be provided. In negotiating this contract, a principal point of contention is likely to be the provision that establishes a procedure for public disclosure. The executive agencies can be counted on to push for the final say as to what information the committee will make public, whereas the committee—if it has any respect for separation-of-powers principles—will resist. Although this and other terms are, in a sense, negotiable, the starting point is implicit: no MOU, no information. Possession, as a CIA official reminded me, is nine tenths of the law. The result, therefore, is that the MOU will likely establish a fairly complex procedure un-

der which both the committee and the executive agency participate jointly in deciding what to make public. In theory, this satisfies separation-of-powers requirements, but in practice it gives the
executive veto power over the outcome of the congressional investigation. By eventually refusing to participate in the preparation of
a "sanitized," unclassified version of the committee's report, the
agency can effectively prevent release of any documented study
which criticizes its activities. Undocumented, a report will be
nearly useless.

Senate Resolution 400. This resolution, passed by the second
session of the Ninety-fourth Congress in 1976, established the
Senate Select Committee on Intelligence (SSCI). During the inquiry by our subcommittee of the Foreign Relations Committee,
the executive branch repeatedly argued that creation of the SSCI
had in effect limited our right to see classified intelligence information because the Senate had now centralized the intelligence
oversight functions in the new committee. This was an erroneous
interpretation by the executive branch. Whatever the merits of the
argument for consolidation, the Senate, in establishing the SSCI,
had made clear beyond question that it did not intend to confer
upon it exclusive jurisdiction over intelligence matters. Section
3(c) of S. Res. 400 provides that "[n]othing in this resolution shall
be construed as prohibiting or otherwise restricting the authority
of any other committee to study and review any intelligence activity to the extent that such activity directly affects a matter otherwise within the jurisdiction of such committee."

Nonetheless, the setting up of the SSCI was used by certain
executive agencies as a pretext for denying key information to the
subcommittee. It must be admitted that, in making this argument,
they found no lack of sympathy among the SSCI's senior staff.
Congress, like any fragmented power, is very open to "divide-and-
conquer" tactics.

The "Third Agency Rule." The so-called third agency rule is a
National Security Council directive, adhered to by all elements of
the intelligence community, which prohibits one agency from dis-

seminating material originating in another agency without the consent of the originating agency. For example, information possessed by the FBI that it has received from the CIA will not be made available to Congress without the consent of the CIA. Such a rule may provide some assurance within the executive branch that sensitive intelligence information will not be passed around haphazardly, but its invocation in response to a request by a congressional committee is frequently for the purpose of delay and obstruction.

Classification. Normally, congressional committees have available to them a variety of sources of outside expertise—think tanks, lobbies, university and law school faculties—which they are accustomed to call upon when their own staff lacks certain knowledge or experience. In the case of a committee investigating an intelligence matter, however, those sources are generally not available. The reason is that the questions about which expert opinion is needed often are so entangled with classified information that they cannot be addressed to persons lacking security clearance. Thus, it may be impossible to solicit expert legal opinion without to some extent revealing the underlying facts, which are classified. As a consequence, some important public policy questions relating to intelligence subjects not only are not weighed and debated in a public forum, but even when they are discussed in a private, governmental forum, expert opinion—particularly expert opinion likely to be critical of official policy—is not available to be taken into account. This is true with respect to basic questions such as whether a certain procedure is typical; whether alternatives exist for accomplishing the same objective; whether a certain activity raises legal issues; and, of course, the most fundamental question, whether a given course of action is wise from a public policy standpoint. The upshot is that certain aspects of intelligence activity may be largely insulated from meaningful review.

The "Sources and Methods" Clause. Section 102(c)(3) of the National Security Act of 1947[1] provides that the "Director of Central Intelligence shall be responsible for protecting intelligence sources and methods from unauthorized disclosure." The terms "source" and "method" are not defined by the act, however, and in the absence of any definition, their elasticity and subjectiveness can be exploited by agency officials looking for some statutory provision to justify nondisclosure to the Congress. With minimal creativity, it can be argued that virtually any set of intelligence information relates to intelligence "sources and methods." It is conveniently overlooked by the agencies that this refers only to *unauthorized* disclosure, which should make the stricture inapplicable to a congressional committee exercising its lawful responsibilities; a good example of how it is abused is provided by the response of CIA officials when asked for certain information concerning that agency's liaison with foreign intelligence services. Initially, some information was made available, without recourse to the "sources and methods" evasion. However, this informaion raised further rather serious questions, which were then put to the agency, whose officials thereupon reversed themselves and declined to make available any further information on those liaisons, claiming that each constituted an intelligence "method."

In a related strategy, Justice Department officials, unable to avail themselves of the "sources and methods" clause, declined to provide the same information because, they said, they had asked the foreign agencies and they objected to disclosure to the subcommittee.

These are some of the reasons, and there are many others, why a skillful bureaucrat need seldom issue a flat refusal to a congressional request for information. It is possible to achieve the same result while maintaining at least the appearance of cooperation.

There are, in addition, factors intrinsic to the legislative process that make effective inquiry very difficult. The chairman of the Subcommittee on International Operations, Senator McGovern, throughout the inquiry, was accessible to, and supportive of, the staff; without his fortitude the amount of information obtained would have been far less. But senators are notoriously busy people who cannot possibly focus on the day-to-day details of an investigation. This makes it more difficult for staff to call upon them for assistance very frequently, and it also makes it more difficult for them to help effectively. We reviewed thousands of pages of documents and conducted transcribed interviews totaling nearly a thousand pages. The more information is involved, the more time it takes to learn and remember how the pieces fit together and to appreciate the gaps that need to be filled. For that matter, even committee staff often find their time at a premium; during most of the inquiry my other duties for the committee continued to consume over half my days.

Finally, for a staff member who intends someday to move, or return, to the executive branch, making waves that rock boats at the State Department, CIA, or Pentagon may not be the best career strategy.

Thus far I have been discussing impediments to effective congressional inquiry into intelligence matters. I do not mean to imply that, faced with these obstacles, a committee is helpless. Far from it. A letter or telephone call from the chairman to the agency head can get results, and the threat of a press release—or press conference—detailing noncooperation may get even better results. Reasoning remains possible, and agency personnel can sometimes be convinced that a coincidence of interests exist between the objectives of their employer and the committee. Divide and conquer is a two-way street: interagency and intra-agency rivalries sometimes can be played upon. Although their own operations are invariably presented (to use Adlai Stevenson's formulation) as shining temples of administrative purity and political probity, it often requires little effort to elicit from executive officials accounts of chronic bungling and outright iniquity on the part of officials of other agencies. And if all else fails, a determined staff member can simply make it clear that he is not going to go away, hoping that agency officials will produce a given document simply to get the matter resolved.

But the "big guns"—the power over the purse, the confirmation power, the subpoena power—can seldom be wheeled out. Generally, these are of use only in response to an absolute executive refusal to cooperate in a specific, material way, but not in a war of attrition waged by officials wise enough not to present a large, unmoving target. Moreover, politicians are conditioned by their craft to make friends, not to seek enemies, so confrontation is extremely distasteful to most members of Congress.

This brings me to what I regard as the most serious impediment to rigorous congressional oversight of intelligence matters: the congressional investigatory process is too vulnerable to pressures emanating from vacillations in the public mood. That vulnerability manifests itself today in the widespread belief in Congress that the subject of intelligence reform has been drained of all political capital; that, indeed, we have entered an era of ever pernicious foreign threats, or, at least, of widespread public perception of such threats, in which any criticism of the U.S. intelligence establishment is made at one's political peril. A *Time* magazine essay illustrates the mood. "This is a troubled world," it declares. "Threatening forces continue to challenge us. . . . In the past, the [CIA] engaged in some practices that are not acceptable in America, but those days are behind us. The CIA has reformed." *Time* concludes that the "oversight committees should be reduced to the two current Select Committees on Intelligence, which, as a matter of fact, have done their job fairly seriously."[2]

It could be that the CIA really has "reformed." It may also be true that the congressional intelligence committees have taken their job fairly seriously. But how does *Time* know? On the basis of what information can *Time* be so sure that institutions almost entirely removed from public scrutiny have reformed and will stay reformed? I suspect that *Time* has succumbed to the proclivity identified by the astronomer Carl Sagan, in another context, to mistake absence of *evidence* for evidence of *absence*. It is an error shared by much of the public and many in Congress.

The sensitivity, or vulnerability, of Congress to every change in the political climate poses the principal obstacle to effective legislative oversight. To a large extent, legislative action and inaction should reflect the popular will. But this is likely to mean that legislative committees responsible for various intelligence oversight functions normally will be only as vigorous as the popular will allows. In practical terms, this means that in periods of relative public indifference, a subpoena will simply not be issued by the committee when the executive refuses to reveal a significant document; no press conference will be called, no letter will be sent by the chairman to the head of the recalcitrant agency; a telephone call will not be made.

In the end, it may be that no structural safeguards can insure responsibility in the operation of the governmental process. It may be that the public temper is all that can ever really be counted upon to prevent the abuse of power. "Democracy," as William James said,

> is still upon its trial. The civic genius of our people is its only bulwark, and neither laws nor monuments . . . can save us from degeneration if the inner mystery is lost. That mystery . . . consists of nothing but . . . common habits . . . carried into public life. . . . One of them is the habit of . . . fierce and merciless resentment toward every man or set of men who break the public peace.[3]

There is no substitute for a vigilant body politic, and in its absence any purely legislative oversight mechanism is but a stopgap. In and of itself, therefore, I doubt that congressional oversight—by *any* committee—is sufficient, and I think that arguments about which committee is best suited to do the job miss the mark. An effective oversight structure must include at least two additional elements: a statutory framework placing clear limits upon the foreign and domestic operations of our intelligence community, and an oversight mechanism that is, to the maximum extent possible, *removed* from the political process.

The need for meaningful intelligence charters has been widely discussed elsewhere. I would only add my voice to those asserting that if we are truly a government of laws rather than men, then laws limiting the agencies' discretion, and not merely words of goodwill uttered by executive officials at closed congressional hearings, are absolutely essential. Those limitations must be painstakingly drafted so as to avoid implicitly or inadvertently conferring authority upon the intelligence establishment to conduct unacceptable activities. On the basis of my experience I believe that they also must unequivocally prohibit our agencies from helping their foreign counterparts to conduct those activities.

As for a politically insulated supervisory process, designing it raises Plato's dilemma: Who can be counted upon to guard the guardians? Obviously, I do not believe that congressional oversight will suffice. Neither do I believe that the mechanism can be placed within the intelligence establishment. In-house review boards, inspectors general, and general counsels vested with oversight functions simply do not have the necessary independence. Agencies with a demonstrated propensity for transgressing boundaries cannot be counted upon to police themselves, to insure that abuses are investigated and statutory guidelines respected. To a lesser extent, the same difficulty arises with the placement of oversight elements elsewhere in the executive branch. They still report to the same authority—the White House—that is ultimately responsible for the activities in question. In short, if the logic of nonpolitical oversight is accepted, it would appear that the process cannot be placed squarely in either political branch.

I have reservations about the creation of entities, such as special prosecutors, that fall within the interstices between the two branches. But it seems to me that in these unique circumstances such a body is warranted. The principal difficulty with them is that they are not accountable. But without the creation of such a body here, unaccountability is likely to persist on a far more massive scale, namely, in the unrestrained exercise of power by the intelligence establishment. It may well persist in any event; various independent regulatory agencies have proven anything but immune to the pressures of cooption. But our experience with the General Accounting Office (GAO), for example, has been largely favorable, and an independent intelligence oversight organization could be based on the GAO model. I do not propose the establishment of a "super National Security Council" to approve individual covert operations or otherwise performing functions properly those of the executive branch. I do suggest that the oversight process would be strengthened by the establishment of an independent body with statutory access to all intelligence information, capable of insisting upon strict compliance with every applicable statute and executive order, able to function continuously, whatever the political climate.

Justice Jackson was doubtless correct when he said that "[t]he chief restraint upon those who command the physical forces of the country, in the future as in the past, must be their responsibility to the political judgments of their contemporaries and to the moral judgments of history."[4] But the difficulty in making such judgments regarding intelligence matters is that the public domain is almost entirely devoid of facts upon which those judgments might be based. That is why I do not believe that the test of effective intelligence oversight can be whether it plays in Pocatello. The agencies to be overseen do not regulate truck widths or set train schedules; they have the capability of radically and permanently altering the political and legal contours of our society. Their activities require the closest possible scrutiny, a scrutiny that cannot depend upon whether vigilance happens to be in vogue in a particular year.

NOTES

1. 50 U.S.C. 403(c) (3).
2. April 30, 1979, p. 95.
3. William James, "Memories and Studies," 1911.
4. *Korematsu v. United States,* 323 U.S. 214 (1944) (Jackson, J. dissent).

8

Human Rights and Constitutional Wrongs: A Case Study of the Origins of Congressional Imperialism *

Thomas M. Franck

INTRODUCTION

IT IS CONVENTIONAL wisdom that, in the conduct of foreign re-lations, Congress should lay down the broad guidelines, leaving the executive to implement them day by day and case by case.

Critics of recent congressional activism charge that this reasonable division of labors has been stood on its head: that, increasingly, legislators have taken over the detailed administration of foreign policy while neglecting the task of creating a legitimating consensus around broadly formulated national goals.

My purpose is to rebut this increasingly common criticism. To do so, I have examined one area of intense congressional activism. In no aspect of foreign relations has Congress been more fully engaged than in the pursuit of basic human rights. It was Congress that made the issue a central component in U.S. relations with foreign powers over the strenuous objection of the administration. True, after broadly defining this new national goal, some legislators then went on to administer the law embodying it; they thereby trespassed on the proper prerogatives of the executive. However,

---

* An earlier draft of this chapter was published by Sweet and Maxwell, London, 1980.

I hope to demonstrate, this was not due to congressional imperialism but to the refusal of the president and the secretary of state to discharge their constitutional obligation to "take care that the laws be faithfully executed." Instead, they engaged in a practice akin to impoundment, boldly refusing to implement the human rights policy enacted by the legislature. When this impoundment ceased, after a new president embraced the law's intent, so did the interference of Congress in the law's execution.

It is my conclusion that most legislators agree with the conventional wisdom and do not wish to be diverted from legislation to implementation. That conventional wisdom breaks down, however, when a president and secretary of state take the position that foreign policy is their private prerogative, beyond the comprehension and competence of Congress.

The human rights experience this chapter analyzes demonstrates that Congress will only reluctantly assume responsibility for the execution of laws, and only after it is convinced that the president is likely to impound, rather than execute, the law of the land. Moreover, the legislators are generally willing to restore presidential prerogatives as soon as this aberration is seen to cease.

Perhaps not so incidentally, the record also demonstrates that the much-discounted folk wisdom of Congress may sometimes comprehend changing realities and become intuitively aware of potential opportunities in the conduct of foreign relations that have escaped our professional policy managers. The priority accorded to human rights by Congress on balance has proven to be in the national interest, while the dire predictions of the executive branch's foreign policy specialists have not been realized.

SYNOPSIS

The Congressional interaction with the presidency in respect of human rights policy occurred in four phases:

First, legislators tried to lay down very general policy guidelines in voluntary "sense of Congress" form. Unfortunately, an administration hostile to their intent merely ignored them in shaping its foreign policy on the basis of what it imagined to be a tough-minded *Realpolitik*.

Second, when it became clear that its policy guidelines were not going to be implemented on a voluntary basis, Congress made them mandatory and more specific.

Third, when it appeared that these mandatory guidelines would not be implemented either, Congress gave itself power to execute the law in direct confrontation with the executive branch.

Fourth, after a new administration demonstrated a willingness to execute the human rights legislation on a case-by-case basis, Congress relinquished its temporary hold on executory powers in favor of those better suited to exercise them.

CONGRESS LAYS DOWN GUIDELINES

As usual, differences over constitutional powers grew out of disagreements over national policy. By the early 1970s, the foreign policy of *Realpolitik* practiced by successive administrations had been elevated to the status of sacred doctrine culminating in wholesale claims of executive privilege and presidential immunity to legal process. The domestic counterpart of all this was the Watergate debacle. In international affairs, the national interest was being defined preponderantly in terms of a static global balance of power between the United States and the Soviet Union. The importance of other states to America depended on how they affected this balance; so did the weight to be given to various substantive concerns, such as the promoting of international economic development. By this system of weights and measures, human rights were of relatively minor importance, for three reasons. *First,* human rights issues were being pressed primarily by minor states of limited importance in the geopolitical equation: nations such as Costa Rica, the Netherlands, and Tanzania. What strategic payoff could we expect from cultivating them? In any event, we already had a political alliance with the Netherlands; we did not need one with Costa Rica; and, no matter what, we could not expect Tanzania to tilt in our direction. *Second,* a human rights policy would risk alienating repressive states that also happened to be loyal allies: Franco's Spain, the colonels' Greece, Marcos's Philippines, Park's South Korea. It could upset delicate and complex political interdependencies without gaining us anything of commensurate *strategic* value. *Third,* as to our opponents, a human rights policy would become a wild card in a game in which only mutual strategic advantage matters. If we were to provoke a confrontation with the Russians, for example, it would be far better to do it over their role in Africa and that of their Cuban surrogates, which is a subject of importance to the United States and appropriate to international negotiations, than over an issue of no strategic significance to us and that is essentially a domestic issue for the Soviets.

It is difficult, today, to recall the prevailing climate in the executive branch during this period. Those few officials within the State Department who talked of human rights and advocated the inclusion of a human rights factor in policy implementation actually risked their careers. They were perceived as softheaded bleeding hearts in a milieu that rewarded stout hearts, hard noses, and a "can do" style.

It was in Congress, particularly in the House of Representatives, that a small coterie of human rights buffs set themselves determinedly against this prevailing *Realpolitik,* thereby offending not only the *macho* of the administration but also of those powerful congressional committees specializing in military affairs and foreign relations. (What began as a revolt by Congress against the president soon became a revolt of the congressional rank and file against their own foreign policy establishment.) Beginning in 1973, events began to drift in the direction of these rebels, perhaps less because of a profound intellectual transformation on Capitol Hill than to a shift in popular conceptual fashion—probably the nearest our nation gets to deep ideological vision and revision. Because of the failure of *Realpolitik* in Vietnam and its disagreeable intrusion into domestic politics, hardheaded amorality was suddenly "out" and public morality "in." The human rights issue conveniently called a lost nation back from Metternich to Jefferson. But while the call was heard in Congress—first by a small group of middle western populists—the executive branch continued to follow the implacable steady-as-she-goes vision of Dr. Kissinger's

Realpolitik. In these circumstances, with the Congress and the administration listening to quite different voices, conflict was inevitable.

Congress determined to assert itself on human rights, as it was also doing in respect of the lingering Indochina conflict, by exercising its "power of the purse," the most effective vehicle for legislative policymaking. The foreign assistance authorization passed in 1973 thus expressed the "sense of Congress" that the president should deny economic and military aid to any foreign government that practices "internment or imprisonment of that country's citizens for political purposes."[1] The administration opposed this policy and made clear that it would not implement it.

Such a "sense of Congress" resolution is the lowest level of legislative command, manifesting a congressional preference without quite creating a legally binding mandate. An attentive administration would have recognized it as a shot across the bow by a no longer supine legislature. Instead, the Nixon administration reacted like a late 1950s Mississippi school board suddenly faced with a busing order. A year after Congress had spoken, a House international relations subcommittee chaired by Representative Don Fraser reviewed the administration's record of implementation and concluded that there had been none—that human rights was simply "not accorded the high priority it deserves in our country's foreign policy." On the contrary, it usually remained "invisible on the vast horizon of political, economic and military affairs."[2] Fraser's report charged that U.S. policy toward South Vietnam, Spain, Portugal, the Soviet Union, Brazil, Indonesia, Greece, the Philippines, and Chile "exemplify how we have disregarded human rights for the sake of other assumed interests."[3] It warned that if the administration did not begin to take seriously the congressional policy directive, Congress itself would take charge of implementing it.[4]

TIGHTENING THE GUIDELINES

Soon thereafter, the legislature tried once more, this time spelling out the "sense of Congress" more explicitly. It specified that "the President shall substantially reduce or terminate security assistance to any government which engages in a consistent pattern of internationally recognized human rights, including torture or cruel, inhuman or degrading treatment or punishment; prolonged detention without charges; or other flagrant denials of the right to life, liberty and security of the person."[5] At the same time, the 1974 Foreign Assistance Act took a first step in the direction of implementing its own policy by voting to end military, and reducing economic, support for Chile while making token cuts in the South Korean program.[6] The administration, which had proposed not a single human rights-motivated aid reduction of its own, vehemently opposed these efforts by Congress to "administer" the law, ritually calling them ill advised and an encroachment on presidential power. Administration officials professed outrage at what they saw to be virtual bills of attainder singling out and punishing regimes that offended the legislators' fine sensibilities.

In the year that followed, the executive branch still continued utterly to ignore the human rights concerns of Congress. At the beginning of 1975, the undersecretary of state did send a telegram to U.S. embassies ordering a report on the status of human rights in each country,[7] and the Agency for International Development promulgated a directive advising field staff to seek out projects with a human rights component.[8] But the administration's 1975 request for new funding authorization, by failing even to mention human rights as a factor in selecting recipients of economic and military assistance, manifested continuing resistance—impoundment—rather than compliance.

Perhaps, in part, this can be explained merely by the bureaucratic stasis that normally follows any external intervention in policymaking. Complaints were common that the Congress had failed to clarify its intentions, leaving harassed officials with such impossible choices as whether to help or punish people living in countries doubly cursed with dire poverty and aggressive regimes. Other administrators pointed to the conflict between the human rights directive and others in the same law mandating support for such new priorities as accelerated food production and population planning.

Some of these complaints were legitimate, and might have been recognized as such by Congress, in 1975, had there been *any* evidence that the administration was, indeed, grappling with the complexities created by the new human rights concern. Instead, Secretary Kissinger made it plain that he resented the legislators' grandstanding, that the matter could not be addressed in the way Congress had done or, for that matter, by any form of legislation. He argued that the nation's human rights concerns should not be set in statutory concrete but, rather, left to the foreign relations specialists, who alone had the information to determine the appropriate strategy in each special circumstance and the skill to weigh accurately the competing U.S. foreign relations concerns. In short, this was an argument for a policy made by men, not laws. Moreover, the administration warned, the ongoing effort to secure greater compliance with minimal rights standards by quiet diplomatic persuasion would suffer if Congress insisted on overseeing that effort publicly. In the world according to Henry Kissinger, a quiet, effective effort by specialists was being threatened by the Capitol Hill carnival. The legislators, on the contrary, saw only noncompliance by arrogant men who treated foreign policy as their exclusive preserve.

As Congress for the first time prepared to write a mandatory human rights law, it became increasingly clear that the executive disagreed not only with the policy the legislature had embraced but also, much more fundamentally, with the right of Congress to utilize legislation, including the power of the purse, to make foreign policy. For years, the powers of the commander in chief had been expanding, under the umbrella of Mr. Justice Sutherland's ill-conceived dicta in the *Curtiss-Wright* case,[9] until presidents had virtually convinced themselves that the Constitution really did give them exclusive power to conduct foreign relations. When Congress had voted to cut off funds for the conduct of hostilities "in, over, or from off" Indochina,[10] even as unassuming and Congress-wise a president as Gerald Ford had boldly ignored that injunction, claiming inherent foreign relations powers that could not be restricted by law.[11] Now, in respect of human rights, the administration was similarly acting on an assumption of plenary powers. It was to this challenge that Congress responded.

CONGRESS ADMINISTERS ITS OWN LAW

Late in 1975, Congress decided to make its human rights policy mandatory and it began by assuming executive noncompliance: such was the condition of interbranch relations in Washington at this time. A floor amendment successfully moved on behalf of House rank and filers by Representative Tom Harkin ordered the president to deny economic assistance to any state engaging in a consistent pattern of gross violations of internationally recognized human rights unless he certified that such aid "will directly benefit the needy people in such country." Anticipating presidential misuse of this escape clause, the Harkin amendment permitted either chamber of Congress to override the presidential certification.[12] In the Senate, too, the backbenchers carried the day, although the "one-house veto" was modified to require a concurrent resolution of both chambers.[13]

In that form, the law was signed on December 20 by President Ford despite his belief, shared by many but not all authorities,[14] that the concurrent resolution procedure circumvents the Constitution's presentation clause in purporting to make law by action of Congress alone.[15] With that, Congress had laid down a mandatory policy on human rights and given itself the power to implement it whenever the executive failed to do so.

By the following year, relations between the branches had further worsened. The State Department had now received, compiled, and analyzed the replies of U.S. embassies to its request for human rights data. Although officials had promised to make these findings available to Congress, what was transmitted as the "Report to the Congress on the Human Rights Situation in Countries Receiving U.S. Security Assistance"[16] was a much-laundered version that named no countries and singled out no practices of governments. It was promptly dubbed the "civics lesson" by scornful legislators[17] who took exception to such bland nonsense as the assertion that while "[s]ome countries present more serious evidence of violations than others . . . we have found no adequately objective way to make distinctions of degree."[18]

"There may be no objective way to determine the degree of violations," Senator Cranston thundered, "but does the Secretary of State have any subjective feelings about what is going on in Chile, Brazil, Korea, Indonesia, Ethiopia and the Philippines today? And can he give us some examples of where quiet, but forceful diplomacy has made a difference . . . ?"[19]

To make matters worse for the administration, the unlaundered in-house version of the report, highly critical of the human rights policies of numerous aid recipients, was quickly leaked to Congress by dissidents within the administration. (The shift in foreign relations powers from the executive to Congress may have been less a result of legislative imperialism than of the White House' inability to prevent its own disaffected bureaucrats from awakening the sleeping dogs of Capitol Hill.) Because the report quoted extensively from embassy replies, it had been suppressed by Secretary Kissinger as too "hot" for Congress.[20] To the legislators, the effort to keep it in the dark merely proved once again that the administration was impounding the law.

Accordingly, tough mandatory human rights procedures were written into the Military Assistance Law in 1976, paralleling and supplementing the previous year's provisions applicable to economic aid. At first, these contained another concurrent resolution provision, but, after strenuous opposition by President Ford, that aspect was deleted.[21] Nevertheless, the new law requires the administration to promote human rights abroad, to deny security assistance to states that engage in gross violations, to provide an annual report to Congress on the status of human rights in each recipient state detailing steps taken by the United States to redress gross violations.[22] Additionally, House or Senate committees are empowered, at any time, to have the State Department assess conditions in specific countries[23] and to justify continuation of aid in the face of serious violations.[24] Failure to comply in effect terminates the aid program in question. (In addition, by Section 617 of the act, Congress by concurrent resolution may end any foreign aid program after eight months' notice.)[25]

During the fall of 1976, Congressman Fraser's subcommittee tested the new reporting requirements, calling for assessments of human rights conditions in Argentina, Haiti, Indonesia, Iran, Peru, and the Philippines. After an initial show of resistance, State agreed to publication of its country reports, which turned out to be surprisingly frank.[26] Since then, annual foreign aid authorization requests are always accompanied by country-by-country reports detailing local conditions and chronicling action to support human rights taken by the United States in the eighty-two recipient states through assistance programs and in quiet diplomacy.[27]

It has become clear that, with the advent of a new administration elected on a human rights platform that essentially adopted the policy set by Congress, implementation would no longer be as serious a problem. To demonstrate its willingness to execute the law, the Carter administration took the initiative by cutting Argentine military sales credits to $15 million from the $32 million authorized by Congress[28] and reducing arms aid to Ethiopia and Uruguay. In 1977 the administration voluntarily rejected a new security assistance agreement with Nicaragua.[29]

Almost as important in demonstrating the administrative shift away from impoundment has been its attitude in situations where human rights has had to take a back seat. When President Carter has wished aid to continue despite human rights violations, his officials have not hesitated to argue in favor of giving priority to other considerations, but have stressed the steps short of an embargo being taken in support of the rights policy. Secretary Cyrus Vance, for example, has defended before Congress our "overriding security commitments" to South Korea[30] but without minimizing the relevance of human rights to the ability of South Korea to rally its people in their own defense. Vice President Walter Mondale, an early congressional human rights enthusiast, has lobbied personally against cuts in aid to the Philippines because of the effect on negotiations for renewal of essential U.S. bases; but he also promised to employ other levers to alleviate conditions under the Marcos regime.[31] Despite such temporizing, most members of Congress now appear convinced that the Carter administration has genuinely embraced the central theme of its human rights legislation, even if sincere men may differ over the best way to implement it in difficult cases. More important, the Carter administration has behaved as if Congress belonged in the picture and ought to be consulted.

This has made it possible once more for the Congress to resist its own zealots, and to relinquish control over case-by-case implementation. During the Nixon-Ford years legislators on the left and right fringes, under the banner of human rights policy, had successfully attacked aid to Angola, Mozambique,[32] North Vietnam,[33] South Korea, Indonesia, Iran, Uruguay, Argentina, Chile, the Philippines,[34] and Uganda.[35] More recently, these efforts to legislate country-specific embargoes have been overwhelmingly defeated. A partial prohibition on military aid to Turkey[36] was repealed in 1978,[37] and most other bans against a named state have either been dropped or modified by giving the president discretion to lift it "in the national interest."[38] Prohibitions on military aid or credits to Brazil, El Salvador, Uruguay, and Guatemala were deleted by 1979,[39] as were those on economic and military aid to Angola and Mozambique.[40] In recent years, Congress has also easily defeated efforts to impose new country-specific restrictions on Syria, Nicaragua, and Afghanistan, leaving it to the administration's discretion to apply the law's broad guidelines.[41] For that matter, the legislature has never invoked the controversial concurrent resolution procedures to terminate any ongoing assistance program.

Similarly, Congress has avoided precipitous action in regard to assistance made available through international financial institutions, despite the fact that during the Nixon-Ford years these had been used to circumvent congressional policy. Between 1970 and 1976, while U.S. aid to human rights violators—Argentina, Brazil, Chile, Nicaragua, Indonesia, Thailand, the Philippines, and South Korea—had declined from $586.9 million to $427.8 million, indirect aid, coming mostly from international lending institutions in which the United States was the principal shareholder, had risen from $1.7 billion to $6 billion.[42] Such "back-door financing" had rightly angered Congress, and by 1975 Representative Harkin had succeeded in amending the authorization for the Inter-American and African Development Banks to require the U.S. directors to use their votes in those institutions against loans and aid to gross human rights violators.[43] In 1977 Representative Herman Badillo got this rule extended to all United States-supported international lending institutions, including the World Bank.[44]

For a time, even President Carter resisted these efforts to tie his directors' hands in setting bank policy. However, when pressed by Congress, Carter undertook to "instruct the U.S. Executive Directors to oppose and vote against" seven specified "gross violators."[45] With that, congressional intervention abated. Senator Robert Dole[46] and Representative Clarence Long have recently failed to persuade their colleagues to withhold funds from international institutions to whatever extent these persisted in making assistance available to human rights violators.[47] Another attempt, in 1978, by Representative Harkin to deny funds to the international banks for use in Nicaragua, the Philippines, Indonesia, South Korea, Uruguay, Chile, and Argentina was buried under a landslide vote of 360 to 41, as were other efforts to enjoin loans to Mozambique and Angola.[48] Congress then dropped all remaining country-specific prohibitions, including even those on Vietnam[49] and Cuba.[50] Meanwhile, the executive has been keeping its side of the bargain by successfully using its weighted vote in several global lending institutions to defeat applications by the more pernicious human rights offenders. Once again, as the moderate congressional majority became convinced that the administration had resumed its traditional constitutional role of faithfully implementing the spirit of the laws, the legislators appear more willing to relinquish the making of day-by-day and case-by-case decisions.

As noted, the administration's new willingness to implement was manifested by the preparation and publication of frank and specific country reports, the selective cutting of assistance, and by use of U.S. voting power in international financial institutions. It was also demonstrated by a significant bureaucratic reorganization that sought to insure that major foreign policy decisions would begin to be made in fuller awareness of the human rights implications.

ADMINISTRATIVE COMPLIANCE

An extensive reorganization of the executive branch was undertaken by the Carter administration to insure that various departments and agencies would comply with human rights laws and implement policy in accordance with relevant congressional guidelines. An assistant secretary of state for human rights was appointed and given a sizable staff. Human rights specialists were added to various bureaus and agencies, including the Agency for International Development and the National Security Council. In April 1977 an Inter-Agency Group on Human Rights and Foreign Assistance was created by directive of the National Security Council to include representatives of the State Department, Defense, Treasury, Commerce, Labor, the Export-Import Bank, and even the Agriculture Department[51] (which, through "food for peace" administers a significant foreign aid program of its own).

The Inter-Agency Group is authorized to "examine our bilateral and multilateral foreign assistance decisions as they relate to human rights, to provide guidance regarding specific decisions on bilateral and multilateral assistance, and in general to coordinate the Administration's position in this area."[52] The group, often operating through a smaller subgroup, has been meeting regularly since its creation. Prior to each session, participants receive a list of assistance issues and proposals currently under consideration, and briefing materials relevant to each project under consideration, including an analysis of a proposed recipient's human rights policies prepared by the State Department's Human Rights Bureau.[53] After full discussion, the group may approve a project because human rights conditions in the recipient country are satisfactory, are authentically improving, or because the program will clearly benefit the needy rather than enhance the power of the government. It may also recommend approval of a project subject to a diplomatic representation emphasizing U.S. human rights concerns. If the group votes against a proposal, it may do so without further comment, or it may recommend a demarche—to be made publicly or privately—explaining how the human rights factor was determinative. Such a statement may or may not encourage reapplication upon the meeting of certain conditions.

The group has already recommended deferral of various AID projects and proposed that the U.S. representative oppose or abstain in the vote on several loans—approximately twenty in the first year—pending in international lending institutions for such countries as Argentina, the Philippines, Ethiopia, South Korea, Benin, Chile, Guinea, and the Central African Empire. Unfortunately, no similar interagency task force exists to bring the human rights factor into play when decisions on military exports and security assistance are pending. Although the Human Rights Bureau is represented on the interagency Arms Export Control Board, that body is not effectively geared to the consideration of human rights concerns. Neither is there a formal procedure for bringing the human rights specialists into treaty negotiations. Thus it was left to Congress—specifically, to Senate Majority Leader Robert Byrd—to wrest quite significant human rights concessions from Panamanian Chief of Government Omar Torrijos as part of the price for ratification of the Panama Canal treaties in 1978. These concessions, having to do with freedom of the press, the return of exiles, elections and the rights of political parties, were an important factor in securing Senate approval for the agreement restoring the Canal Zone to Panamanian jurisdiction.[54] Similarly, when the White House in 1978 submitted two human rights conventions for Senate ratification, its counsel, Robert J. Lipshutz, sent along proposals for reservations to be added by the Senate that had not even been seen by the State Department's Human Rights Bureau. The assistant secretary for human rights considered opposing them in public testimony before the Senate Foreign Relations Committee. Again, the Human Rights Bureau was unpleasantly surprised when President Carter personally congratulated Nicaraguan dictator Anastasio Somoza, in July 1978, for certain human rights reforms at the very time the bureau was maneuvering to kill a proposed military credit for that regime.[55]

Despite these lacunae and lapses, the administration is today infinitely better prepared and motivated to administer the broad outlines of human rights policy conceived by Congress than a few years ago. The executive branch now normally works with, not to circumvent, the legislature. In his 1978 report to Congress, Secretary Vance promised "to give far higher priority to human rights considerations in the formulation of American foreign policy" even while reserving the right, in specific instances, to risk inconsistency for the sake of overriding security concerns. The Congress has been increasingly responsive to this new approach and has tended, often after bitter internal fights with the irreconcilables in its ranks, to restore to the presidency those functions that are rightfully its.

CONCLUSIONS

The assertion by Congress of the power to administer the laws it made in the field of human rights was not an indication of constitutional overreach, or of a new doctrine of power distribution among the branches. Rather, it was an ad hoc response to a momentary disorder in the system, caused by the impoundment of lawfully enacted foreign policy by an administration that had increasingly placed itself—in doctrine and practice—beyond the reach of law.

Even in "normal" times, however, there may be instances when Congress attempts to legislate foreign policy on a case-by-case or country-specific basis: usually when a large, domestic, single-issue constituency or ethnic lobby makes a successful effort to arouse the legislators. For example, U.S. producers of commodities have waged a fierce campaign to have Congress prohibit the use of loans or other assistance by international financial institutions to help poor Third World countries produce commodities for export that compete with American production.[56] But even the few ethnic lobbies that have been truly influential in the field of foreign policy have lost more battles of late than they have won. Congress refused to back them against the president to block arms sales to Saudi Arabia and Turkey in 1978. Most legislators simply do not want to be drawn into the business of tinkering with the details, preferring to lay down the guidelines and using their investigative powers to oversee the administration's faithful execution of them. The experience of implementing country-specific decisions on foreign assistance has given legislators a taste of intense lobbying by single-interest groups and equally determined counterlobbying by the White House and other executive agencies. Most have not enjoyed the heat, nor do they relish devoting the time and effort needed to master the highly complex content of even relatively minor issues with little political payoff. Providing there is convincing evidence of implementation rather than impoundment, there is a perceivable tendency—admittedly a slow one—to trust the administration to administer.

NOTES

1. The Foreign Assistance Act of 1973; P.L. 93-189, 87 Stat. 714, §32, 22 U.S.C. §2151 note.
2. U.S. House of Representatives, Committee on International Relations, Subcommittee on International Organizations and Movements, *Human Rights in the World Community: A Call for U.S. Leadership*, Mar. 27,1974.
3. *Ibid.*, p. 9.
4. *Ibid.*, p. 3.
5. The Foreign Assistance Act of 1961, as amended; P.L. 87-195, 75 Stat. 424, §502B. The amendment was added by the Foreign Assistance Act of 1974; P.L. 93-559, 88 Stat. 1795, §46.
6. Foreign Assistance Act of 1974; P.L. 93-559, 88 Stat. 1795, §§25-26.
7. U.S. Department of State, Unclassified Telegram to All Diplomatic Posts, No. 012320; Jan. 17, 1975. See also U.S. Department of State, Unclassified Airgram to All Diplomatic Posts, No. A-1045; Feb. 14, 1975.
8. U.S. Agency for International Development AIDTO Circular A 687, unclassified, airgram, Dec. 9, 1975.
9. 299 U.S. 304, 57 Sup. Ct. 216, 81 L. Ed. 255 (1936).
10. Foreign Assistance Act of 1973; P.L. 93-189, 87 Stat. 714, §30, 22 U.S.C. §2151 note.
11. See T. Franck, *After the Fall: The New Procedural Framework for Congressional Control Over the War Power*, 71 A.J.I.L. 605, 614–21 (1977).
12. S. Rep. No. 94-406, H.R. 9005, Oct. 1, 1975, § 309 at 35.
13. International Development and Food Assistance Act of 1975; P.L. 94-161, 89 Stat. 849, §310, amending the Foreign Assistance Act of 1961 by including a new §116.
14. See the essay in this volume by Professor Bernard Schwartz, *supra*, Chapter 5.
15. See T. Franck, *supra* note 11 at 627–34.
16. U.S. Senate, Committee on Foreign Relations, Subcommittee on Foreign Assistance, *Report to the Congress on the Human Rights Situation in Countries Receiving U.S. Security Assistance*, Foreign Assistance

Authorization: Arms Sales Issues. Hearings, 94th Cong., 1st sess., between June 17 and Dec. 5, 1975, pp. 376–80.

17. The second communication pertaining to the country reports was a "Prepared Statement by James M. Wilson, Jr., Coordinator for Humanitarian Affairs, Department of State," *ibid.*, pp. 463–67.

18. *Ibid.*, pp. 377–78.

19. U.S. Senate, Senator Cranston, *Cong. Rec. S.* 37603 (Nov. 20, 1975).

20. Interview with Les Janka, senior staff member for congressional relations, National Security Council, Washington, D.C., June 23, 1976; Interview with Ambassador Robert J. McCloskey, assistant secretary of state for congressional relations, Washington, D.C., June 24, 1976.

21. The White House, Message of May 7, 1976. *New York Times*, May 8, 1976, p. 1: Ford vetoes foreign aid bill in part due to restrictions, e.g., Congress blocking power. House of Representatives, 94th Cong., 2d sess., Rep. No. 94-1272, *Conference Report* on H.R. 13680, pp. 50–51.

22. 22 U.S.C. §2304(a), (b).

23. 22 U.S.C. §2304(c) (1) (A).

24. 22 U.S.C. §2304(c) (1) (C).

25. 22 U.S.C. §2367.

26. *New York Times*, Jan. 2, 1977, p. 1.

27. The 1978 report ran to 426 pages. U.S. Department of State, *Report* Submitted to the House Committee on International Relations and Senate Foreign Relations Committee, *Country Reports on Human Rights Practices*, 95th Cong., 2d sess., Joint Committee Report, February 3, 1978. See also U.S. Department of State, *Report* Submitted to the House Committee on International Relations, *Human Rights Practices in Countries Receiving U.S. Security Assistance*, 95th Cong., 1st sess., April 25, 1977 (hereinafter *Human Rights Practices in Countries Receiving U.S. Security Assistance: 1977*).

28. *New York Times*, Mar. 1, 1977, p. 6.

29. *Ibid.*, Apr. 6, 1977, p. 3.

30. *Human Rights Practices in Countries Receiving U.S. Security Assistance: 1977*, pp. 12–13, 17–18; *New York Times*, Feb. 25, 1977, p. 1.

31. Interview with Mr. John Salzberg, staff consultant, House International Relations Committee, Subcommittee on International Organizations, Washington, D.C., June 2, 1978.

32. Foreign Assistance and Related Programs Appropriations Act, 1978, Foreign Assistance Act; P.L. 95-148, 91 Stat. 1230, §114 (hereinafter the "1978 Act").

33. *Ibid.*, §107 and Foreign Assistance and Related Programs Appropriations Act, 1979, P.L. 95-48, 92 Stat. 1591, §108, 22 U.S.C. §§2169, 2211, aid to Cambodia, Laos, Uganda, and the Socialist Republic of Vietnam.

34. Not all these attacks were successful. Iran, Indonesia, and the Philippines emerged relatively unscathed. The aid prohibition on Argentina is contained in 22 U.S.C. §2372. The prohibition on Uruguay and Ethiopia is found in the 1978 Act, *supra*, note 32, §503A. Limitations on Argentina, Brazil, El Salvador, and Guatemala are in *ibid.*, §503B. An additional prohibition on Chile is found in the International Security Assistance and Arms Export Control Act of 1976; P.L. 94-329, 90 Stat. 729, §406. The mild prohibition on the Philippines is in the 1978 Act, *supra*, note 32, §503C.

35. *Ibid.*, §107.

36. 22 U.S.C., §2370(x) (1).

37. International Securities Assistance Act of 1978, of Sept. 26, 1978, P.L. 95-384, 92 Stat. 730, §13(a) revising 22 U.S.C. §§2370, 2373, 2751, 2776.

38. E.g., 22 U.S.C. §620(f) (communist countries).

39. Prohibitions contained in the 1978 Act, *supra* note 32, §503B, have been deleted from the Foreign Assistance and Related Programs Appropriations Act, 1979, P.L. 95-481, 92 Stat. 1591, Oct. 18, 1978.

40. U.S. House of Representatives, Committee on Conference, *Conference Report, Making Appropriations, Foreign Assistance, Fiscal Year, 1979*, Rep. No. 95-1754, 95th Cong., 2d sess., Oct. 10, 1978, p. 14. International Security Assistance Act of 1978, Sept. 26, 1978, P.L.95-384, 92 Stat. 735, §10(a), amending 22 U.S.C. §2346b.

41. Rep. No. 95-1754,*supra*, note 40, pp. 10, 18.

42. *New York Times,* July 17, 1977, p. 7.

43. Debate on H.R. 9721, U.S. House of Representatives, *Cong. Rec.*, H. 39399 (Dec. 9, 1975); see also U.S. Senate, Rept. No. 94-673, 94th Cong., 2d sess., Mar. 1, 1976, pp. 13, 25. The law is: 22 U.S.C. §283y; P.L. 94-302, May 31, 1976, 90 Stat. 592 (repealed Oct. 3, 1977).

44. International Bank for Development and Reconstruction, P.L. 95-118, 91 Stat. 1067 of Oct. 3, 1977, §701(f).

45. Letter to Hon. Clarence Long, Chairman, Committee on Appropriations, Subcommittee on Government Foreign Operations, from The President, The White House, unpub.

46. Amendment No. 300 to H.R. 5262, 95th Cong., 1st sess., May 19, 1977.

47. *New York Times,* Oct. 19, 1977, p. 10.

48. *Congressional Quarterly,* Aug. 5, 1978, p. 2012.

49. U.S. House of Representatives, Committee on Conference, *Conference Report, Making Appropriations, Foreign Assistance, Fiscal Year, 1979*, Rep. No. 95-1754, 95th Cong., 2d sess., Oct. 10, 1978, p. 17.

50. *Ibid.*, p. 18.

51. Since August 1977 the "food for peace program" administered by the Agriculture Department is required by law to apply human rights

standards and to deny aid to violators except where it directly benefits needy people. International Development and Food Assistance Act of 1977; P.L. 95-88, 91 Stat. 533 at 545–46, §2031. This is now §112 of the Agricultural Trade Development and Assistance Act of 1954; P.L. 83-480, 68 Stat. 454, as amended, 7 U.S.C. 1712.

52. U.S. Department of State, Memorandum: "The Interagency Group on Human Rights and Foreign Assistance," Mar. 9, 1978, p. 4, unpub.

53. Interview with Mr. Mark Schneider, deputy assistant secretary of state for human rights, Washington, D.C., June 15, 1978.

54. See T. Franck and E. Weisband, *Foreign Policy by Congress*, Oxford University Press, 275–76 (1979).

55. *International Herald Tribune*, July 29–30, 1978, p. 5.

56. Foreign Assistance and Related Programs Appropriations Act, 1979; P.L. 95-481, 92 Stat. 1591 of Oct. 18, 1978, §§608–10.

9
Confidentiality and Executive Privilege

George W. Calhoun *

> Three may keep a secret, if two of them are dead.
> —BENJAMIN FRANKLIN
>
> It's a great kindness to trust people with a secret.
> They feel so important while they are telling it.
> —ROBERT QUILLEN

G OVERNMENT SECRETS. Who "owns" them? Quite obviously the government does; but who in the government? Surprisingly, the answer is important, for in it lies one possible way friction can be reduced between Congress and the president

If the heads of each of the three branches that make up the government were asked, they would undoubtedly claim they "owned" all of "their" documents. But Congress (and to a lesser extent

* The author, George W. Calhoun, recently served as Special Counsel to the Attorney General to represent the Department of Justice (including the Federal Bureau of Investigation) in connection with an investigation conducted by the Subcommittee on International Operations, Senate Foreign Relations Committee, into the alleged activities of agents of certain foreign intelligence services within this country. The following are some insights growing out of that and other experiences spanning the better part of a decade.

The views expressed herein are not intended to reflect those of the Department or, necessarily, others with whom the author spoke in preparing these comments. Nevertheless, the author would like to express his appreciation to the numerous officials both within and without the executive branch who took the time to share their views on the subject discussed in this chapter.

courts) feel they also have a right to get copies of any executive branch's files they want. Needless to say, there are those in the executive branch who do not agree, so when a demand for confidential executive information from Congress is received, it is almost always met with at least some resistance; and that reaction increases the chance the president will ultimately refuse to honor the demand by filing a formal claim of executive privilege.

This chapter will review, generally, that prospect and, particularly, the practical, day-to-day problems that can crop up, why they occur, and some solutions that are being or might be used to resolve them.[1] Specifically, it will concentrate on some of the "personal" factors and attitudes that can precipitate friction and resistance between the two branches—mainly the attitudes of executive and congressional personnel who process such demands—and then examine an important ameliorating force that tends to minimize the risk of constitutional confrontation. Finally, there will be exploration of means by which both branches can reduce conflict in the future.

Fights between Congress and the president over access to secret information are really quite rare, but when trouble does occur, it usually starts as a result of a number of deep-seated feelings held by those charged with the responsibility of protecting the information.

Aside from the fear that confidential information will be compromised, one of the most important motives for refusing access is the prevalent, but rarely disclosed, belief of many in the government that each branch *owns* the information it develops. In the executive branch, this feeling is particularly strong because the nature of its work requires it to generate more confidential information than the other two branches combined.

This is not to say that the others have no "secrets." Indeed they do. The judicial branch, for example, generates confidential information when its judges discuss their prospective opinions in chambers.[2] The remainder of the courts' work, though, is almost always made public as a matter of course—for example, pleadings filed by the litigants (except in those few cases where secret or *in camera* pleadings are filed in cases involving such things as the national security);[3] the ensuing trials (with certain limited exceptions);[4] and opinions (again, except in very rare cases involving, for example, national security matters).[5] The judicial process then is one that does not ordinarily generate much confidential information.[6]

Much the same could be said of Congress.

Its members generally work directly with the public (citizens, lobbyists, and consumer groups); they hold open hearings to consider legislation; they engage in public markup sessions (during which they revise proposed legislation); and they make speeches and cast votes, virtually all of which are public. Still, like courts, Congress generates some confidential information—for example, when its members meet in caucus or "executive" (an interesting adjective when used in this context) session—but the bulk of their work is generally open to the public.

The executive branch, in this respect, is quite different. Much more of what it must do has to be done in private: it presents, for example, matters to grand juries; assembles confidential investigative files in criminal matters; compiles files containing personal information involving such things as census, tax, and veterans information; and health, education, and welfare benefits, to mention a few. All of these activities must, of necessity, generate a considerable amount of confidential information. And personnel in the executive branch (which is much larger than the other two combined) necessarily prepare many more confidential memoranda. Finally, they produce a considerable amount of classified information as a result of the activities of the intelligence community.[7]

When the three branches are compared, then, the conclusion would have to be that the bulk of secret government information is developed by the executive. And because the disparity is so great, many people feel that confidential information is really something that "belongs" to the executive, as (by analogy) opinions are traditionally thought to "belong" to courts.

A second aspect of this feeling of ownership is the friction that comes about when demands for access to confidential information become a one-way street. Every day Congress and the courts require the executive to supply them with many of its confidential files, but the executive has rarely, if ever, attempted to get the other branches' private files in return. This imbalance has prompted resistance on the part of some in the executive branch, the more so as there is a perceived tendency, once information is supplied, to yield to demands for additional access.[8]

There is another, more personal property concept that comes into play when decisions are made whether to respond to congressional demands, but before discussing that, it would be helpful to pause and define some conceptual boundaries necessary to our analysis.

It would be futile to try to review here every demand for confidential information Congress has made in the past, and respective responses of the executive, for the scope of the subject is immense. In order to reduce the subject to manageable proportions, we will focus solely on one salient set of problems: those which have arisen in connection with the sharing of classified information.[9] As background, it would be helpful to review the process by which classified information is generated and protected.

The primary participants in the classification process, the operational or line personnel, are a group of people who will be given the title here of "classifiers" (though the full range of their duties is in reality far greater than that). Classifiers have three basic duties. First, they must develop sources and methods for gathering secret information their respective department or agency needs to perform its duties. Second, they must insure that these sources and methods are protected so they can continue to supply the needed information. And third, they must see that the process they use to disseminate the collected information will insure that it remains secret. In order to accomplish the last two goals, classifiers start with a cardinal rule: they limit the distribution of classified information to as few persons as possible, and then only to those who have a "clearance" and a legitimate need to know it.

In order to identify those people, classifiers have established a security system that regulates, among other things, the numbers and identities of individuals who will be granted access to such information. When classified (or, for that matter, any other confidential) information is developed, it is regularly shared with those who the classifiers feel have an interest in such matters; for example, the intelligence community or prosecutors.[10]

When an individual or organization outside this normal distribution system takes steps to get the information, some institutional resistance normally begins almost as a reflex. Along with concern that valuable information will be leaked, causing damage to the national security, there is another consideration that comes into play, something that could be called a personal, property interest. This feeling is instilled in everyone during their early childhood.

Who does not remember the childhood singsong: "I know a secret, I know a secret"? That taunt said a lot: it told the listener, "I am better than you, because I know something you don't know." So very early, children learn that secrets are special; the holder of the secret is important, and he has the power to make other people important by telling them the secret. It is his benefice to share with whomever he wishes. He designates his friends by confiding in them and his enemies by refusing to do so. The holder of a secret also has a sense of pride that is prompted by a feeling of being trusted, and when someone's vanity prompts him to reveal the secret, others who have protected it feel a sense of betrayal. No one keeps a secret as well as a child.[11]

With the passage of time, childhood bromides[12] are put aside, but not the feelings they instilled, particularly the idea that a secret conveys power and something of a property interest. Inevitably, this basic human experience plays a part in the decision-making process when demands for access to secret information are received. There are other constraints, which are also not of their choosing, on classifiers' powers to make these decisions.

Recent events have, for example, made it clear their power to protect their secrets has been seriously weakened: not only do they face a variety of "demands" for their data, but they are beleaguered with a host of vexing (and often unauthorized) disclosures, many of which go unchallenged by anyone.

On the demand side, prosecutors are being required to give criminal defendants access to sensitive information, supposedly to allow them to defend themselves but usually in the hope that if the government is required to reveal its secrets to a criminal defendant, it will dismiss the indictment rather than disclose the information.[13] And the public and the news media are making ever increasing demands for secret information under the Freedom of Information Act.[14] If this were not enough, there are a host of problems with unauthorized disclosures as well: newspaper and magazine leaks,[15] espionage cases,[16] books and articles by "private" writers,[17] cases of former intelligence community employees writing books or articles disclosing sensitive information,[18] and former employees taking classified material home with them for a variety of reasons.[19]

As seen from inside the executive branch, all of these events have raised the specter of the nation's wall of security crumbling, of serious erosion of the power of classifiers to protect the information they develop. Quite naturally, classifiers are not overjoyed at the prospect of having to grant even greater access to "their" secrets.[20]

Other personal considerations that affect the outcome of this process include the feelings some classifiers have about their jobs.

Recent changes in public perception of the intelligence community have had a telling effect on their self-esteem, and in some cases, those changes have made classifiers more defensive about what they do. In the past, for example, the public, raised on heroic tales of undercover agents and espionage in the nation's cause, tended to view security work as exciting and thrilling. Classifiers could expect to command respectful silence with the single remark, "I'm sorry, but it is secret." The revelations of Watergate, the Rockefeller Commission Report, and the COINTELPRO investigation have tarnished that image, revealing that classifiers do not often resemble the glamorous James Bond but, instead, engage in tedious, systematic collection of bits and pieces of information in the hope of putting together a larger jigsaw picture that may be helpful to the nation's defense. Not only is this a less glamorous image, but the investigations also revealed that, in a few cases, those who dealt in classified matters were abusers of civil rights and hiders of illegal activities: in other words, people the citizenry ought not to trust. This decline in their personal stature has made some classifiers as defensive of institutional as of national interest and less inclined to reveal any more about their work than they have to, particularly to an adversary—Congress—that has taken their agency to task on a number of occasions in the recent past. And that brings up the problem of trust.

Classifiers, in deciding whether access to sensitive information should be allowed, are particularly sensitive to the element of control. This is a particular problem where Congress is concerned.

Releasing information to Congress, for many classifiers, is tantamount to setting a ship afloat at sea without benefit of motor, rudder, or sails. They feel that once the information is launched in the direction of Congress, there is really no further control a classifier can hope to exert over its ultimate destination. The speech and debate clause of the Constitution effectively prohibits any intrusion by the executive or the courts into so-called legislative affairs.[21] In other words, if members of Congress decide to make secret information public during a congressional debate, a court will not order them to stop and the speech and debate clause forecloses prosecution by the executive branch. Classifiers fear this prospect, for if there is anything that troubles classifiers almost as much as making sensitive information public, it is giving it to someone over whom they have no control, someone who can reveal the information at will.

Not surprisingly, then, classifiers do not always relish the prospect of having to comply with a congressional demand for classified information. Unfortunately, there are other feelings that can cause friction, one of the most widely held of which is the idea that Congress intrudes into areas traditionally thought to be the executive's domain. Many people in the executive branch view the role of Congress as something of a navigator and the president as the captain of the ship of state. In other words, Congress determines the general course, and the president has the task of seeing how and when the legislative objectives are reached. Within the past decade, however, Congress has expanded its powers, primarily through a claim of "oversight" responsibilities, so that now it claims it, too, can make decisions as to which way the ship will go, how fast, and how far.[22] What this means from a practical standpoint is that Congress, by "oversight" can control much of what most executive departments and agencies do.

A consequence of this expansion of oversight[23] is that congressional demands for sensitive informaion have increased even more. Oversight tends to generate more oversight, and the appetite for confidential information grows even as it is being satisfied. To the executive this is very troubling, for very intense oversight appears to insinuate wrongdoing.

While some friction among the branches is good, when it begins to take intensely adversarial forms the effect is to instill more recalcitrance. A number of classifiers currently feel that congressional demands for sensitive information are primarily motivated by a desire to indict, embarrass, or divide the executive; others think there is a post-Watergate desire to topple another president, that Congress is really more interested in running the country than legislating, or that a particular member is simply looking for headlines to get reelected. Some classifiers believe that most of their problems arise from congressional staff members who were selected because of their notorious hostility to the interests of the executive branch. These perceptions of bias become acute when, as an investigation comes to a close, there is increasing congressional staff pressure on the executive to produce ever greater amounts of information. This last-minute rush is widely perceived by classifiers as an effort by congressional staffs to justify their investigative efforts to their principals.

The growing proliferation of committees claiming to have jurisdiction over the same sensitive information also causes problems. Today, multiple demands are being made on the executive for the same documents, and such widespread dissemination invites leaks. In one recent Senate investigation, classifiers were caught in the middle of a battle between an oversight committee and an investigating committee as to which had "primary" responsibility for a particular subject and, therefore, the right to be first to receive a sensitive item.

Classifiers also complain, in recent years, about the weakening of the power of committee chairmen. They tend to resist a request for access to information when the chairman appears no longer able to carry out promises to protect its confidentiality.[24] Another concern is that the chairmen and members are so swamped with responsibilities that they tend to rely ever more on activist staff, becoming virtually their captives and rubber-stamping their wishes and automatically endorsing their demands. Finally, classifiers criticize the lack of an institutional mechanism in Congress to resolve disputes over access; they sense that each member is an independent agent in an unstructured free-for-all where no one is really in charge. The executive organization is traditionally thought of as a pyramid with the president, the ultimate decider, at the top, whereas Congress is seen as a collegial body made up of many pyramids, depending on the context or the perspective from which it is viewed; for example, as a group of committees, political parties, or ideological groups. However it is viewed, no one in Congress seems to be able to exert the comparable power the president has over the executive branch.

Many, if not most of these perceptions are oversimplifications that border on error, but since perceptions constitute a kind of subjective reality, they have an important influence whether accurate or not.

If the executive bureaucracy's perceptions of members of Congress and their staffs cause possible friction, the problem is compounded by the reciprocal phenomenon: the way the Hill perceives the shortcomings of the executive branch.

For a brief period of time, it seemed to many that Watergate was a harbinger of things to come, an era of unprecedented confrontation among the branches. Revelations of those abuses, coupled with the Church and Pike investigations of the intelligence community, and the impeachment hearings all led some in Congress to conclude that the executive branch was using the classification system to cover abuses of power, if not outright illegal activity. This is not an entirely new suspicion. A little over thirty years ago, for example, young Congressman Richard Nixon complained about President Truman's claim of executive privilege:

> That would mean that the President could . . . arbitrarily issue an Executive order in any . . . case [thereby] denying the Congress . . . information it needed to conduct an investigation of the executive department and the Congress would have no right to question his decision.[25]

Today, one would hope the dispirited era of Watergate has passed; yet some members and staff still feel that the executive has not yet learned to work closely with, and to trust, the Congress. They complain that the executive branch fails to tell Congress about its problems sufficiently ahead of time so that *joint* corrective action can be taken—it tends instead to wait for the news media to uncover its difficulties (or for Congress to discover them), and that in turn forces Congress to develop a "watchdog" approach to the executive.

If Congress and the executive share an attitude, a feeling, it is distrust of the other.

Another source of irritation is a contradiction in the executive's own rules defining for its personnel the procedures for responding negatively to a congressional demand for information. In the early 1950s, former Attorney General Brownell issued an opinion saying that heads of departments or agencies were authorized, on their own, to refuse to provide Congress information if they so decided. Later, directives were issued by a number of presidents detailing the procedure by which the president's approval would be required before a demand could be refused. Unfortunately, the later directives did not expressly overrule the Brownell procedure, so some "confusion" remains whether the president's personal approval is required in every case. Efforts over the past quarter century to clear up this confusion by rescinding the Brownell opinion have been unsuccessful. This conflict has resulted in refusals at (or even below) the cabinet level, and they have led some members of

Congress to doubt whether the executive is legitimately declining requests for information or if it is deliberately ignoring the very rules presidents have issued to govern its actions.

Others have expressed criticisms that confrontations are escalated unnecessarily—that the executive cries before it has been hurt—and that the executive takes advantage of certain institutional conflicts in the structure of Congress. For example, we are accused of deliberately trying to circumvent unfavorable congressional requests by giving the principal committee that oversees such information the documents first (indeed, in some cases ahead of time) and then declining to permit access by a second requesting committee, directing it instead to go to the "superior" committee.

Criticisms have also been voiced that the executive will admit of little, if any, legitimate congressional interests in such things as foreign affairs; rather it perceives Congress' concern as an intrusion (or nuisance) into an area regarded solely as a presidential prerogative. The executive is also regarded by some as being too imperial, especially in not taking congressional investigations seriously enough in the past, particularly the Church and Pike committees' investigations. Finally, there is a view that the executive has too great a concern for precedent, the fear of establishing a rule by releasing a particular item of information that will always dictate the outcome of any later decisions that have to be made in response to congressional demands.

As with the negative perceptions of Congress held by the classifiers, the validity of these congressional perceptions may be in doubt; that they are genuine feelings is not. They do seem to influence the reaction of congressional staff members when they meet resistance from the executive bureaucracy.

The competing, if not conflicting, forces brought to bear by these different interests, attitudes, feelings, and perceptions suggest an almost inevitable series of confrontations. Fortunately, there are a number of ameliorating factors. One of the most important of these is a self-imposed constraint on the executive. When it decides to refuse a demand for information from Congress, there are exacting procedures that must be followed before executive privilege may be asserted.

In order to understand how a claim of privilege comes to be made, one must trace the process from the beginning. When sensitive information is received by a classifier (from an informant or undercover agent) and its use is intended to extend beyond the recipient's office, it is usually reduced to writing (in an investigative or intelligence report); and if it is national security information, the document is stamped with a notice of the classification level the classifier feels appropriate. The notice is put at the bottom of each page, and it reveals who classified the document, the basis (reason) for the classification, and the time that must pass before the document is automatically declassified. (Under current regulations, classifications must be justified periodically or the information will be made public.) Once this process is completed, copies are sent to the particular "community" members that have an interest, and the original is stored in the classifier's files. Later, if someone else wants to see it, he must prove that he has a proper security clearance and a legitimate need to know the information.

It is important to reiterate that the classifier makes the initial judgment about where copies of the document will go later—in other words, who will be given access to it. (He must also be consulted before any further dissemination or declassification occurs by the components to which he has previously given access.) The classifying officer, then, has a "property interest" in the documents he generates; and though he may leave office, his successor will retain the power to decide whether a particular piece of information from that office remains classified and whether it can be disseminated further. The significance of this step in the process, at least as it pertains to congressional requests, cannot be understated: the classifier has the first word on whether the information sought should be given to Congress. And, more often than not, his opinion is influenced to a considerable degree by the factors, the perceptions, discussed earlier. In addition, he will be influenced by the nature and context of the request, its scope, and the "track record" of the requester in handling secrets.

Because the information involved is secret and not available to the investigating committees, the committee has no way it can describe exactly what they need. This forces them to cast the widest net, to be very general and broad in shaping their initial requests. Usually they will say something like: "give me everything you have involving this subject." Classifiers, on the other hand, resist any unnecessary access to their information, so they inevitably approach requests of this breadth by immediately looking for ways to avoid even so much as conducting a search for the requested information. Accordingly, they will usually take as their opening position that the request is too broad. Usually, agreements can be worked out in most instances that narrow the request to information concerning only certain aspects of the subject. Still, problems do arise.

Because some congressional staff members do not know how executive records are kept, even seemingly limited requests for information can require excessive searches. A committee may ask, for example, for all documents covering a certain period, whereas the executive's files may be set up by name or subject, not by dates. Once again the problem is usually resolved by negotiation. The bureaucrat tries to educate the staffers to the recordkeeping constraints and tries to determine precisely what the investigators really want.

Sometimes, however, the investigators may balk. Fearful of tipping their hands, overlooking something, or having it appear that executive branch personnel are dictating the scope of their investigations, members and their staffs are very reluctant to pinpoint their requests too closely. Thus begins what may be a real confrontation.

When the latest version of the request arrives and it is decided it will be refused, the "proprietor" usually prepares a position paper marshaling the reasons why a search for the information should not be conducted, or, if one has already been conducted, the reasons why the information should not be turned over to Congress. Then, if the person designated by the executive to coordinate such matters—the "policymaker"—decides that the information should not be "released,"[26] the prospect of a formal claim of executive privilege's being filed begins to loom. The matter is not necessarily at an end, though, for any refusal to provide information sought by Congress has to be accompanied by a claim of executive privilege made on the personal approval and over the signature of the president (assuming, for the moment, that the aforementioned Brownell opinion is not being employed).[27]

Fortunately for all concerned, there is no joy in this prospect, for the demands made on the president's time are so great that access to him must be very limited; consequently, there is considerable reluctance on everyone's part to seek a personal audience if it can be avoided. If for no other reason than this, formal claims of privilege are rarely sought.

Another deterring factor is that whereas presidents of necessity have their difficulties with Congress, they do not like others to start fights for them. A claim of executive privilege clearly poses that risk, and every president knows Congress could "retaliate" by delaying the passage of important administration programs. That specter also dampens the ardor of many people to embroil the president in another fight with Congress. Another factor taken into account by the policymaker is the possibility that someone up the line, even the president himself, may reject the advice and refuse to make the claim. If the policymaker is overruled, his ability to continue to work effectively with Congress on the investigation involved will be seriously impaired. For these reasons, there is considerable concern that the executive privilege process be used sparingly.[28] The internal executive procedures exert pressure on those negotiating with Congress to resolve the conflict through a compromise that satisfies the needs both of the investigators and the "proprietors" while also preserving the prerogatives of the two branches.

There is another reason, perhaps growing in importance, why the privilege is not used as often as it was in the past. It can be argued that executive privilege is something that does not belong to the president and that it is not a privilege. Rather, it is at most a concession of failure on the part of two branches to resolve a difficulty and an invitation to a court to step in and decide the matter. On this point, the court in *United States* v. *American Tel. and Tel. Co.* seemed to agree when it encouraged further negotiations between the branches, signaling it felt they had not done enough.[29]

Policymakers, in seeking to avoid a congressional or judicial showdown, have a number of options. They can simply choose to provide the information, as requested, over the objections of the classifier. That course has at least two potentially serious risks: (1) there is the chance that extremely sensitive information can be "released," unnecessarily; and (2) it invites the ire of classifiers, whose bureaucratic support has to be relied upon by the very official who has "arbitrarily" overridden their advice.

They can also try to get Congress to consider alternatives. In some cases the committee can be told the information will be given to an oversight committee—the committee to which Congress itself has given principal responsibility for the subject being investigated—and the requesting committee will then be asked to go there for the information. This approach is generally not successful, since oversight committees usually will not allow access to highly sensitive information unless the investigating committee accepts certain rigorous limitations, ones even the executive rarely requires, and this makes it extremely difficult for the committees to use the information. For example, the committee in possession may insist that the documents in question be read in their special room and refuse to permit the taking of notes.

Still another option is to invite the ranking and minority members of the investigating committee to come to the agency or department for an oral briefing on the requested information, preferably without their staffs being present. Finally, a designated trusted staff member may be briefed.

If all these efforts fail, the head of the department or agency, or one of its ranking officials, will usually try to arrange a meeting with the chairman of the committee, and perhaps the ranking minority leader, to underscore the executive's concerns. Matters rarely get to this point, however, for most high executive officials are acutely aware of the powers of Congress and have little interest in becoming directly involved in a conflict over documents. Where such meetings do occur, accommodations are generally reached, usually in the form of the executive's agreeing to provide some of the documents, with summaries or briefings to cover the rest.

If this, too, fails, the head of the department or agency must advise the attorney general of the confrontation and request that he initiate the procedure for obtaining a formal claim of executive privilege from the president. If the attorney general feels that no satisfactory resolution can be reached and that the matter ought to be presented to the White House, he will usually transmit it first to the counselor to the president. Later a meeting may be held that involves the president, the counselor, the attorney general, the department or agency head, and any necessary executive branch employee.

With the exception of what must of necessity be considered an aberration—the era of Watergate—refusals invoking formal claims of executive privilege have been few, and this is primarily due to the procedure involved in getting a claim "approved."

It is not due, it should be added, to doubt about the legality or constitutionality of this "ultimate weapon" of the president. The Supreme Court has only recently affirmed the constitutional basis of the privilege. In *United States* v. *Nixon,* the Court stated:

> The privilege is fundamental to the operation of government inextricably rooted in the separation of powers under the Constitution.[30]

In perhaps an even more relevant opinion, the D.C. circuit court in *Senate Select Committee* v. *Nixon* suggested that congressional requests for information, in the face of an assertion of executive privilege, are not as "strong" as those of the judiciary in a criminal proceeding or of a grand jury. In the former, the privilege can prevail; in the latter, it will usually fail.[31]

This may well be the reason Congress has wisely chosen not to contest such claims in court—the *AT&T* case and the Erwin committee challenges mentioned above were two rare exceptions— Congress has apparently learned that a judicial challenge to a claim of executive privilege is a risky business: they can lose not only the decision, as in *Senate Select Committee* v. *Nixon,* but some of their power, in the process, to the courts.

As in any other human endeavor, improvements in the relationship between the executive and legislative branches of government are heavily dependent on the motivations and intentions of the individual personalities involved, factors not easily controlled. There are, however, steps that can be taken to increase the flow of information between the two branches and minimize friction.

One way Congress could help would be to address one of the main concerns of classifiers by centralizing requests for sensitive information. It could accomplish this by establishing, for example, an "Office of Executive Affairs," through which all demands for sensitive or classified information would be made to the respective executive agencies and back through which the requested information would be provided. The office could be responsible for maintaining the security of classified information by providing storage facilities, reading rooms, and other features designed to safeguard the integrity of the classified data. It would also promote efficiency in expanding requests by first determining whether the information had previously been provided to another congressional committee.

There are drawbacks to this kind of system from the intelligence community's perspective. The intelligence community "compartmentalizes" information so that if a particular area is compromised, the damage will be limited by the compartmentalization. While the classified information here would be centralized, the stronger security precautions of the office should provide sufficient protection against the risk of compromising what is received. The House and Senate intelligence select committees are already fulfilling a large part of this function, so that the additional risk in creating an office of this kind ought to be minimal if proper procedures are followed, procedures to which the intelligence community should be permitted to contribute.

Congress could also help smooth the process by resolving conflicts of jurisdiction among the various congressional committees, perhaps by creating a special joint investigative committee which could resolve committee disputes or, if necessary, handle all investigations involving sensitive information. If, during an investigation, a committee determines that it will need access to classified information, it could consider shifting that aspect of the investigation to the joint investigative committee that would have the proper procedures and staffing to handle such problems. And if all of these requests went to one place in the executive branch, that is, the Office of Legislative Affairs in the Department of Justice, an additional benefit would be that the executive branch would be able to insure its answers were properly coordinated, thereby minimizing much of the contradiction and confusion which presently exists when differing answers are given by the various executive components as a result of each agency's interpreting a particular request a different way.

Some thought could also be given by Congress to its security system, or more accurately, the absence of it. The executive classification procedures include the appointment of a security officer and a well-defined system for classifying information, transmitting it with receipts, storing it in proper facilities, and assuring that it goes only to those who have a need to know, with complete control reposing in the official who originates and classifies a document. As a result, those who have classification authority in the intelligence community can feel free to share secret information, for the community members trust their counterparts, a trust prompted in large measure by the fact that they share each other's secrets. That, coupled with the protections provided by their security systems, which have many similar (and familiar) characteristics, means the bonds of their trust are quite strong. Congress, in sharp contrast, enjoys neither the benefit nor the trust engendered by a security system. Admittedly, the intelligence oversight committees have procedures for receiving and storing classified information, but Congress itself has no security officer nor overall system for classifying, storing, disseminating, or declassifying information. And there is no particular individual who can be looked to by the executive branch to allay their concerns about releasing secret information to Congress.

Thus, one of the ways Congress could ease some classifiers' concerns would be to establish a security system similar to that of the intelligence community, and to which it could relate. Formal procedures could also be established by which Congress itself would classify information. Currently, the power to classify information is only an inherent power of the executive branch, not specifically provided for by the Constitution or statute, yet recognized both by congressional legislation and judicial decision.[32] By Executive Order 12065, the president extended this power to the departments and agencies but not to Congress. Thus, as matters currently stand, when Congress classifies a document, it does so either without expressed authority or, at best, on a "quasi-derivative" theory: by "borrowing" the executive's classification power.[33] In view of its importance to any effective security system, Congress may want to regularize its classification power by giving it a firmer basis in law or procedural rules.

Congress might also consider establishing a procedure whereby reconsideration could be sought when there is disagreement with a subcommittee or committee chairman over a question of access. As things presently exist, the chairman is the ultimate decider for Congress, notwithstanding the fact that he may be the chairman of a minor subcommittee. In the executive branch there are ways to get reconsideration at ever higher levels. It might be helpful to have some similar means by which a dispute with Congress could be rethought at various levels, perhaps by the full committee, the oversight committee, or the full House or Senate itself, as the seriousness of the problem requires.

Efforts could also be made to minimize the needless participation of staff members in meetings involving highly sensitive information. At present, when a briefing is offered to a committee or subcommittee chairman, the chairman is frequently accompanied by a host of staff members, only a few of whom really have a need to know. This disregard of the "minimize distribution" and "need-to-know" principles inevitably raises concerns on the part of those presenting the briefing, for the information is being spread too widely. Again, the answer may be to provide for a decision by the full committee in case of a dispute over the staffers to be briefed. In any event, the committee should give the executive notice of which staff it feels must participate.

There are also measures that can be taken by the executive branch to reduce friction.

It would be helpful for each department to authorize a bureau to arbitrate disputes over production of documents, thereby reducing the need to involve operational people, the head of the department, and the attorney general. This kind of "Departmental Review Committee" would have the necessary clearances and the expertise to provide the needed objectivity for a reasoned decision.

Another improvement would be for the executive branch to require department and agency heads to notify the Justice Department in all instances where compliance with a Congressional request is not effected within thirty days of the deadline set in the request. This would allow the attorney general to monitor potential conflicts at an early stage and to enter the discussions before positions on both sides have become intractable.

Finally, one approach that has proven quite effective in two of the most recent investigations—the House Assassination Committee and the McGovern Subcommittee on International Operations—is for the investigators and the department being investigated to work out, at the beginning, a mēmorandum of understanding setting forth the purposes of the investigations, the kinds of information that will be sought, what will be done with the information, and the protections the committee will employ to make sure the information is not distributed unnecessarily. Our relatively short experience with such a system of ground rules has shown that they can ease executive concern that the congressional investigators will seek carte blanche to review the files. It has also been helpful to the committee in demonstrating that the agency being investigated has recognized its need to know information pertinent to its investigation.

CONCLUSION

Let me end with a disclaimer. My comments may be misleading in three ways: if they suggest inordinate congressional demands for access to classified information, or that there is constant friction and struggle between the two branches, or that the struggle which does exist can be resolved only by adopting my suggestions. It may be useful to restate that the overwhelming majority of requests made by congressional committees for access to information do not involve classified information, and even when they do, they are freely complied with, more often than not.

But conflict does occur. Perhaps it could be eliminated almost entirely if Congress would recognize the sincerity of the executive's concern that confidential information given to Congress will be made public and would address itself to that fear. By taking steps that would effectively protect against unauthorized disclosures, Congress could virtually eliminate executive resistance. Admittedly, it is unrealistic to expect a fully "secure" Congress, which would require the exercise of a far greater control over the actions of members than they are likely to tolerate, or than is constitutionally permissible in view of the speech and debate clause. Perhaps, too, the only true guarantee of secrecy is the grave.[34] Still, I have tried to advance suggestions that would at least mitigate the risk to security.[35]

NOTES

1. Traditionally, claims of executive privilege have been studied from a historical perspective, that is, a recounting of all the occasions in the past when Congress sought information the executive did not want to produce. Two excellent examples of that approach are a book by Raoul Berger, *Executive Privilege: A Constitutional Myth* (Cambridge, Mass.: Harvard University Press, 1974), and an article by Archibald Cox, "Executive Privilege," 122 U. of Pa. L. Rev. 1383 (1974). The approach here will be more from a pragmatic rather than a historical perspective.

2. See, e.g., Statement of the Judges, 14 F.R.D. 335 (1953), though Bob Woodward and Scott Armstrong's recent book, *The Brethren, Inside the Supreme Court* (1979) raises some question whether this is still true.

3. *Halkin v. Helms,* 598 F.2d 1 (D.C. Cir. 1978); *United States v. Butenko,* 494 F.2d 593 (3d Cir. 1974).

4. *Gannett Co., Inc. v. Daniel DePasquale,* 99 S. Ct. 2898 (1979), barring reporters from certain pretrial proceedings.

5. In a recent espionage case, *United States v. Enger and Chernyayev,* Cr. No. 78–149 (D. N.J. 1978), judicial concern for confidentiality prompted the court to take the unusual step of issuing a "secret" memorandum of opinion which neither side was permitted to see, but which was intended to be reviewed by the appellate court in the event the case was ever appealed. For reasons not important here, it was not.

6. Indeed, there is a considerable reluctance on the part of most courts to do so, the extent of which was demonstrated recently in a case involving the publication of allegedly classified H-bomb material. There, the Court of Appeals refused to permit even so much as part of an oral argument to be made in private. *United States v. Progressive Magazine,* 467 F. Supp. 990 (W.D. Wisc. 1979).

7. The "community" consists of the Federal Bureau of Investigation, National Security Agency, Central Intelligence Agency, State Department, and Department of Defense, and its primary mission is to gather national security information.

8. In addition to this difference between Congress and the executive, it is also important to remember that when a fracas does occur, the judiciary is, as a practical matter, superior to the others. Recently squabbles developed between Congress and the president over access to confidential information in Watergate and the judiciary decided who prevailed. To that extent, it might be said that none of the branches are equal. This really should come as no surprise though, for two hundred years ago John Adams suggested this is the way it should be when he said, "The judicial power ought to be distinct from both [the other branches] so that it may be a check upon both."

9. There is some dispute whether the "iron curtain" of executive privilege blocks access more in the criminal investigation area than in the classified information arena, but the point is really not important here, for they have many common denominators that constitute the heart of the discussion that follows.

10. The FBI will, for example, send NSA or CIA intelligence information it discovers that pertains to their operations, even though access to the information may never have formally been requested.

11. *Le Miserables,* Cosette, Bk. VIII, Ch. 8.

12. "A secret is like a dollar bill; once broken, it is never a dollar again." *Affurisms: Josh Billings; His Sayings* (1865).

13. This tactic is a shade lighter than blackmail; it is called "graymail," and it has been employed in a number of prosecutions— i.e., *Helms, Gerrity, Berrellez,* and the *L. Patrick Gray* cases.

14. U.S.C. 552.

15. E.g., the Pentagon Papers; a recent Article on "How a Hydrogen Bomb Works" in *Progressive Magazine;* and a disclosure by Jack Anderson of a highly classified Senate document, the so-called McGovern Report.

16. *United States v. Humphrey,* 456 F. Supp. 51 (E.D. Va. 1978); *United States v. Enger and Chernyayev,* Cr. No. 78-149 (D. N.J. 1978); *Boyce,* No. 77-3336 (9th Cir. 1979); *United States v. Madsen,* No. 79-130-A, (E.D. Va. 1979); *United States v. Kampiles,* No. 78-2646, (7th Cir. 1979).

17. Howard Moreland's article on the H-bomb.

18. Victor Marchetti and Philip Agee, both of whom are former CIA agents.

19. Edwin Moore (CIA) and Graham Martin (former ambassador to South Vietnam).

20. Again, it must be remembered that classifiers "allow" access either voluntarily or when someone asks to be "granted" a clearance and access, thereby recognizing implicitly the power of the classifiers to say no if they are so inclined. Congress demands access, and when it does, admits to no such power in classifiers. This much Congress made clear when, in two cases (the Church and Pike reports), congressional committees made public secret information over the express objection of the agency involved.

21. Senator Gravel made this much clear a number of years ago when he read, and with impunity, documents the executive branch had previously classified.

22. A recent example of how deep into the executive's domain Congress is willing to reach is demonstrated by the fact that the Department of Justice' Appropriation Authorization Act for 1979 contains a requirement that the executive "explain" to Congress the degree to which the executive is declining to prosecute cases, why, what can be done to improve its percentage, and what it can tell Congress to assure that its decisions are consistent with "national policy." This mandate essentially requires the president to "audit" the degree to which he is taking care to see the laws are faithfully executed and to report the results to Congress. Now it would seem the Congress is "overseeing" the president.

23. Today there are almost seven times the number of oversight committees as there were five years ago, and there is a mounting concern about the growth of the congressional bureaucracy during the past decade. During that period, House subcommittees rose from 108 to 146.

24. Under House Rule XI, Section 706(c), a House member must make any documents he receives available to anyone in the House who wants them, regardless of whether they are classified or not. This has forced at least one member to request to visit the executive office, stand by a table while someone else opened an envelope, removed its contents, turned the pages (while it was being read), and then returned it to the executive department, thereby providing the information the member needed but permitting him to say that he had never had "possession" as it is defined under the House rule.

25. 94 *Cong. Rec.* 4738 (1948).

26. This is a most interesting word when used in this context, since it is generally used to refer to cases where the executive is considering a request to "release" information, e.g., make it public. It is, in other words,

an excellent example of the principle that adverbs are often as important as the assertion.

27. See, e.g., Statement by the President, Mar. 12, 1973; and Memorandum for the Heads of Executive Departments and Agencies, "Establishing a Procedure to Govern Compliance with Congressional Demands for Information," Mar. 24, 1969. As the Berger book listed in note 1, *supra*, makes clear, this procedure has been honored in its breach.

28. No record seems to have been kept that lists all prior claims of executive privilege (but cf. *United States v. Nixon*, 487 F.2d 700, 732–33 [D.C. Cir. 1973]), undoubtedly because some claims were made without using the term, whereas in others refusals to provide information have been made under the rubric of executive provilege when the president has not in fact signed such a claim—e.g., the Brownell approach.

29. 551. F.2d 384, 394 (D.C. Cir. 1977).

30. 418 U.S. 683(1974).

31. 498 F.2d 725 (D.C. Cir. 1974).

32. 50 U.S.C. 783(b), the Freedom of Information Act, and in a number of judicial decisions, e.g., *Goland v. CIA*, 607 F.2d 339 (D.C. Cir. 1978); *Halkin v. Helms, infra; Gravel v. United States*, 408 U.S. 606 (1972); and *Gravel v. United States*, 408 U.S. 606, 637–38 (1971).

33. This touches on a point made earlier, and that is that while confidential information is thought by many to belong to the executive, all classified information at this point "belongs" to it. So demands for that kind of information are really demands for executive branch "property."

34. *Don Quixote*, Pt. II, Bk. IV, Ch. 62, p. 862.

35. There is, on the other hand, at least one good reason why even they should not be undertaken though—as one wag once remarked—"If it ain't broke, don't fix it." For more than two hundred years Congress and the president have been able to perform their respective constitutional responsibilities, and although in the process they have generated friction, they have in the main functioned quite successfully. If the past is a prologue of the future, it might be better in the final analysis to leave the entire matter alone and let the political forces at play dictate the outcome of each of these "problems" on its merits. That approach has insured, at least in the past, that each competing interest will be served to the extent it should be, and maybe that is all for which one should really hope.

Part III

Prescriptions for Partnership between President and Congress

I O

Legislating and the Conduct of Diplomacy: The Constitution's Inconsistent Functions

Lee R. Marks

T RADITIONALLY, the respective roles of the Congress and the president in defining and executing policy have been different for foreign policy than for domestic matters. The Congress has traditionally prescribed in detail the laws that govern domestic programs. The day-to-day conduct of foreign policy was generally left to the executive. Congress asserted itself on major issues—largely through the exercise of the Senate's treaty responsibilities—but did not often legislate specific policies.

Congressional restraint with respect to foreign policy was not dictated by the Constitution. The few provisions in the Constitution that address foreign policy allocate responsibility fairly evenly between the legislative and executive branches. Congress alone is authorized to regulate commerce with foreign nations and to define and punish piracy and offenses against the law of nations (Article I, §8). The president alone receives ambassadors and public ministers (Article II, §2). The power to make treaties and appoint ambassadors, public ministers, and consuls is shared (Article II, §2).

The president enjoyed some measure of deference in foreign policy—at least until the last quarter century—largely because it was believed that conducting relations with other nations was an executive function. As the State Department's legal adviser patiently explained to the House Ways and Means Committee in 1940:

> The conduct of the foreign relations of this country is in its nature essentially an executive function. The President could not successfully deal with them, if every agreement made by him on any and every question or subject of discussion between this and foreign governments required the approval of the Senate before becoming effective. Such a procedure would so hamstring the President as to render the conduct of the foreign relations nigh impossible.[1]

Now, however, the balance has shifted. In foreign affairs as in domestic affairs, the discretion of the executive branch is being narrowed by detailed legislation. Increasingly, Congress is legislating tactics and prescribing by statute specific solutions to specific foreign policy problems. In doing so, Congress is neither asserting its own interests effectively nor advancing the United States' ability to conduct a consistent and coherent foreign policy.[2]

The 1960 edition of *Legislation on Foreign Relations,* an annual compendium of laws affecting foreign policy published by the Senate Foreign Relations Committee and the House Committee on Foreign Affairs totaled 519 pages. The 1975 edition was 1856 pages. The 1978 edition took three volumes and totaled 2299 pages.[3]

Some laws represent an effort to legislate the resolution of a specific foreign policy issue. The Byrd amendment on Rhodesian chrome, the Case-Javits amendment, and §408 of the Department of State Authorization Act for fiscal years 1980 and 1981 reflect the continuing effort by Congress to influence U.S. policy toward Rhodesia. Many statutes require that foreign economic and military aid be terminated if a recipient country engages in conduct that Congress disapproves of, such as harboring terrorists or acquiring nuclear enrichment technology without safeguards. In some cases, Congress has subjected U.S. companies (including their foreign affiliates) to rules of commerce in the international marketplace that reflect primarily our domestic values. The Foreign Corrupt Practices Act and the Arab boycott legislation are examples. And, in some cases, the legislation is procedural, requiring prior notice to Congress of proposed activities and the submission of reports to Congress. No one has calculated the precise figure, but hundreds of reports are ground out annually by the Department of State for the Congress pursuant to statute. Some of these generate interest, such as the human rights reports produced for each country receiving foreign aid, but most are ignored.

The sheer quantity of legislation that affects foreign policy is illustrated by the problems encountered when the United States normalized relations with the People's Republic of China (PRC). As of January 1, 1979, the United States recognized the People's Republic of China as the "sole legal government of China" and established diplomatic relations with that government. We also acknowledged the Chinese position that Taiwan was part of China, but President Carter announced that in the future, "the American people will maintain commercial, cultural, and other relations with the people on Taiwan without official government representation and without diplomatic relations." The people-to-people relations the president had in mind included virtually all government programs then in effect (except for military sales). To continue these programs on an unofficial basis, a new private instrumentality was to be established. The instrumentality, incorporated as a District of Columbia nonprofit corporation on January 10, 1979, was the American Institute in Taiwan.

The precedent for the distinction between "official" relationships with the PRC and "unofficial" relationships with the "People on Taiwan" had been set in 1971 by Japan.

For diplomats, the "Japanese solution" made sense. If it seemed logically anomalous to continue relationships with Taiwan, although unofficial, while recognizing the PRC as the sole legal government of China, what of it? Creative anomalies, like delicate ambiguities, make for sound diplomacy. For State Department lawyers, however, the solution was a nightmare. By skirting the issue of what, exactly, Taiwan was—other than the place where the people on Taiwan lived, as one wag put it—the terms of normalization called into question the applicability to Taiwan of dozens of statutes.

Almost all statutes authorizing programs with other countries define eligibility through the use of such terms as "foreign country" or "government." Clearly, Taiwan could not be a "country" or "government" if the PRC was the sole legal government of China. In the absence of new legislation, we could not continue nuclear assistance under the Atomic Energy Act of 1954 or programs under the Mutual Educational and Cultural Exchange Act of 1961. EXIM financing and OPIC insurance were impossible, as were programs under the Export Administration Act, the Arms Export Control Act, or the Foreign Assistance Act of 1961. Foreign military assistance and international security assistance were out, as was cooperation under the National Fisheries Center and Aquarium Act, the Solar Heating and Cooling Demonstration Act, and the National Science Foundation Act of 1950, as amended. So, too, for the Fisherman's Protective Act of 1967 and the Marine Mammal Protection Act of 1972.

If we acknowledged the PRC claim that Taiwan was part of China, was Taiwan a "non-market economy country" for purposes of §§402, 403, 407, and 409–11 of the Trade Act of 1974? Or, alternatively, a "non-state controlled economy country" for purposes of the Antidumping Act of 1921? A country "dominated or controlled by communism" for purposes of §406 of the Trade Act? A "friendly nation" for purposes of the Mutual Security Act of 1954 or the Export Administration Act of 1969? Was Taiwan perhaps an "organization or association acting for or on behalf of a foreign government" (the Johnson Act, 18 U.S.C. §955) or a "department, agency or independent establishment of a foreign country" (Foreign Military Sales Act)?

Similarly, some laws authorize programs that can be carried out only in countries with whom we maintain diplomatic relations. And §620(t) of the Foreign Assistance Act prohibits assistance to any country with whom we have severed diplomatic relations. By normalizing relations with the PRC, had the United States "severed" relations with Taiwan? The Arms Export Control Act and the Atomic Energy Act of 1954 require specific assurances from officials of countries to whom arms, nuclear materials, and the like, are sold. If Taiwan was not a "country," could it have "officials"? Under the Immigration and Nationality Act, there is a visa quota for each country. The courts used to look to the Department of State for suggestions of foreign immunity, but in 1976 Congress codified the doctrine in the Foreign Sovereign Immunities Act, in terms that excluded Taiwan.

It took thirty-four pages just to list the number of statutes affected by the normalization of relations with the PRC.[4]

These problems, and others, were cured by the Taiwan Relations Act, P.L. 96-8 (1979), but only after a strenuous effort to identify the issues and draft language that would preserve the substance of our programs and relationships in Taiwan on terms compatible with normalization.

The proliferation of statutes affecting foreign policy is understandable. The legislation concerning Taiwan was an instance of a law in the area of international affairs initiated by the executive, a law that was necessary and proper. But its extraordinary length testifies to the need to amend a vast jungle of *other* legislation, much of it of less evident necessity or propriety. This is part of the general inflation of laws and regulations that has occurred in recent years. In the name of reform, progress, and due process, we are rapidly subjecting every aspect of our political, social, and commercial life to regulation. For every abuse, some interest group wants a legislative solution; Congress has become increasingly accommodating.

Moreover, the lines between foreign and domestic policy are no longer so sharp as they once were. We could once make fiscal and monetary decisions independent of external circumstances, but we are now part of a world economic system. Currency exchange markets are forcing our present anti-inflationary policies, and international conditions require us to coordinate macroeconomic policy with other industrial nations. Historically, trade was the only economic activity clearly involved with foreign policy. Now decisions about agricultural surpluses, strategic stockpiles, commodity agreements, relationships with OPEC countries, and the modernization of NATO forces shape our domestic economy as much as they do our foreign policy. The decision to halt grain shipments to Russia in response to the invasion of Afghanistan is a current example. And because these decisions affect jobs, prices, and earnings, they are of intense concern to members of Congress.

In the period since World War II, foreign economic and military aid has been an important part of our relationships with a large number of countries, particularly the developing countries. We have used the ability to increase or withhold aid as an instrument of foreign policy. This has inevitably drawn the Congress more deeply into foreign policy because it is, in effect, being paid for by the taxpayer and because foreign aid involves Congress' most cherished function—the power to appropriate. Congress is generally reluctant to defer to the expertise of the executive branch, but least of all when it comes to spending money.

Television and jet planes have played a part. Foreign policy was once regarded as an exotic art best practiced by those with expert qualifications. It seems less exotic when members of Congress and their constituents routinely travel abroad. Television made the Vietnam War as immediate and sharp as our urban riots. And the powerful drive to build respect for human rights into foreign policy has been fueled by television and media reports of torture, imprisonment, and so on. Congress has also reacted to the excesses of the CIA and FBI and the inflated executive claims of power to commit and use troops abroad during the Vietnam War. The War Powers resolution (P.L. 93-148 [1973]), the Hughes-Ryan amendment (§662 FAA), and the so-called intelligence charter legislation (S. 2525) are among the specific responses.

S. 2525 may well be a permanent casualty of the Iranian crisis, which will surely diminish enthusiasm for curbing the CIA. But, as introduced, S. 2525 contained 263 pages of definitions, procedures, limitations, prohibitions, and standards governing all intelligence activities, civilian and military, in this country and abroad. It may be healthy to bring spies in from the cold; subjecting them to a statute only slightly less complicated than the Internal Revenue Code is overkill.

And, finally, the absence of both strong presidential leadership and strong congressional foreign policy leaders has encouraged large numbers of members to sponsor foreign policy causes and made it relatively easy for many of them to succeed.

That the population explosion of laws affecting foreign policy is understandable, or that many of the laws are well-meaning, does not make the process less mischievous. Congress must be a partner in charting the basic directions of foreign policy, but the day-to-day execution of policy cannot be legislated.

When Congress legislates, it acts prospectively, narrowly, and inflexibly. Foreign policy legislation invariably addresses a single issue: our distaste for secondary boycotts directed against Israel, for Turkish intransigence in refusing to compromise on their military solution to the Cyprus problem, or for many regimes' violations of human rights. The Evans amendment prohibits Export-Import Bank credits for any sales to South Africa unless the South African borrower certifies to the U.S. secretary of state that it complies with the antiracialist employment practices set forth in the "Sullivan code." And the Jackson-Vanik amendment makes trade relationships with Eastern Europe, China, and the Soviet Union dependent on their respective emigration practices and on their willingness to provide assurances about these practices to the president. These laws not infrequently become part of the problem they seek to cure. What has delayed normal trade with the Soviet Union is not emigration—Jews are currently emigrating in record numbers—but Soviet unwillingness to genuflect before Congress by providing the public assurances required by Jackson-Vanik.

Foreign policy problems—like domestic problems—typically involve conflicting variables and competing interests; they can seldom be resolved by assigning absolute priority to a single issue. Flexibility and timing are critical in dealing with concrete problems, but these are almost impossible to achieve through legislation. Secrecy is often vital but almost always sacrificed when solutions are legislated. When we threaten a discretionary sanction in private a foreign leader can back down in private; if the same sanction is imposed by statute, the foreign leader must accept the demand made by the law or publicly capitulate. The essence of negotiation is uncertainty; particularly in a complex multilateral negotiation, each party must have some apprehension about the objectives, determination, and capacity for action of the other party. Uncertainty is the very thing legislation is intended to cure.

Suppose Country A is secretly acquiring nuclear enrichment technology, not subject to safeguards, in what appears to be a clandestine effort to acquire a nuclear weapons capability. The United States wishes to discourage Country A. What we should do depends on many factors: What other interests do we have with Country A? Which carrots and sticks are likely to prove effective? Which may exacerbate this situation? What other nations can we enlist in a common effort? Is Country A a major supplier of an important strategic material? What political or economic issues do we now confront with Country A? What domestic leadership does Country A have? How will it be affected by any action that we take? How useful or important is it to strengthen or weaken Country A's leadership? Is Country A in the "front line" of defense against a current Soviet campaign of expansion? One could articulate more questions to be addressed in formulating a plan to discourage Country A. Congress, however, has already dictated a plan. Section 669 of the Foreign Assistance Act requires that all economic, military, and security assistance be terminated for a country that receives nuclear enrichment technology in these circumstances.

Suppose that Country B is a haven for terrorists but covertly acts as a moderating influence on more radical countries in its region and is about to become an important source of energy that will involve substantial U.S. investment. Depending on the facts, one could conceivably decide that as much as we deplore terrorism, on balance it best serves U.S. interests to maintain good relations with Country B rather than to permit its attitudes toward terrorism to dominate our relations. Here, too, however, Congress has preemptorily dictated what our response must be. If Country B grants "sanctuary from prosecution" to any individual or group that has committed an "act of international terrorism," §602A of the Foreign Assistance Act requires that the president terminate all assistance to Country B for one year; §509 of the Foreign Assistance and Related Appropriations Act of 1978 requires that Export-Import Bank credits be denied.[5]

The issue is not whether we should withhold aid from a country that seeks to acquire atomic bombs or to harbor terrorists. In a particular case, withholding aid or threatening to do so may be appropriate. But that is a decision to be made at the time, based on all the facts, not abstractly in advance.

How much discretion to leave to the executive is an issue with respect to domestic policy as well as foreign policy. Virtually all legislation requires allocations of responsibility and power between branches of government. Foreign policy, however, has characteristics that justify greater congressional restraint and greater deference to the executive branch.

The process of governing is different from the process of conducting foreign relations. The imperatives of regulating a society are not the same as the imperatives of international survival.

Moreover, we generally have more knowledge, more ability to predict consequences, and more clarity about our objectives when we act domestically than in foreign policy. Even laws governing domestic policies sometimes turn out differently than we expected, but it is much harder to predict the consequences of laws that purport to affect other cultures. And, if a domestic law generates unexpected consequences, there is likely to be a constituency with political power pressing for remedial legislation.

Some characteristics of legislation that are essential in governing the domestic body politic are far less applicable when dealing abroad. The government must treat all of its citizens alike, absent rational and clearly articulated bases for differential treatment. There is no such need to deal alike with foreign countries. Similarly, law brings predictability and certainty to events, characteristics less helpful in dealing with other countries than in governing domestic affairs.

Americans feel strongly about many values. We are committed to freedom, nonproliferation, fairness, prompt compensation for expropriated property, human rights, competition, full disclosure, the right to emigrate, and the promotion of our exports. We abhor torture, discrimination, commercial bribery, apartheid, terrorism, and secondary boycotts. We prefer elected presidents over dictators and self-determination over annexation. Each of these values (and more) is enshrined in our statutes. Each has its congressional partisans. Each has laid claim, at one time or another, to being our highest priority. In most actual world crises, they cannot all be pursued simultaneously; sometimes none is attainable except at an exorbitant cost to our national security or self-interest.

Other countries have different values and their own priorities. Many Third World countries take issue with us on almost all our values; even our closest allies find us moralistic on the question of bribery and obsessive on issues of competition and disclosure. Moreover, other countries have their own domestic political problems, foreign policy concerns, shifting alliances, obsessions, and idiosyncrasies. With each of these countries, we have numerous political and economic interests whose relative importance is in flux.

Few foreign policy decisions are self-evident. The difficult decisions are close. As much as we may want crisp, definitive solutions, obfuscation and delay often serve our interests better. To decide in advance that under no circumstances will we provide foreign assistance to a nation that fails to halt the export of heroin to the United States, or harbors terrorists, is to make prospective judgments about our net interests—in a future, unforeseeable set of circumstances—that can be right only by coincidence, if at all. To prohibit any foreign assistance for training or advice to the police of a foreign country, or for any program of internal intelligence, may be virtuous with respect to Latin America but dangerous in the case of Italy, which is plagued by leftist terrorism.

What is the effect of all this legislation?

Politically, it varies. Some legislation has handicapped our ability to conduct a consistent, coherent foreign policy. Soviet limitations on the emigration of Jews may have been immoral or cruel, but it was irrational to condition our economic relationships with communist nations on that single issue. Efforts to restore economic and political stability to Turkey, critically important because of its location, have been hampered by congressional responses to the Greek lobby. For the most part, however, the political impact of the statutes has probably been less dramatic; they may be more an irritant than a major factor in determining policy.

Economically, we have responded to large balance-of-payment deficits and diminishing productivity by tying one hand behind our backs. Export-Import Bank financing was intended to benefit U.S. business enterprises, making them competitive with those of other industrialized states which provide similarly generous credit to foreign purchasers; it is now seen as a favor to be dispensed only to foreign nations that deserve it—not including South Africa, countries that harbor terrorists, or countries that consistently violate human rights.

By conditioning Export-Import financing on the good behavior of foreign countries, prohibiting commercial bribery, and preventing compliance with boycotts (among other measures), we have proved our virtue. We have also helped British, French, Japanese, and German firms beat out their U.S. competitors. We have not noticeably improved morality abroad.

One can recognize that bribery is accepted practice in some parts of the world without condoning it. The sensible way to deal with bribery would have been through international agreement, a goal vigorously pursued by the State Department in recent years. Enactment of the Foreign Corrupt Practices Act made it more difficult to achieve international consensus, since it provided the other putative parties to such an agreement with a competitive edge over the United States.

The legislation affects process as well as substance. The role of lawyers in deciding foreign policy issues becomes greater, and questions of policy become transmuted into questions of statutory interpretation. And because the need for flexibility is so great, the temptation to interpret legislative commands narrowly is overwhelming. No matter how detailed the legislation may be, there remains ample room for interpretation. What is "legitimate self-defense" or "an act of international terrorism"? How long is "promptly"? State Department lawyers are both able and no less anxious than lawyers generally to serve their clients' interest. Some interpretation can almost always be found that will avoid strict compliance with a statutory command. That process, however, is itself corrosive both because it creates an adversarial relationship between the executive and legislative branches and because it leads inexorably to more legislation, more efforts to interpret it away, and so on in an inextricable, self-generating circle.

This is not a plea for congressional abstinence in foreign policy. The Constitution is right to make foreign policy a shared function. A nation's foreign policy must be soundly rooted in the attitudes and values of its people, and it must reflect as best it can the underlying currents and moods of each decade. No president can long sustain a policy that does not command basic congressional support. To be effective, however, Congress must deal with broad issues, not tactical decisions, and it must resist the temptation to remedy every perceived abuse with a new law and to resolve every disagreement with the executive by a new statutory command.

It is a cliché to say that we live in a difficult, complex, dangerous, and shrunken world and that it requires the utmost skill and resolve to sustain our moral, economic, and political strength. But it is also true. This, then, is a plea for congressional self-restraint.

NOTES

1. Statement of G. H. Hackworth, legal adviser, Department of State, before House Ways and Means Committee, Feb. 1, 1940. 5 Hackworth, *International Law* 397.

2. Congress and its members affect foreign policy through hearings, speeches, informal persuasion, and active participation in events, as well as through legislation. A headline in the *Washington Post* (Oct. 28, 1979) declared: "To Save SALT, Sen. Byrd Huddled in Secret with Soviet [Ambassador Dobrynin]." This paper focuses on legislation.

3. Not all of the increase is attributable to new laws; the scope of the publication has expanded as well.

4. Hearings before the Committee on Foreign Relations, U.S. Senate, 96th Cong., 1st sess., 243–76.

5. These sections, and most similar statutory constraints, permit the president to continue assistance if he finds that the national security so requires, and certifies his findings in writing to the Congress. In some cases, the Congress may by resolution override the president. National security waivers, in practice, do not solve the problems. First, for a conscientious administration it is frequently difficult to make the required findings. Particularly in light of past abuses justified in the name of na-

tional security, a president would have to hesitate before certifying to the Congress that cutting off assistance to a particular country would have a "serious" or "significant" impact on the national security of the United States. Second, the very act of certifying in writing to the Congress that a violation has occurred, together with the president's findings, has political consequences. The certification when it becomes known escalates the dispute.

I I

Downtown Perspective:
Lessons on Liaison with Congress

J. Brian Atwood

T HE FOURTH year of the era of accommodation was 1980. The ardor of the congressional revolution has cooled some. The executive has found ways to defuse issues of prerogative. A new set of rules governs the relationship between Congress and the executive branch in the formulation of the nation's foreign policy. After almost a decade at the barricades, battling over turf within the Constitution's "twilight zone," the two branches are now for the most part working on the substance of America's world role rather than on the form of their relationship with one another.

The image of a pendulum swinging between the White House and Capitol Hill is dated; a series of statutes insures congressional involvement whichever direction the political winds seem to be shifting. The discussion now focuses on the quality of the contribution Congress makes to the many issues that constitute the international agenda.

During the first three years of the Carter administration, Congress was highly active, providing a national forum for the debate of controversial issues and rendering judgments on a variety of proposals. In approving the Panama Canal treaties; in proposing to sell aircraft to Israel, Egypt, and Saudi Arabia; and in lifting of the Turkish embargo, Congress providing important backing for the president's policies in Latin America, the Middle East, and the eastern Mediterranean. In enacting legislation supportive of the administration's nonproliferation, arms sales, and human rights policies, Congress offered an added degree of legitimacy to these important global policies. In the Iran and Afghanistan crises, Congress joined the president in a powerful display of national unity.

There were many convincing indications that the system could function well, even with an assertive, decentralized Congress and an increasingly complex set of issues. There were also areas of serious concern. Perhaps most troubling was a tendency to undercut diplomatic strategies that depend for their success on flexible, sometimes rather subtle tactics. Many in Congress found it politically appealing to advocate the forceful assertion of American military, economic, and political power, as it was used in the 1950s. To a significant extent, they reflected the frustration of our people as we confront an often chaotic world, much of which seems to be homing in for an attack on the American life style.

Whether the political trends are toward "internationalism" or not, Congress will provide, for the foreseeable future, the principal forum for the national debate over America's world role. That Congress is now eager to provide that forum is a product of its own revolution, begun in the Vietnam years. That Congress has the information to perform its role more constructively is the result of a conscious effort by the executive branch to seek accommodation. What follows is a personal account of the circumstances that brought about an era of accommodation between the branches.

1975: THE WATERSHED YEAR?

After two years of frustrating political and legislative defeats, Secretary of State Kissinger was ready in January 1975 to turn at least momentarily from the world scene to his relations with Congress. In a speech before the Los Angeles World Affairs Council, he called for "new principles of executive-legislative relations—principles which reconcile the unmistakable claims of Congressional supervision and the urgent requirements of purposeful American world leadership."[1] It was not clear in 1975 whether

Kissinger felt congressional "supervision" and "American World Leadership" were at all compatible. Some felt he yearned for a new "Vandenberg era," a time when congressional-executive comity was found in highly personal relationships between the secretary of state and certain "responsible" leaders, such as Arthur Vandenberg, chairman of the Senate Foreign Relations Committee during the Truman administration. Whatever Kissinger's underlying motive, Capitol Hill took notice of this first official acknowledgment that a change in approach was needed to deal with the shift of power congressional opposition had wrought.

In the two years preceding this speech, Congress had reacted to an effort by the executive to usurp its constitutional position by using its power of the purse with a vengeance. Combat activity in Indochina was terminated and an arms embargo imposed against Turkey. Congressional investigators were exploring the netherworld of the "clandestine" operation. And with the passage of the War Powers Resolution over a presidential veto, Congress made known its desire to participate in decisions of war and peace. To the secretary of state the need for a new approach was apparent in 1975.

But it would take more than a clarion call to bring about the "national partnership" Kissinger wanted. Reconciliation did not come in 1975. A full year later, Deputy Secretary Robert Ingersoll would tell the same Los Angeles organization that 1975 was a year of "conflict and tension between executive and legislative branches on foreign policy issues."[2] Congress had terminated assistance to Vietnam and Cambodia, prohibited our involvement in Angola's civil war, fretted over "secret agreements" in the negotiation of the Sinai accord, and given itself a veto over major arms sales. The congressional revolution seemed barely to skip a beat.

The confrontation between the branches was a boon to advocates on both sides. Reams were written on the respective war powers of the two branches; on impoundment; on the "advise and consent" and "necessary and proper" clauses of the Constitution; on statutes governing a recipient nation's use of U.S. arms; on the doctrine of "executive privilege"; and, ultimately, on the grounds on which a president could be impeached. The partisans drew their lines clearly and distinctly. These were matters of *fundamental* import, involving interpretations of the Constitution. Each decision, for good or ill, constituted a *precedent*. Compromise was fine for a lesser order of issues; it was not possible when the *powers* of the *presidency*—or of *Congress*—were in question. Secretary Kissinger's speech did not begin to penetrate this rigid, unyielding preserve of the constitutional advocate. These lawyers, scholars, and bureaucrats saw themselves as the guardians of the powers and rights of future presidents—and future Congresses.

The reconciliation effort was as much hindered by the rules and practices of the bureaucracy as by strict interpretations of the Constitution. Never mind the call for a new national partnership, certain information simply would not be shared with Congress. There was a valid reason for denying certain documents: a drafter might never again feel unconstrained in offering his or her best advice. Congress, on the other hand, wanted the best evidence available. Members wanted to know who said what to whom and when. Watergate had done that. Congress wanted to be a real partner, and its committees wanted an opportunity to review *all* the options.

For many downtown this was getting a bit too close for comfort. One executive branch memorandum on congressional relations, written in 1976, reflects a common reaction: "we would not favor the general presentation to Congress of the range of options considered by the Executive Branch in the process of making policy determinations." Many a battle was fought over a congressional request for an "internal" document. At the barricades, threats of subpoena and executive privilege were frequent echoes of the adversary relationship that had developed. Kissinger's speech could not erase the mistrust. That would be broken down only over time.

FIRST STEPS

Progress was made on some fronts. Perhaps the most concrete example was the decision to upgrade the Office of Congressional Relations at the State Department, to increase its numbers and enhance the quality of its professional team. An important indicator of progress toward accommodation was the choice of Robert McCloskey to work with Congress. Only a few months earlier in 1975, McCloskey had been brought back from Cyprus, where he had been our ambassador, to resume control of the Public Affairs Bureau. He had been a credible spokesman for the Department during the difficult years of the Vietnam War. He had earned the secretary's trust, so much so in fact that when he took over as the assistant secretary he wore three important hats: assistant secretary for congressional relations and public affairs and chief U.S. negotiator for the Spanish Bases agreement. McCloskey's portfolio alone was enough to convince his Hill clients that the secretary of state was taking them seriously.

McCloskey wanted a highly professional staff to work with Congress. He expanded his legislative management officer corps from six to eleven. He brought in top Foreign Service Officers to work the front lines on the Hill. And he insisted that his office—H, as it is called in Departmental parlance—move to the center of the policy formulation process.

Most important, McCloskey decided that it was futile to try to turn the congressional tide by standing before it and commanding it to recede. He began the slow process of pulling the defenders of prerogative back from the ramparts. It was not an easy task. The lawyers saw each attempt at compromise as undercutting precedent. And the diplomat saw his preserve being invaded by beings motivated not by "professionalism," but by politics.

SPANISH BASES: A NEW APPROACH

One of McCloskey's first challenges was set down by the leader of the effort to place an embargo on Turkey, Senator Tom Eagleton of Missouri. McCloskey was beginning negotiations with Spain to guarantee continued use of military bases in that country. It was a rare instance when the assistant secretary for congressional relations had policy control over an issue of great interest to Congress. The Hill watched closely how McCloskey met his first test.

When the existing agreement with Spain had been reached five years earlier, in 1970, the administration created a procedural firestorm in the Senate by choosing to submit it in the form of an executive agreement, rather than as a treaty subject to the advice and consent of two thirds of the members. The Foreign Relations Committee severely criticized administration witnesses for presenting the Senate with a fait accompli. Senators Fulbright, Case, Javits, and others on the committee took the view that the "advise and consent" clause meant little if it did not apply to the agreement of Friendship and Cooperation between the United States and Spain. But the congressional revolution had not yet peaked in 1970, and despite its misgivings, Congress eventually authorized funding for the Spanish agreement.

Now in 1975 Eagleton was raising the issue again, at the outset of negotiations for a new five-year pact. Writing to McCloskey, he urged him to use the treaty form. He expressed his general agreement with the principles announced by the two sides as the framework for negotiations, and he suggested that he could support a new agreement, *were it to be submitted for approval as a treaty.*

McCloskey wasted little time in arranging a meeting with Eagleton to discuss the proposition. He could not commit the administration on the form the agreement would take, but he would consult with Eagleton closely as the negotiations progressed. The treaty option would remain, in the lingo of Pennsylvania Avenue, "on the front burner."

He kept his word. Nearly every month, McCloskey provided a full accounting of the difficult negotiations. It was a candid, open consultation, and it paid off—both at the negotiating table and subsequently in the Senate.

On November 20, 1975, Francisco Franco finally succumbed to a long illness. The death of the generalissimo, Spain's ruler for more than thirty years, presented a whole new set of variables just at the moment the United States was negotiating the single most important aspect of the bilateral relationship. The world wanted to know the direction the newly crowned king, Juan Carlos I, would take Spain. The countries of the European Community reacted predictably, refusing to upgrade relationships until Spain was clearly embarked on a democratic course. Many liberals in the United States recommended taking similar steps to place our relations in a state of suspension, as a way of pushing Spain toward democracy. They were strongly opposed to concluding a largely military agreement—an extension of the Franco era arrangements—at such a decisive moment in Spain's history.

Eagleton was troubled as well, but he knew that McCloskey was not ignoring the internal developments in Spain. Indeed, the negotiations had been purposely stalled in December as both sides assessed the situation. In the interim, the signs were not bad in Spain as the king sought to strengthen his hand by placing moderate generals in key positions. There was a long way to go, but the king's democratic intentions were becoming increasingly clear.

When the negotiations resumed in January, the United States proposed that the international agreement under negotiation be presented to the respective parliaments as a treaty. It was a terribly attractive offer to the representatives of the post-Franco Spanish government, which yearned for the symbolic benediction that a solemn treaty approved by two thirds of the Senate would provide. So attractive was it that the United States was able to use it to gain reductions in the amounts proposed by Spain as remuneration for the use of its territory. When the treaty was signed on January 24, the course Spain would take in the post-Franco era was still very much undecided.

In April, with the treaty now in the Senate, Eagleton sent his legislative assistant to Spain to examine the evolving political situation. What he found confirmed the administration's judgment that Spain was moving cautiously but steadily toward a democratic system. Pressure from Europe was not helping—traditionally such pressure had caused Spain to withdraw into a shell of chauvinism. It was a judgment call, but what Spain seemed to need most was a vote of confidence.

On June 21, 1976, the U.S. Senate passed its resolution of advice and consent to the treaty with Spain by a vote of 84 to 11.[3] That resolution contained a declaration sponsored by Senator Eagleton expressing the hope and intention that the treaty would "serve to support and foster Spain's progress toward free institutions." A few liberals voted against the treaty on the grounds that

Spain had not yet achieved the democratic objective. Most Senators yielded to the judgment of colleague Tom Eagleton, who had become the Senate's most credible spokesman on the relationship between Spain and the United States.

Almost a year earlier, Bob McCloskey had responded to Eagleton's challenge with the tactics of accommodation. He and the administration of Gerald Ford reaped the benefits. More important, the system had worked to advance both U.S. interests and the development of democracy in Spain. It was now a little more likely that the concept of a national partnership between Congress and the executive would become a reality.

A NEW ADMINISTRATION

In June 1975, Professor Louis Henkin, writing for the "Murphy" Commission on the Organization of the Government for the Conduct of Foreign Policy looked toward a new administration and the prospect for a full reconciliation between the branches:

> . . . A new Congress and a new President [should] enter negotiations with a view to reestablishing general relations on a cooperative, less distrustful, less adversary basis, not to vitiate separation but to make it work better; to attempt to resolve issues of constitutional principle, singly or in a "package deal," or to arrange to live with them; to experiment with new institutions and procedures as regards foreign relations in general and selected issues in particular.[4]

Henkin characterized his model relationship as "cooperation-in-separation." He saw a need "to inform Congress effectively of American foreign relations on a continuing basis, and to allow Congress to participate in the process of formulating and implementing foreign policy before it must act formally." Henkin pictured the separation of powers "not as an adversary game"; he felt that "each branch should have the information it needs to exercise that separate, independent judgment."

The inauguration of a new president in January 1977 offered the opportunity to defuse the confrontation and to accelerate the move toward accommodation. A new set of policymakers came into the executive branch unencumbered by the narrow political and legal interpretations of the past decade. The new president, Jimmy Carter, viewed his office through the prism of Vietnam and Watergate. He vowed to work with Congress in a spirit of openness and candor. He wanted a real partnership with Congress in the formulation of American foreign policy. Not having battled Congress over issues of prerogative, chances were good that he would succeed.

It was not an easy transformation. Bureaucratic inertia and an entrenched, skeptical Congress slowed the process of reconciliation. Traditionalists in the diplomatic corps were not eager to concede that Congress should, under the Constitution, exercise separate, independent judgments on foreign policy matters. Their constant plea for "flexibility" fell on deaf ears. Congress continued to enact laws that seemed to place the diplomat—and the country's foreign policy—in a straitjacket.

A newly elected president of the majority party should have given confidence to those members of Congress who had led the congressional revolution against the last two Republican administrations. But it was the Democrats who had grown the most skeptical. It would take more than a member of their own party to change the deep-seated suspicion that had characterized their view of the executive branch.

Liberal Democrats continued to challenge the executive, if not Jimmy Carter personally. These fellow Democrats took the position that they were helping the president implement his policies. Presidential initiatives on human rights, arms sales, and nonproliferation—cornerstones of Jimmy Carter's global approach to foreign affairs—appealed to the liberals. But they saw these policies in absolute terms, and when they perceived deviations they led the effort to "hold the President's feet to the fire." Assuming that counterpressure was needed to deal with a recalcitrant bureaucracy, these members fought to legislate policies into rigid, unyielding formulas. Their vigor in pursuing an objective was in many instances as great as it was at the height of the Vietnam War.

A major effort would be required to establish some common ground between those who had fought the battle of the branches in the Congress and the new team in the executive. The initiative came from the administration. At the State Department, Secretary

Vance made clear his intention to share fully with Congress information on foreign policy matters. At his confirmation hearing, Vance told the Foreign Relations Committee: "I do not believe that we can develop or properly implement American foreign policy without the closest cooperation between the two branches of the Government." Not only did he pledge cooperation; he also added a new variation to the pledge when he said, "we are going to seek out your view . . . because we need those views."[5]

This was what Congress wanted to hear. But how would the new administration translate its words into action? Ways had to be found to lend credibility to the vows of the principals. The first step was to acknowledge the legislative landmarks of the congressional revolution and, despite qualms in some cases over their constitutionality, to express a general willingness to be constrained, politically, if not legally, by their provisions. Thus, the president indicated his willingness to abide by congressional determinations made pursuant to the War Powers Resolution, the Arms Export Control Act, and the Foreign Assistance Act.

Troublesome constitutional questions would not go away, but new approaches were devised to avoid conflict. In July 1977, for example, after much internal debate, administration witnesses told the Foreign Relations Committee that the president would "follow the provisions of the existing [War Powers] Resolution." They went on to say that the resolution, "conscientiously applied, is an effective instrument for insuring that the Nation will not be committed to war without adequate deliberation and participation by both Congress and the Executive." The committee, and particularly Senator Javits, a principal author of the war powers legislation, expressed pleasure over the forthcoming approach. As Javits put it: "I am delighted. We are now faced with a problem of the trees, not the forest. You all have seen the forest."[6]

POSITIVE ACCOMMODATION

The new administration had only to review the record of the previous five years to appreciate the need for accommodation on procedural questions. Time after time an alienated Congress had voted no to administration proposals, for procedural rather than substantive reasons. As Franck and Weisband have observed in *Foreign Policy by Congress:*

> . . . intricate policy decisions were made largely as fall-out in a battle over Constitutional prerogatives. It stood to reason that conflicts over the respective powers of the branches were to be avoided.[7]

But though this was a necessary insight, it constituted a largely negative perception of the congressional role, that is, avoid conflicts over prerogative and stop getting hit over the head. It had become increasingly clear in the post-Watergate period that Congress had to be a major part of the leadership equation as our nation addressed a complex set of domestic and international issues. Observing this change, the perceptive opinion tester, Daniel Yankelovich, observed that "not only had automatic support for presidential policymaking dwindled, but public opinion data have indicated that the American people are eager to have more say—both directly and through their surrogates in Congress—in the formulation of foreign policy."[8]

Furthermore, in an era of increasing vulnerability, when more subtle diplomatic tactics were required, an active, involved, and understanding Congress seemed necessary to augment the executive branch's efforts to gain public support. With most issues on the foreign affairs agenda no longer yielding to pure assertions of power, the challenge was to find ways in which Congress could be persuaded to act in support of executive branch decisions. A new kind of collective leadership was needed to implement decisions that frequently reflected a least-worst option. Congress had given itself a codeterminant role—some say more out of anger than design—and now an administration found it desirable to share in substantial ways a portion of the burden of leadership.

CONSULTATION

The most dramatic manifestation of this new approach was not in immediate public view. The internal process by which the executive branch makes foreign policy decisions was transformed to accommodate more fully congressional perspective and other domestic factors. It was not an overnight transformation but came gradually as the president, the secretary, policymakers, and mid-level officers began to see real value in listening to the voices of legislators before final decisions were taken.

Hearing those voices is an art, not a science. The word "consultation" has many meanings. In its purest form, the executive seeks the advice and counsel of the Congress in the formative stages of policy development, before positions harden around a particular option. This definition is most difficult to sell within the executive branch. Nevertheless, the new administration, in a number of cases, brought Congress into the act at an early stage.

Consultations conducted during this "formative" phase naturally were among the more successful. Members of Congress know when they are brought in at the takeoff of a policy initiative. One such consultation involved efforts to apply the administration's nonproliferation policy to Pakistan, a country that was bent on purchasing a reprocessing plant from which weapons-grade material could be produced. For about a two-year period the administration consulted both formally and informally with members of the two foreign affairs committees, laying out the options for approaching this complex task. What was the best way to convince Pakistan to forgo its plans? How could this be done in a manner that would preserve our relationship with Islamabad? How would the Symington and Glenn amendments, calling for a cutoff of assistance if a country is found to be importing such technology, play a role in our overall strategy? These questions continue to be examined in consultations between the executive and Congress.

There are other examples of the "formative" consultation. After the civil war in Lebanon, the State Department examined with both foreign relations committees whether we should help the Lebanese government rebuild its army. Options for dealing with the Morocco situation and the difficult problem created by the war in the western Sahara were fully explored. Our policy toward Yugoslavia and our arms supply relationship with Egypt were other examples. Each of these consultations produced an exchange of information that served to improve the quality of the policy decisions.

The administration did not always succeed in involving Congress at the earliest stage. In some cases it was driven by events toward a particular option, though the details were not fully formulated. The overall objective was clear in these cases, but decisions had not yet been made on how to get there. SALT, the Panama Canal treaty, troop reductions in Korea, and the setting of assistance levels in negotiations for base rights in various countries were situations in which Congress, while not in on the ground floor, provided excellent advice.

A third variation occurred when the good intention of consultation slipped into the expediency of notification. Given the harried state of the world, the administration was not able to avoid giving legislators last-minute notice of an impending course of action in place of real consultation. This type of "consultation" has been well received when it was clear that little or no opportunity existed in which the administration could seek advice and counsel. In some crisis situations, there was widespread understanding of the need to hold information closely. However, if there was no good reason, a last-minute notice could yield sharp criticism and more second-guessing than would have ensued under better-managed circumstances.

This was very much the case when the administration announced that it was normalizing relations with the People's Republic of China. The president had made it clear from the outset that he would normalize relations with the PRC sometime during his administration. Still, the administration chose in this instance to provide Congress only a few hours' advance warning of this long-awaited change in policy.

A variety of foreign policy and political considerations went into the decision not to consult, not least being an awareness that subjecting the decision to the consultation process might have complicated the effort to reconcile the divergent positions of the two countries on the status of Taiwan. The policymakers were well aware of the views of members on this fully debated and emotional issue, but the details of how the administration would work out its policy were not yet decided. Consultations over these aspects of the decision were forgone, and not without cost. The subsequent consideration of the Taiwan Relations Act—the bill to establish the legal foundation for our continued relations with Taiwan—was a long and arduous process. The final bill emerged with a firm congressional imprint, inspiring a negative reaction from the PRC government. This rather prominent omission held important lessons for an administration that otherwise had a good record.

Consultation has been called "the sacred principle of congressional relations."[9] Yet consultations with Congress on national security matters were rare before 1975; what did occur was limited to the "trusted" few. Paradoxically, it is an indication of the current administration's relative success in establishing new practices and higher expectations that a failure to consult, today, would create complications of such proportions that the policy initiative itself would be at serious risk.

Perfection has by no means been reached. It remains understandably difficult to convince those who must deal with a multitude of variables in the decision process to add yet another. Despite all the enlightenment over the importance of a partnership with Congress, the concept of seeking advice and counsel from an institution as adversarial and political as the U.S. Congress remains difficult for the "traditionalist." Frequently, the decision to consult is based on tactical considerations; the desire to see a particular policy implemented is often the motivating factor. With Congress in a position to block initiatives, consultations are justified on a variety of purely pragmatic grounds: to insure support, to confirm estimates of congressional attitudes, to assure that members are informed on an issue that will ultimately attract their attention, and to meet specific requests for information. Preserving and improving the cooperative relationship remains the underlying goal, but, quite frankly, very few specific decisions to consult are based on altruism.

DOWNTOWN: THE FEAR AND THE HOPE

Great progress has been made in recent years in balancing the relationship between Congress and the executive. The difficult questions about American foreign policies are debated more thoroughly now than they were in 1975. The process of executive-congressional codetermination provides real opportunities to share in the task of educating the public and to gain important, manifest backing for presidential policy. Never is the country more effective on the world scene than it is when the executive and Congress are seen to join in a particular initiative. Some of the debates along the road of codetermination have created problems. Our relations with Panama, the PRC, and some other countries have been strained during these legislative battles. But the final outcome has generally served to strengthen the administration when it came to apply the newly agreed policy and to grapple with difficult issues of implementation. A majority vote in the two houses of Congress is a powerful source of legitimacy for our foreign policy.

Nevertheless, there are storm clouds on the horizon that bear watching. The levers of congressional power which were fashioned to deal with Vietnam and Watergate are increasingly being utilized by those whose major thrust is to appeal to fears created by our nation's more vulnerable world position. Initiatives which are designed to preserve the maximum portion of the U.S. position in international negotiations over regional or global matters are characterized by some in Congress in such terms as "appeasement," "sell-out," or "weakness." More troubling, the demagogues seem to have many more responsible fellow members on the run, and, consequently, issues that in normal times would be handled with ease push Congress to the edge of the precipice.

The legislation to implement the Panama Canal treaties was a case in point. The House at one point actually defeated the conference report on the Panama bill. It didn't seem to matter that the treaties were already the "law of the land"; or that our nation was obliged under international law to implement them; or that a failure to implement might have cost us the newly acquired right to operate the Canal to the year 2000. After much rethinking and maneuvering, disaster was averted, but the call was too close for comfort.

In a dramatic floor speech in which he urged his colleagues to support the Panama bill, Majority Leader Jim Wright cited threats of reprisal members were receiving from well-financed right-wing organizations. Wright recalled passages from Walter Lippmann's pessimistic examination of parliamentary democracy in *The Public Philosophy*. Lippmann had characterized elected legislators as "insecure and intimidated men" who have a compulsion to make the "big mistakes that public opinion insists upon," particularly in the foreign policy area. Wright mentioned a number of private talks he had had with colleagues in which they said they understood why the legislation was necessary, but could not vote for it because of constituent pressure. The majority leader appealed to those members:

> Permit me to say as kindly and gently as I possibly can . . . you sell America short. If you do not believe that you, in frank and candid explanation, can show them why this is in America's interest . . . well then, let us face it: You do not really believe in the fundamental premise of a representative democracy.[10]

The House, in one of its finest moments, rose to the occasion and passed the bill. But our system should not have to depend on brilliant appeals to conscience at the edge of the precipice. Congress now has the responsibility to share in decisions that will dictate the future course of our nation's foreign policy. Votes on foreign policy issues are invariably difficult; there are few political benefits in supporting foreign aid, or the Panama implementing legislation, or arms sales to Arab countries, or SALT II. Yet the difficult issues cannot be avoided. The hope is that they will be faced with the confidence that the American people will respond to "frank and candid explanation."

The congressional revolution was fought as much to require Congress to accept its constitutional responsibilities as to curb the imperial presidency. The stakes are high, now that Congress has injected itself so forcefully and irrevocably into the process of making foreign policy decisions. The executive must continue to pursue a policy of accommodation, improving its consultation and information-sharing techniques. But the best institutional relationship in the world cannot compensate for an absence of political courage.

As Elihu Root has observed: "While there is no human way to prevent a king from having a bad heart, there is a human way to prevent a people from having an erroneous opinion."[11] Only a Congress and a president working together are capable of steering our people away from "erroneous opinion" in a world of difficult choices. That task will require understanding, and it will require leadership. Such is the challenge we face in this, the fourth year of the era of accommodation.

Notes

1. Address by Henry A. Kissinger, Secretary of State, before the Los Angeles World Affairs Council, Jan. 24, 1975.

2. Address by Robert S. Ingersoll, Deputy Secretary of State, before the Los Angeles World Affairs Council, Jan. 22, 1976.

3. See *Congressional Record* p. S. 19390 (June 21, 1976).

4. Commission on the Organization of the Government for the Conduct of Foreign Policy (June 1975), vol. 5, appendices, pp. 9–21.

5. Hearing before the Committee on Foreign Relations, 95th Cong., 1st sess., on Nomination of Cyrus R. Vance to be Secretary of State, Jan. 11, 1977, pp. 5 and 13.

6. Hearings before the Committee on Foreign Relations, U.S. Senate, 95th Cong., on *A Review of the Operation and Effectiveness of the War Powers Resolution*, July 13, 14, and 15, 1977, pp. 187–212.

7. Thomas M. Franck and Edward Weisband, *Foreign Policy by Congress*, (Oxford University Press, 1979), ch. 7, p. 158.

8. Daniel Yankelovich, "Farewell to 'President Knows Best,'" *Foreign Affairs* 57, no. 3 (1979): 670–71.

9. Douglas J. Bennet, "Congress and Foreign Policy: Who Needs It?" *Foreign Affairs* (Fall 1978): 45.

10. *Congressional Record* pp. H-8521, H-8522 (Sept. 26, 1979), speech by Congressman Jim Wright (D-Tex.).

11. Elihu Root, "A Requisite for the Success of Popular Diplomacy," *Foreign Affairs* (Sept. 15, 1922): 5.

I2

Can Congress Come to Order?

Senator Gary Hart

NOT LONG AGO, a distinguished European man of letters spent some time in Washington, and, at the invitation of a member of the Senate, devoted a day to observing the Congress in action. He had an opportunity to sit in on a meeting of the Senate Foreign Relations Committee and, in the afternoon, to see the House debate a foreign policy matter on the floor. At the end of the day, his senatorial sponsor asked him what he thought. He responded, "It was chaos—but not enough to create a world."

To the outside observer, Congress' approach to foreign policy issues can seem more chaotic than creative. Even the member, familiar with the labyrinth of formal and informal congressional procedure, often comes to feel that a given congressional action is more the product of chance combinations of unrelated factors than of well-considered actions aiming at a clearly perceived goal. In fact, this is often the case.

As it is supposed to be. Congress is, by design, a confederation, and not surprisingly, its decision process reflects the constantly shifting coalitions that are inherent in confederations. Each member has his own power base—his own constituency. Constituencies differ not only in geographic location but in ethnic makeup, in perception of economic and other interests, in attitudes toward national self-definition. As was intended, the member is influenced by the perceptions of his constituency. He seeks to balance those perceptions with his own personal views of what is best for his constituents and for the nation.

This balancing is a dynamic process. So is the interrelating of one member's final balance of these factors—his position—on a given issue with the positions of other members. And so, equally, is the interrelating of positions on one issue with positions on other issues.

Chaos, indeed. To the philosophe, the final picture is highly distressing. There are no neat lines of authority or argument to diagram. Cause and effect are not easily discernible, and the final effect of an action may be unpredictable and remote. The philosophe recoils from immersing delicate yet critical foreign policy issues in this procedural witches' brew.

What explanation has the Congress for this sorry state of affairs? Its defense is to point out that in its contradictions, its logically extraneous considerations, its multitude of seemingly irreconcilable interests, the Congress mirrors the nation.

A foreign policy that does not ultimately accommodate—not necessarily mirror, but accommodate—the nation, the perceived interests of the population, becomes a foreign policy of the philosophes and the philosophes alone. History has seen such policies. Kerensky had such a policy in 1917 when he promised to continue fighting the Germans. Mussolini had such a policy in World War II when he led his nation into an aggressive war. The United States had such a policy in the 1960s when it argued no sacrifice was too great to maintain a pro-Western government in an obscure corner of Southeast Asia. The point is simple: a foreign policy that lacks public understanding and at least acquiescence cannot be sustained under pressure.

So, if Congress is not always logical, it reflects the reality that the nation is not always logical. The prudent men—fortunately, most of them were not philosophes—who wrote our Constitution did not foresee a logical Congress, but rather a representative Congress. However, after the experience of the national confederation, they did see the need for an element in the government that could respond more to reason and less to the pressures of confederate processes. To that end, they created an executive branch. Could they return today, I doubt they would be shocked by the disorder in the Congress. But the current dissolution of the executive branch into a network of particular interests, each fending increasingly for itself with little regard to the whole, might occasion some thoughtful comment from them.

In all fields, including foreign policy, the executive branch is today less a unity than an administrative grouping of actively diverse interests. ACDA disagrees with the Pentagon and with NSC and takes its disagreements to the Hill and the press, seeking allies and support. The Defense Department happily undermines OMB with any congressional committee that will listen. The services individually do the same to the Office of the Secretary of Defense. Neither hesitates to venture into the field of foreign policy, suggesting particular views of the international environment, in seeking to enhance its budget. The State Department feuds in legendary fashion with NSC. Secretaries of state of recent memory have gone one way while the rest of the State Department went another, all quite publicly. Perhaps our question should be, not can the Congress come to order—it was never intended to be orderly— but rather, can the executive branch?

The disorder in the executive branch compounds that in the Congress. The contending interests in the executive avidly seek allies in the Congress—allies against other elements in the executive. We end up with alliances that span both branches: the House Subcommittee on Arms Control is an ally of ACDA, the Seapower Subcommittee of the House Armed Services Committee is an ally of Admiral Rickover, and so on. These alliances add to the disorder of our foreign and defense policies. They also render somewhat ironic presidential condemnations of congressional disunity.

In truth, in both the Congress and the executive branch minimum levels of cohesion are required. Today, they are missing. The minimums were intended to be different for the two different branches of government. But it is a difference of degree. The Congress is by nature chaotic in its process, but it should not be totally chaotic in its products, its decisions, and legislation if the national interest is to be well served. The executive branch should not be monolithic, lest it shut out new ideas and become stagnant, but it is charged with maintaining internally and promoting externally a basic coherence of policy.

We need a new basis for cooperation between the legislative and the executive, a basis that would permit each to put its own house in order and then to work together in the national interest. Often this need is approached with suggestions for procedural changes. Some believe new procedures within and between the two branches of government can lead to a new foreign policy harmony within the context of power sharing, of congressional participation in foreign policy decisions.

Certain changes in procedure in both branches would undoubtedly be beneficial. However, what is needed is not primarily a change in procedures nor a "crackdown" on dissent in the executive branch, but a new consensus on fundamental foreign policy goals and strategy. A new consensus would provide a basis for both the executive and the Congress from which to deal with the diverse problems we face as a nation. By giving both branches common objectives and a common frame of reference, it would lessen the concern of both branches over the relative power of each and improve the climate for congressional participation in foreign policy decisions. It would give the constituents we represent a framework within which to judge the issues and our handling of them.

A consensus need not stifle creativity. Rather, it can help channel thinking in useful ways. It can insure that something creative does emerge out of the chaos of congressional procedure.

It is of course easy to call for a new foreign policy consensus. It is rather more difficult to find the basis for one. But I do not think the task is impossible. A unique opportunity to work toward such a consensus has grown out of the debate on SALT II and the resulting public attention to defense and foreign policy issues.

As the SALT debate has shown, a new consensus is not likely to emerge through a wholescale adoption of the traditional "liberal" or the traditional "conservative" viewpoint, but rather through a combination of elements of both into something essentially new. The public has shown no inclination to return to the cold war on the one hand nor, on the other, to adopt a policy of disarmament, appeasement, and isolation.

Rather, the American people appear to have grasped two fundamental points, points that may provide the basis for a new consensus. The first is a result of the war in Southeast Asia. We now recognize American power is not infinite. We cannot seek to impose our will throughout the world without regard to our own limits. The second, which has shown through the debate on SALT II, is a healthy skepticism toward the Soviet Union. To be skeptical is not to say the United States and the Soviet Union cannot work together under some circumstances. A majority of the American people probably supports some form of arms limitation agreement with the Soviets. But it does realize that the basic national imperialism of the Soviet Union remains a powerful and dangerous force.

A renewed appreciation of the Soviet threat is a "conservative" contribution to the potential new foreign policy consensus. For some time, our attention has been diverted from the Soviet threat for a variety of reasons: attempts through "détente" to alter Soviet behavior by negotiation and bargaining; the correct realization that many of our foreign policy objectives relate less to the Soviet Union than to Third World powers, acting independently; focusing our policy of containment on an increasingly ill-defined philosophical system called communism rather than on Soviet national imperialism; and last, but not necessarily least, Americans' dislike of drawn-out, "solutionless" situations—our characteristic desire for the "quick fix," and our loss of interest when there is no such thing.

Unfortunately, Soviet imperialism remains a danger of our time. Its origins are diverse: traditional Great Russian chauvinism, communism as interpreted by the leadership of the Communist Party of the Soviet Union; competing institutional interests of elements within the Kremlin, particularly the military; and the desire of the Soviet Union for "300 percent security," for a world not only where no one *does* threaten them but where no one *can* threaten them— a world where Soviet power is indisputably preeminent.

Our traditional strategy in containing Soviet expansionism can generally be described as a "direct approach." We have sought to counteract Soviet moves with direct action by the United States, either in the local theater where the Soviets are active, or in bilateral relations with Moscow. We have seen U.S. action as the best counter to action by the Soviet Union.

This direct approach evolved in the late 1940s, when the Soviet Union expanded the areas under its influence or control. At that time, a direct approach was the best counter to Soviet expansionism, for two reasons.

First, the power of the United States was far superior to that of the Soviet Union. As remains the case today, we were superior in virtually every nonmilitary area—though our margin of superiority was greater then. Militarily, the Soviets were stronger in only one way: the Red Army in Europe was more powerful than that of the United States and Allied conventional ground forces in that theater.

In every other military area—strategic forces, naval forces, air forces, military technology—the United States was clearly, measurably, and generally overwhelmingly stronger than the Soviet Union.

Second, there were really only two powers in the world in the late 1940s: the United States and the Soviet Union. Japan and Germany were in ruins. The other nations of Western and Eastern Europe had been devastated by war and occupation and required all their resources for reconstruction. China was in the midst of a bloody civil war. Nations such as Iraq and Egypt, which are important regional powers today, were backwaters. Much of Asia and Africa were still colonial dependencies of European states. In this environment, only the United States had the power to resist the Soviet Union effectively.

But—and this realization is a "liberal" contribution to the potential new foreign policy consensus—since that time, the world has changed dramatically.

The United States retains its superiority over the Soviet Union in most nonmilitary areas. Particularly in our culture, with its strong emphasis on personal and economic freedom, we have retained a tremendous advantage. Not only is the cultural superiority of the West evident to most neutrals, both the substance and the outward symbols of Western culture are widely sought within the U.S.S.R.

However, the Soviet Union has virtually eliminated American advantages in military power. American strategic monopoly was followed by American superiority, then by parity. The Soviet navy may today be more capable of carrying out its missions than is the U.S. Navy. The Soviets have answered our superiority in tactical aviation with a massive air defense system of a type proven highly effective in the 1973 Mideast War. The technological level of Soviet equipment in the field is increasingly equal or superior to our own.

In the one area where the Soviets were superior in the late 1940s—ground forces in Europe—they remain superior today.

Another international development, less frequently remarked, has been of at least equal importance. At the same time Soviet power has increased substantially relative to American power, the capability of other nations has risen relative to the two superpowers. As we discovered in Vietnam, and as the Soviets have discovered in Egypt, in Romania, and in their relations with China, lesser powers can rebuff and defy a superpower. We are returning to a more normal historical situation than the superpower/nonpower dichotomy of the late 1940s. As has been the case through most of history, a small power can defeat a great power in the small power's own backyard.

There appear to be two fundamental reasons for this development. The first is the spread of modern warmaking capability into all regions of the world. Nations with natural or industrial resources—with wealth—can and do equip themselves with modern tanks, warplanes, and missiles. Nations without wealth but with strategic position—the Yemens are good examples—are equipped gratis by major powers.

In the late 1940s, only the United States, the U.S.S.R., and perhaps Great Britain had effective modern conventional forces. Today, Iraq has two thousand tanks and China has ten thousand. Peru has more tanks than the intervention forces—airborne and marine corps—of the United States or the Soviet Union. The same is true of Algeria, Argentina, and Cuba, among others.

It would be difficult militarily, as well as politically, for either of the "superpowers" to project forces successfully against a growing number of small powers.

The second fundamental reason for the shift in power has been the spread of nationalism. As the Vietnam War demonstrated, the infliction of massive devastation on a small power by a great power may not destroy the will and resistance of the small nation if its nationalism is sufficiently strong. The Soviets know very well if they invade Yugoslavia they face a protracted "people's war," fueled by the nationalistic spirit of the Yugoslavs.

The day when a great power could defeat the army of a small power, occupy its capital, and end the war is passing. Even after the army is defeated and the capital occupied, the small power has the ability, through the nationalism of its people, to carry on a protracted campaign of terrorism, sabotage, and guerrilla warfare. The cost of such a conflict to the great power will increasingly exceed the possible gain.

The protection these two developments give to smaller powers against military threats from the United States or the Soviet Union enable the smaller nations to take advantage of their strengths in nonmilitary areas. Most important among these, in many cases, is the control of vital natural resources, such as oil.

In effect, both the liberals and the conservatives have been right. The threat of Soviet expansion is still very real and must be countered. But the United States no longer can or should attempt to be the world's policeman. We need a new foreign policy, one that combines these liberal and conservative realizations. We need a foreign policy—which I believe could be a consensus foreign policy—that seeks to use the rise in power of the nongreat powers to counter the expansionistic tendencies of the Soviet Union. Such a policy would be well described by the term used by the Chinese for their foreign policy: resisting hegemony while not seeking hegemony.

The United States has no need to seek hegemony over other nations. With our economic, cultural, and political advantages, other nations will generally want to work with us. Our technology is eagerly sought by virtually the entire world—including the Soviet Union. Our political freedoms are the envy of most other peoples.

In contrast, the Soviet Union has virtually nothing to offer except military strength. Other than arms, few of its exports are attractive. The Soviet Union is ill equipped to cooperate economically with other nations or to contribute to the development of other countries. It remains outside the world economic system; the ruble is not convertible; and the Soviets lack organizational capability to share technology. While varieties of socialism and even communism are of interest to some developing states, Soviet model state socialism is increasingly recognized for what it is: a new tsarism, where a small political and managerial elite lives very well but where the legitimate desires of the majority of the population for a higher living standard cannot be met, and greater cultural and political freedom will not be granted.

Accordingly, the Soviet Union does seek hegemony. It has few "carrots" to offer; it must seek to use the "stick." Its behavior not only in Eastern Europe but toward countries such as Egypt and Somalia reveals the heavy-handed nature of Soviet "friendship." The nations of the Third World increasingly recognize Soviet policy for what it is: neocolonialism of the worst sort.

This situation gives the United States a natural advantage. The nationalism that is the dominant characteristic of most of the world's nations will automatically lead most of them to oppose Soviet hegemonism. Soviet neocolonialism has almost consistently been rejected as firmly as was Western colonialism. The rejection of the Soviet Union will not be because of U.S. pressure on smaller nations. It will be an autonomous act.

Our job is not to convince other nations to reject the Soviet Union. Rather, it is to be willing and able to help them reject it successfully if they choose to do so, despite Soviet pressure: to resist hegemony while not seeking hegemony. Four specific policies would seem to be needed to accomplish this. As in the case of the overall policy, these combine "liberal" and "conservative" elements, suggesting a basis for consensus.

First, we must let the smaller nation define its relationship with the United States.

Adopting a policy of permitting another nation, particularly a Third World nation, to define the nature of its relationship with the United States may at times run counter to some short-term U.S. interests. Some U.S. corporations may not feel their interests are best served by such a policy. At times, U.S. foreign aid may appear wasted, in that it may seem that a United States-designed program could make more efficient use of the monies provided.

Ultimately, however, such short-term gains are illusory. As the American people perceive, we have too often poured resources into a nation only to find, not gratitude, but anti-Americanism as our reward. Why? Because in the eyes of the recipient our aid was neocolonialist in nature, as we defined the programs to fit our perception of morality and efficiency. Such an approach, however penny-wise, will almost always prove pound-foolish.

If we permit other nations to define our mutual relationship, we will find ourselves having different approaches in different countries. Some nations will want only government-to-government assistance; others, only private investment; and still others, a mixture of the two. We must accustom ourselves to such flexibility.

Other nations will have to understand that our resources are limited both in total quantity and in type. We cannot meet endless requests; we cannot provide certain types of assistance, such as U.S. military forces or commitments, except in a very few cases such as NATO.

Second, we must develop more associations and fewer alliances.

During the late 1940s and early 1950s, we forged a chain of bilateral and multilateral military alliances. They established the United States as the *primum mobile* in resisting Soviet expansionism with local nations providing military bases for U.S. forces in return for an "umbrella" of U.S. protection. These alliances are increasingly inappropriate in a world where resistance to Soviet expansionism will be primarily a product of local nationalism rather than American initiatives. Too often they have been elevated into moral imperatives, no longer questionable in terms of our national interest, the interests of the other nations involved, or the objective of containing Soviet expansionism. We might do well to remember the words of Gen. Charles de Gaulle, who remarked that "nations have no permanent friends, only permanent interests."

Instead of military alliances, a new policy consensus should emphasize associations, primarily nonmilitary in nature. They would be flexible, designed to change as the circumstances of the parties changed.

Third, whereas the defense of a smaller state will primarily be the product of its own efforts, the United States will need a military capability to limit Soviet options in dealing with smaller states. Primarily, this means the United States must have preeminent naval power. Most of the nations of the world do not share a land border with the Soviet Union. The Soviets can threaten them directly only by sea. If the United States is the dominant naval power, it can interfere with or block most direct Soviet threats to other states. This would inherently limit Soviet options.

Of course, most Soviet threats will not be direct, and resistance to indirect pressures, military or other, must come from the local state. But it would clearly contribute to the security of other nations if America had undeniable control of the sea.

Fourth, we must avoid involvement in the internal affairs of other nations.

In the past, and perhaps even at present, we have placed ourselves in opposition to local nationalism through well-intentioned but inept attempts to tell other people what was good for them, to define their needs. An indiscriminate and crude Wilsonianism has led us to present ourselves as the model society, to prescribe to other people how they should structure their economies, reform their political structures, and even fight their wars. We have done this even with our allies among the developed countries.

In the long run, this approach usually fails, for two reasons. First, we can seldom understand the complexities of another society well enough to prescribe effectively for it. We apply our moral principles or our sociological analyses, and in either case the programs dictated by our approach founder on complex factors we do not understand. Even with our European allies, we often fail to understand their particular needs and perceptions, especially in defense matters.

We fail also because we become the neocolonialist, the white overseer come to direct the natives. Even the best intentions and the best analysis of another nation's needs will create only failure if they appear in a neocolonialist light.

We can ally ourselves with local nationalism only in situations where that nationalism is coherent and definable. In situations of internal conflict, that is rarely the case. However attractive or necessary it may seem at the time for us to involve ourselves in a nation's internal struggles, we must avoid the temptation. Angola is an example of such a situation, where we were wise not to intervene, and where the Soviet Union and its Cuban surrogate may find, in time, that their intervention has not helped their cause.

Ultimately, the goal of our new consensus policy should be to create a *polycentric* resistance to Soviet imperialism. This is a major change from our cold war policy, where resistance to the Soviet Union was seen as being a product of U.S. action under U.S. direction.

The time is ripe for such a policy. We have seen the ultimate failure of a United States-centered policy in Vietnam. We have also seen the emergence of independent local resistance to Soviet expansionism. The most dramatic example to date was the defeat of the Soviet proxy invasion of Zaire. A consortium of local powers— Zaire, Morocco, Egypt, and the Sudan—acting from a basis of shared nationalistic fear of Soviet imperialism, and supported by a European power, France, defeated the Soviet proxy forces. The United States was only marginally involved.

Would this new policy just be a return to the cold war? I don't believe so. We must recognize that our differences with the Soviet Union are so basic that we have few common objectives of fundamental importance. That does not mean that there will not be times when we are prepared to do the same things for different reasons. There are areas in which our interests overlap, and we should be alert to possible agreements that serve the interests of both countries—particularly if we can reduce the danger of direct military conflict.

Even in areas of sharp competition some agreements on ground rules are possible. Despite the Afghanistan invasion, Soviet leadership still appears to be committed to a political strategy of keeping international tensions within manageable bounds—not because it is abandoning its objectives, but because it recognizes that such a policy is the most prudent way to pursue them. We have therefore identified a number of arms control measures that could serve the interests of both countries. SALT II could have been the most substantial recent accomplishment, but, despite its tabling, negotiations continue in Geneva on a comprehensive test ban agreement and control of chemical and radiological weapons, and in Vienna on control of antisatellite arms. These negotiations offer the hope of a more secure future for both nations.

A new consensus foreign policy based on the concept of resisting hegemony without seeking hegemony could, I believe, bring the Congress and the executive branch to order. It could even bring order to another area of major contention, defense policy.

A principal realization emerging from the SALT II debate is the need for new terms of debate on defense issues. It makes little sense to continue to argue in terms of doing more of the same or less of the same, which are largely the terms of the present debate.

By the time the increase of 3 or 5 percent in defense spending now called for is spread between strategic and general-purpose forces, between all four services, between R&D and procurement, operations and maintenance and manpower, the net effect will be slight marginal adjustment of various military balances and very little adjustment of the net balance. We have forgotten, in our defense budget, a basic principle of war: concentration. We have spread ourselves so thin, by trying to do everything, that even substantial sums of additional money are not likely to allow us to do many things well.

At the same time, calls for less defense effort make little sense. The Soviet military challenge is real.

We must stop debating whether more is better or less is better. Only better is better. There is no merit in buying more forces or weapons that are not likely to be effective on the probable battlefield: more nuclear-powered cruisers, more foot infantry divisions, more A-10's or F-18's. The task is to find a basis for determining just what "better" really is. We need a basis for establishing some priorities in defense. We need some means of concentrating our defense efforts where they will do the most good. We need a strategy, a strategy that will enable us to see what qualities our military should have.

A foreign policy of resisting hegemony without seeking hegemony suggests a military strategy. Specifically, it suggests a maritime strategy. As I have already noted, if the United States were to have obvious and undisputable naval superiority, Soviet military and diplomatic options in dealing with third nations would be limited. A goal of maritime superiority in turn would give us the basic tool we need for setting defense priorities. We would no longer have to argue for or against 3 or 5 percent across-the-board budget increases, where every institutional interest will get its customary slice of the pie. We would have our needed point of main effort: our naval forces.

The logic behind a maritime strategy is compelling even today, without a consensus on foreign policy. By geography, we are an island. Our most vital interests are primarily "rimland" interests. Our economy is dependent on seaborne trade and, particularly, on seaborne importation of raw materials. Our principal alliances have meaning only if we control the sea. Japan, our number one trading partner, is dependent on sea communications even within its home islands. Although our focus on NATO has been on ground forces for the central front—at the price of inefficiency in resource allocation, since it takes three army divisions to maintain one in Europe because of the need for a rotation base—NATO is as dependent on Western control of the sea as on a balance of forces in Europe. And although the Europeans can provide divisions on the ground in Europe, only the United States can mount the needed worldwide effort to counter growing Soviet seapower.

A maritime strategy would also concentrate our efforts in forces compatible with our economic strength. Our national strength is capital, not manpower. Manpower is very expensive for us, whereas it is cheap for our adversaries. But capital goods are comparatively inexpensive for us. In 1978 I issued, jointly with former Senator Robert Taft, Jr., of Ohio, a white paper on defense that calls for a maritime strategy. In that white paper we stated:

> Because we can match our potential opponents only through qualitative superiority, it is of critical importance for us to concentrate our defense expenditures in those areas where, out of each defense dollar, the minimum goes for manpower and the maximum is available for capital expenditure; i.e., for research and development and the procurement of weapons systems. Expenditures for land forces fail to meet this requirement: out of each dollar going to the Army, 59% must be spent for manpower costs; out of each dollar of naval expenditures, only 33% is for manpower.

A maritime strategy would also help us avoid a return to conscription. Land forces are inherently manpower intensive. In contrast, our naval forces could be expanded substantially in fighting power without a great increase in manpower. In 1964, the navy had 917 ships in the active fleet, compared with 462 today. But it had only 143,000 more personnel. The ability of a navy to support 100 percent more ships with only 27 percent more personnel shows that concentrating our efforts in naval power would reduce overall manpower requirements.

While the logic of a maritime strategy is strong today, it would be compelling if we reached a foreign policy consensus along the lines suggested in this paper. Our policy would not be to involve ground forces overseas to fight others' battles for them but to create a general condition in which the Soviet Union found its options limited in taking actions against others. Dominant U.S. seapower, would provide that limit, and only dominant seapower, not landpower, could provide it.

If, in turn, we achieved a consensus on a maritime strategy, our defense debate would achieve badly needed focus and cohesion. We would have a guiding principle in defense matters, as we would in foreign policy matters. We could escape the marginal investment for marginal effectiveness trap in which we now find ourselves, where no matter who wins the defense debate, the effect on our military capability is small. Without a unifying strategy in defense as in foreign policy, we will continue to find ourselves splintered to the point of chaos, in both the Congress and the executive branch.

In sum, can the Congress come to order? It cannot achieve the degree of order intended for it—order in final product rather than in procedure—without some new policy ideas. In the absence of a new consensus, neither the Congress nor the executive is likely to progress beyond the current struggles of special interests for short-term gains with no regard for the larger picture. For there will be no larger picture.

We cannot expect a consensus to be formed around any of the current entrenched viewpoints. Nor should we think that desirable. It is as fruitless to debate cold war versus détente in foreign policy as it is to argue the relative merits of Herbert Hoover and FDR in economics. In all fields, the time has come, not just for new answers, but for new questions, leading to new consensus. Those elements of current viewpoints that remain applicable will continue, but in new combinations for new objectives. With new consensus, our traditional procedures, including the intended disorder in Congress, can be workable and can continue to perform the vital functions for which a certain amount of disorder is necessary.

Will Rogers once commented, "the country has come to feel the same when Congress is in session as when the baby gets hold of a hammer." We cannot take the hammer away from the baby. But we may, with a new consensus, be able to concentrate its energies on things that need an occasional hammering.

13

Congress versus the Defense Department

Representative Les Aspin

THERE IS A popular image of the Pentagon sending platoons of military lobbyists festooned with ribbons up to Capitol Hill to lobby for its favored weapons system.

Actually, the Defense Department doesn't lobby as much as the popular perception would have it. Essentially, the Defense Department relies on three preexisting and permanent factors to forward its cause—jobs, an appeal to emotion, and a monopoly on expertise.

First, there are jobs. Each major weapons program carries with it the promise of greater employment for several congressional districts. The military doesn't really have to lobby hard; it knows there will be several very concerned congressmen out there doing the job for the Pentagon. In fact, if the navy wanted to shut me up, it could do so ever so effectively by assigning a fleet to Racine, Wisconsin. Jobs for homefolks are always of the utmost importance to congressmen who want to remain in Congress.

Second, the Defense Department relies heavily on an appeal to emotion. Every new weapons proposal comes wrapped in the flag and inscribed, "If we should ever get involved in another war, this airplane (ship, tank, missile, et cetera) will be essential to save the lives of thousands of our boys." It's very hard for a congressman to vote against "the lives of our boys." The biggest emotional kick, however, comes from the periodic revelations of growing Soviet military prowess. The Pentagon feeds the image of the Russian bear as ten feet tall. Each new weapon proposed by the Pentagon is necessary, therefore, to meet the threat posed by some new Russian advancement. The Defense Department has been accused over the years of revealing horror stories of Russian military developments to influence congressional votes. Melvin R. Laird, when he was defense secretary under Richard Nixon, replied, not without reason, that: (a) he couldn't time revelations, since there was a vote almost every month on some defense issue in Congress; and (b) while liberals might object to his talking about a new Russian carrier, they couldn't dispute the fact that the Russians were building a new carrier. Laird is correct. The Russians do conveniently help the Pentagon sell its programs. All the Pentagon has to do is package the announcements in the most dramatic way.

Third, the Defense Department relies on expertise, or rather Congress' lack of expertise. All congressmen learn a fair amount about social security because every time they return to their districts they are surrounded by senior citizens and must respond to a myriad of questions about social security. All congressmen learn a fair amount about sewer programs and community development block grants and housing programs because mayors and county board members back home are always seeking the congressman's aid in getting funds from federal programs in those fields. But rarely does anyone not serving on a defense-related committee learn much about weaponry. Even those members with large military constituencies don't necessarily learn much about weapons; what they hear are angry questions about commissary subsidies and changes in the military pension program. So the armed services and their supporters in Congress make full use of the jargon of the profession to frighten off potential critics. Senators Barry Goldwater (R-Ariz.) and Howard W. Cannon (D-Nevada), who are both pilots and staunch airpower advocates, regale their colleagues with stories about the fighter planes they have test flown replete with the jawbreaking jargon of the profession. Other members sit in awed silence, unable to respond because they lack the expertise and the jargon.

This does not mean that critics of some military program must simply throw up their hands and give in to the weight of jobs, emotion, and the military's monopoly on expertise. Most commonly, critics throw themselves into the battle and try to grapple directly with all three issues. For example, the critics will pour over reams of documentation, learn the Pentagon's jargon, and be able to face the generals toe to toe. Critics can and do develop expertise. The only problem is that the critics become so enmeshed in the jargon and the fine points that nobody but the generals are listening. It's like a debate between presidential candidates who spout out numbers by the hatful to a public growing somnolent by the digit.

The record of opposition to established defense policy is not one to inspire anybody to make a career of questioning the established wisdom of that agency.

The real battles over weapons and defense policy are not fought out in Congress, in the public arena, but in the Pentagon itself. It is in that "Puzzle Palace on the Potomac," as the career military dubs the Pentagon, that the decision is made as to whether a new helicopter takes precedence over a new tank. It is in that "Disneyland East" that the decision is taken whether investment for conventional warfare should take precedence over investment for strategic warfare.

Despite all the traditional talk about the power of the purse, Congress really doesn't use the purse strings to exert authority. Congress rarely does more than nibble at the edges of the defense budget.

History bears me out on this point. No major weapon has ever been defeated on the floor of either house. The closest call was the 1969 vote on the antiballistic missile (ABM). The effort to kill the ABM failed on a tie vote in the Senate. It is easy to forget that the ABM debate was a unique political event. Several influences converged: critics argued that the ABM would not work, and numerous opponents were ready to come to Washington to explain to congressmen why it would not; peace groups said the ABM was destabilizing and were concerned enough to lobby intensely; hostile constituent pressure (almost unheard of on a weapons system issue) was brought to bear by people living near proposed ABM sites; and, finally, the weapon was not then in production, so that members of Congress did not face pressures from large numbers of workers fearful of losing their jobs. The ABM controversy brought together a constellation of forces that is not likely to be repeated by chance and is almost impossible to put together by design.

Opponents of the B-1 were never able to marshal all these forces. It is worth noting that only two days before President Carter decided to kill the bomber in 1977, the House voted 243 to 178 to support it. And even after Carter came out against the B-1, the House sustained his position by the narrow margin of 202 to 199. Even with the administration opposed to the B-1, that weapon had sufficient appeal (not to mention backing from business and labor groups) to come within 3 votes of a majority.

Congress actually does very little to pare the defense requests of any administration. Each year I have the Library of Congress review the congressional action on the defense budget. The first time the Library reviewed budgets was for the six fiscal years from 1971 through 1976—years when antidefense feelings in the country were at their peak, and Congress and the executive branch were controlled by different parties. The total dollar reductions imposed on the Defense Department came to 6.3 percent of the cumulative requests—much higher than the norm before or since. The study then analyzed the kinds of reductions that were made and found:

1. Nine percent of the cuts were in noncritical areas such as reductions in servants for generals, in the number of public relations men at the Pentagon, and in funds for the construction of new commissaries.
2. Thirty-five percent were illusory cuts or simply financial adjustments, such as the elimination of aid for South Vietnam after Saigon had fallen and of funds that the services had testified were no longer needed because of changed circumstances.
3. Twenty percent were not cuts but postponements; for example, if a program was experiencing development difficulties,

Congress dropped funds for procurement until the problems were resolved.

4. The remaining 36 percent of the cuts (or just 2 percent of the total requests) were in areas that could actually affect defense policy.

However, as the Library pointed out, even this overstated the substantive reductions: "For instance, the elimination of a weapon system is always treated as substantive rather than noncritical [for purposes of the study] even if the system is in fact ineffective, duplicative of other systems, etc." The study concludes that congressional reductions in the defense budget between fiscal year 1971 and fiscal year 1976 were "less critical than might be supposed by a superficial presentation of the total reductions. . . . Congress has exercised only a limited influence on U.S. policy and the military force structure."

What limited budget impact Congress has had comes from the defense-related committees. When defense appropriations bills come to the floor, the House and Senate normally do little more than tinker with them. In the last two decades the House, in floor action, has cut a net of only .04 percent from the appropriation bills brought before it. The Senate has cut only .06 percent. And in half those years, at least one house made no change whatsoever in the sums proposed by the appropriations committees.

I am not saying that the classical method by which legislative bodies have exerted their power over the executive since the barons cornered King John at Runnymede is a complete myth.

The authority to draw tight the purse strings is a real one. And no executive agency can ever allow itself to forget it—not even the Pentagon. This power, however, is all too often reflected in the penchant to spend every penny appropriated. Many agencies discover toward the end of the fiscal year that they haven't spent much of their appropriated funds. There is then a mad dash throughout Washington to spend to the last mil. If an agency spends only 80 percent of its appropriations this year, it can expect that Congress will appropriate only 80 percent as much next year.

This is not what the power of the purse was supposed to mean. It is a twisted version of a grand theory dating back over the centuries. Congress does retain this power and can wield it any time it wishes. The problem is that it doesn't wish much.

Whereas Congress as a whole shies away from frontal assaults on the defense establishment, the defense committees—the two armed services committees and the two defense appropriations subcommittees—do not have that problem. They are hobbled, however, by constituent interest.

When congressmen are elected, one of their first priorities is to insure their reelection. Chances for reelection are not enhanced by concentrating on national legislation. Junior members—and to a great extent senior members as well—are reelected on the basis of what they do for their constituents. This involves both smaller chores, like resolving social security problems for senior citizens, and larger economic concerns of the communities they represent, such as arranging federal financing for a new dam.

Congressmen elected from districts with special economic interests are likely to gravitate to committees that have some influence over those interests. A congressman from the wheat belt will try to get on the Agriculture Committee; one from a fishing port will want a seat on the Merchant Marine and Fisheries Committee; and the congressman from Cape Canaveral will want to be on the Science and Technology Committee. Congressmen from areas with major military bases or defense industries usually turn up on the Armed Services Committee. It is not by coincidence that all three of the representatives from the Norfolk, Virginia, area— home of the largest naval complex on the East Coast—serve on the House Armed Services Committee. Also on the committee is a congressman from the San Diego area, which has the largest concentration of military personnel in the country, and one from the San Antonio area, with the major concentration of air force personnel. The largest Marine base is at Camp LeJeune, North Carolina, and the congressman representing that district also serves on the committee.

Preference for specific committees is based not only on economics but also on ideology. Conservatives concerned with national security tend to think in terms of military solutions and therefore seek seats on the Armed Services Committee, whereas liberals with international concerns gravitate to the Foreign Affairs Committee.

There is one further problem. Although it is not generally realized, the congressional armed services committees authorize only about one third of the defense budget, mostly in procurement, research and development, and military construction. (The other two thirds go mainly for manpower and day-to-day needs such as fuel and utilities.) Indeed, when the armed services committees were formed in 1947, the only part of the defense budget they specifically authorized was that for military construction (about 3 percent of the total). Since 1961 the armed services committees in both houses have extended their authority, first to procurement, then to research and development. And it is likely that their authority will gradually be extended in the years to come.

As a result of this historical development, members of the armed services committees tend to define their job, not in terms of overseeing the defense budget per se, but rather in closely scrutinizing parts of it. Absorbed in minutiae, most members of the committees do not consider alternatives to proposed defense programs because they simply do not regard themselves as responsible for the budget and defense program as a whole.

Take a major personnel issue, for example, like the Defense Officer Personnel Management Act, known simply as DOPMA. The bill would control promotions through the field-grade officer ranks and also set a policy for restricting the numbers of officers in those ranks.

DOPMA was proposed by the Pentagon in 1974. It languished annually in the House Armed Services Committee. The bill was not unimportant. By lowering the proposed ceilings on these ranks, we could limit the ability of the services to assign officers to many chores beyond the pure military. If there weren't so many colonels in uniform, there wouldn't be so many colonels available to assign to foreign policy issues, where they now make their weight felt. (The military has done a far better job of mastering the fine points of foreign policy than the foreign policy establishment has done of mastering military issues. To a certain extent that's true because there are many more available military officers than Foreign Service Officers.)

But it is hard to develop much interest in wending one's way through such a thick and dull piece of legislation as DOPMA. I must frankly admit to heavy eyelids every time I even hear the acronym DOPMA. When the House Armed Services Committee was finally able to stay awake long enough to pass the bill, it didn't really address the fundamental questions posed by the bill. Its two main changes were: first, decreeing that there should be a one-star admiral's rank; and second, providing certain benefits for optometrists in uniform (one member of the subcommittee being an optometrist himself). Minutiae reigned.

We should not expect too much of Congress when it comes to the formulation of defense policy. But there is no reason to sob resignedly over this. Congress does have a major weapon in its armory, one that is too frequently ignored by the public, the press, and academia. And that weapon is procedure.

If there is one word that describes the essence of Congress, that word is "procedure."

Congressmen love procedure, perhaps because so many of them are lawyers. "Closed rules," "open rules," "motions to table," "consent calendars," "union calendars"—this is the stuff of which congressional decisions are made.

To understand the congressman's penchant for procedure, one must understand how it benefits him—and the nation. In the first place, procedure allows Congress to construct a majority and to make progress. In an institution with many factions, one of the few things members can regularly agree on is the procedure for resolving an issue. So, very often procedure becomes substance.

Second, procedure allows congressmen to mask many of their votes and often their true feelings about an issue from their constituents. The first end the Vietnam War vote in the House of Representatives, for example, came on a motion to instruct the conferees to insist on the House version of the Defense Authorization Bill in the light of the Legislative Reorganization Act of 1970. A congressman could vote as he chose and leave his constituents scratching their heads.

Often the procedural approach helps a congressman come down on both sides of an issue—a most comfortable position for any officeholder who is daily faced with conflicting demands from his constituents.

For example, in the fall of 1979 the House of Representatives was called upon to vote on the resumption of peacetime Selective Service registration. The mail was pouring in from liberal groups and college campuses saying this legislation was a greater affront to civil liberties than Idi Amin. But the mail was also rolling in from conservatives and national security advocates saying that the legislation was the only thing that would keep Russian tanks off the White House lawn.

Congress came riding to the rescue down the median strip between these two conflicting positions. The House approved an amendment, first, stripping from the bill the section restarting registration, and, second, inserting in the bill a section calling for a presidential study of various mobilization questions.

Congressmen who supported the amendment were then free to return home and tell those who opposed registration that they had voted to kill the registration proposal, while later in the day they could tell those who advocated registration that while particular provisions of the registration proposal were defective, your congressman voted to require the president to look this registration question over and come back with a better proposal that will save this nation from the encroaching Russians.

Every profession has devices to keep kibitzers and amateurs at arm's-length. Procedure does that for Congress. When confronted by a constituent demanding to know why he voted against funding for the B-1 bomber, the congressman can always say, "Well, it was brought up under a closed rule and that, of course, is just intolerable because it prevented a full and fair debate. We couldn't vote for it under those circumstances." He has the advantage, for although the constituent may know more about bombers, the congressman definitely knows more about closed rules.

Third, procedure allows Congress to defy the executive without confronting executive branch expertise. In 1972, for example, after the SALT I agreement was signed, Defense Secretary Melvin R. Laird handed the two armed services committees his recommendations for additional weapons that would be needed as a result of SALT. One of the items in Laird's package was added money for the hard-target reentry vehicle (HTRV), which faced heavy opposition in the Senate. The House Armed Services Committee reconvened and opposed the SALT additions. The Senate Armed Services Committee, however, decreed that the request had arrived too late for hearings and dropped the HTRV from the bill. When the conference committee met to iron out the differences between the two versions, the HTRV was rejected—not on the merits of the case (even though the principal people involved understood the issue), but on the procedural ground that only one house had considered the matter.

An incident described by David Halberstam in *The Best and The Brightest* * illustrates the congressional instinct to avoid direct confrontation with the executive and achieve objectives through procedure. The issue was whether the United States should intervene in Indochina in 1954 on behalf of the French. At President Eisenhower's suggestion, Secretary of State Dulles met with the congressional leadership, including Senator Lyndon Johnson, then the minority leader. According to Halberstam, the president wanted to get a resolution from Congress, permitting the use of naval and air power to save the embattled French units at Dienbienphu. Johnson, who was unenthusiastic about Congress taking responsibility for another war so soon after the end of the one in Korea, also did not want responsibility for denying the President the authority to resist communist expansion. So he posed a series of procedural hurdles. Had Dulles consulted with our allies? When it turned out that he had not, it was agreed that Congress would reconsider the matter after the secretary had secured a reasonable measure of North Atlantic support for a venture to relieve the

*New York: Random House 1973, pp. 140–46.

French. It was known to Johnson, and probably also to Dulles, that the allies, and particularly the British, whose influence and role would be crucial in any consultation exercise, were distinctly unenthusiastic. By being led to the consultation, a perfectly reasonable procedure in itself, Dulles had been put in the position of being turned down not by Congress but by Westminster.

Procedure, then, can be and is used by Congress to avoid direct responsibility. Congressmen have recourse to procedure, not only to mask their votes and achieve objectives without confronting the executive, but also to protect themselves politically. Congress as an institution does not like to be caught out front.

So it is that the decisive votes on a multi-billion-dollar defense budget, which contains money for such diverse items as antitank missiles, a naval base in the Indian Ocean, and medical care for more than a million retirees will most likely be held on nominally procedural questions, such as thresholds, ceilings, and cutoff dates. The most capable legislators understand this, perhaps instinctively. Congress establishes thresholds which require, for example, that when x occurs, then y must happen; when a certain point is reached, then the president must report to Congress (the War Powers Bill is an example). Congress established ceilings requiring, for instance, that spending for certain functions cannot exceed a specified amount ($2.5 billion for military assistance service funded, or $500 million for transfer authority). And Congress established cutoff dates (e.g., the flight pay for colonels and generals who do not fly stops May 31, or the bombing of Cambodia ends August 15). Congressmen are most comfortable dealing with national security matters in procedural terms; there they are the experts.

All this may be discouraging to those who look to Congress as a source of leadership. Very often these people think that if Congress could get more information or be reformed in some way, it would assume a leadership role. But the problem is not information; in many ways Congress now has more information than it can digest. In any congressional office reams of documents arrive every day and most are tossed in the round file. Only to a limited extent does

Congress digest information and decide issues on a rational basis. It is primarily a political arena, a place where issues are debated in a political, not an academic or rational context.

Focusing on procedure tells us a good deal about what Congress will not do; we must also look at what it can and will do. As I see it, Congress performs three basic roles fairly well.

The first and most obvious is as a conduit for constituent views. It is, in fact, the only federal institution where the people's wishes are pumped directly into the system. For example, it is an important sounding board, revealing how effectively federal programs function or how a proposed course of action will be received. As a sounding board, it is not perfect; special interests are overrepresented, and its votes do not always indicate the general will. Still, what is debated on the floor of Congress is important, and the mood of Congress, reflected in these debates, is rarely very far from the mood of the country at large.

The second role of Congress is as general overseer of government policies and resource allocation. In this role its actions are not unlike those of a board of directors. With very few exceptions, Congress is not where policy is initiated. Most congressional committees or subcommittees have no overall plan or policy to pursue in their area of concern. The Compensation Subcommittee of the House Armed Services Committee, for example, has no guiding policy about the structure of pay and allowances in the armed forces. The subcommittee rarely initiates legislation; it reviews, questions, and periodically modifies what the executive proposes. In performing this role, subcommittee members enjoy certain advantages. Often they have years of experience and know what has been tried before. They have communication lines to branches of the armed forces that provide them with information the executive may have neglected; and they are more sensitive than a Pentagon manager to conflicting pressures that build up around any policy change.

Congress' third role is to act as guardian of the processes of government—that is, to establish and protect procedure. In many ways this is the most intriguing of the three roles. By establishing new procedures, which are ostensibly neutral, Congress often is able to effect substantive changes.

A good example is the National Environmental Protection Act (NEPA). Congress required that for any major federal project that would significantly affect the quality of the environment, an environmental impact statement had to be written by the agency undertaking the project. This provision would force federal agencies to consider the environmental impact of a project before it was carried out. What happened, of course, was much more fundamental. Environmental groups around the country found they could use NEPA to bring suit against any federal agency that did not comply fully with its procedures. Once an environmental impact statement is written, environmentalists use it as a source of objections to the proposed project. The impact statement forced federal agencies into discussions with environmentalists and where the environmentalists were able to make a convincing case, it became politically difficult to ignore them.

As a result, NEPA brought a new group, environmentalists, into a decision-making process from which they previously had been excluded. A long series of projects regarded as dangerous to the environment—from nuclear reactors to public works (one of the most famous being the Cross-Florida Barge Canal)—were halted. By establishing this new procedure, Congress wrought changes more significant than it might have voted in dealing with each project individually.

New procedures established by Congress produce substantive change by changing the decision-making process or bringing new people into it. Sometimes the direct impact of such legislation proves less important than the indirect results. For example, Congress in 1961 passed the Symington amendment, which required that in allocating foreign economic aid, consideration be given to the resources that a recipient country assigns to defense. If a country's defense spending were excessive, the president should withhold aid. The direct impact of that amendment was nil; no country's aid was withdrawn for spending too much on the military. But the indirect impact was considerable. A committee chaired by the Agency for International Development (AID) now had to be included in policy decisions that until then had been managed solely by the Pentagon. It was included because, should Congress wish to investigate compliance with this amendment, AID would then be asked if it had been consulted. As an indirect result of the Symington amendment, a new group of people with a wholly different outlook was brought into the decision-making process.

Historically, Congress has used a vast number of procedural devices to alter the decision-making process. Structural change is one. Congress has established organizations and abolished them; it has increased their influence by having them report directly to the president, or decreased it by having them report to a third-ranking official. If Congress does not think that arms control, for example, is being given sufficient consideration by the executive branch, it can create an agency with independent access to the White House, as it did with the Arms Control and Disarmament Agency (ACDA). If it considers human rights a neglected factor in foreign policy decisions, it can legislate into existence an assistant secretary of state with staff and power to insinuate those concerns into the entire departmental process.

A second procedural device is to require certain findings before specific programs may be carried out. The Walsh Act of 1935 required that before the administration could transfer destroyers to another country, the navy first had to certify they were not needed. Senator David I. Walsh, the author of the act, feared that President Franklin D. Roosevelt was about to give destroyers to Britain and thus drag the United States into another European war. While the senator's purpose was to prevent President Roosevelt from giving destroyers to Britain, he assumed Congress would be reluctant to give that order directly. He thus decided on a procedural device that would be acceptable to Congress. As Senator Walsh no doubt anticipated, the navy was not willing to declare it had too many destroyers.

A third procedural device is for Congress to designate specific officials to make certain decisions. Placing responsibility for a decision in an office with predictable political or organizational interests naturally influences the decision. The act that established the Naval Petroleum Reserve, for example, requires that any decision to release petroleum from the reserves must be approved by the secretary of the navy. Any navy secretary is reluctant to make such a determination.

Finally, Congress can involve already existing groups in government decisions by making them part of a new procedure. This might be a citizen group (such as the environmentalists in the NEPA case), an agency of government, or perhaps even Congress itself. Sometimes the people brought into a decision do not belong to an identifiable group. For instance, under the provisions of the War Powers Act, if the president commits American forces to hostilities abroad, he must report to Congress within forty-eight hours his reasons for doing so, and at the end of sixty days he must withdraw those forces unless Congress votes to continue the commitment. By establishing this procedure, Congress had made itself the final arbiter on whether troops should be used. But, as we have seen, Congress is never happy in such a role and is most unlikely to challenge a president in such a foreign policy decision. Indeed, liberals objected that the War Powers Act was too weak: bringing Congress into the decision would not change anything because Congress would simply rubberstamp whatever the president had already decided to do.

But the liberal objection overlooks the effect of this bill on decision making in the executive branch. When the president considers sending troops somewhere, he and his advisers now know that the decision will provoke an intense debate for up to sixty days. Congressional committees will hold hearings; newspapers will write editorials; "Meet the Press" and "Face the Nation" will cross-examine government spokesmen; there will be network specials, demonstrations, and letters from constituents. The predictability of all this commotion is bound to strengthen the hand of those in the president's council who oppose military intervention. They can now object, not with their own arguments, but with the kind the president will inevitably have to face. Congress' ultimate verdict is not the most important factor; what is important is that the president and his advisers know their policy will receive intense public scrutiny. They will be much less inclined to embark upon a military adventure without a very strong case for it.

The ways in which Congress has used procedure in the past suggest that procedural changes offer the best hope of attacking many of today's problems, including defense issues.

Procedure is not the end all and be all, of course. Just as Congress applies its brains to procedural ways to control the executive, so the executive works hard to limit the power of the hidden hand of Congress.

Congressional efforts to make some agency more important by requiring that it report to the president can obviously be subverted by a president who simply chooses to ignore that agency. When Congress has required that two agencies representing divergent views both get a crack at making policy, it has not been unheard of for an administration that wants Agency A to win to appoint a lightweight to represent Agency B.

There will never be a way to prevent the imagination of man from trying to undo the work of the imagination of others. The point is not that procedural approaches are infallible but that they work so very often. Yet the procedural tack is generally the last rather than the first approach liberals will take when grappling with the Defense Department.

Take the weapons procurement system. Critics generally appear on the scene only after a particular weapon has gone through years of research and development, and long after it has developed a constituency.

One of the major problems in controlling procurement of new weapons is the "requirements" syndrome. Every weapon requested by the military services is quickly defined as essential to fulfilling their military mission. Weapons systems become "requirements" very early in the process—well before Congress ever sees them as specific budget items. By the time Congress comes face to face with a new weapon, service and bureaucratic momentum is already behind it, contractors and unions are interested, and it is probably too late to stop it. What is needed is a vehicle for bringing other decision makers into the process sooner, perhaps a procedure requiring the president to act on major weapons in the early stages of development. Legislation could also mandate that advice be submitted to the president from experts who do not have a parochial interest in a follow-on system for every weapon in the inventory.

One procedure for dealing with the weapons requirement syndrome might be the following: the president is required by Congress to give his approval before any research and development money is spent, on any weapons system to cost more than x billion dollars. Before making his decision, the president receives the independent views of the secretary of defense, the secretary of state, each of the service chiefs, the head of ACDA, and the president's science adviser. Each would be required to: (1) estimate the long-term cost of the weapons system; (2) estimate costs of alternative ways to accomplish the same mission; and (3) evaluate the new system's impact on future arms control agreements. If this procedure, or something like it, were established, some of the most expensive and most destabilizing weapons proposed might be stopped before they gathered irresistible bureaucratic momentum.

Of course, new procedures do not guarantee correct decisions. All one can seek to guarantee is that more critical minds will have some influence before crucial decisions are made. It is also possible that the executive branch will subvert a procedure once it is established, although doing so would have its political risks and costs. Influencing decision making through procedural change may seem to be influencing it at the margin; certainly it operates one degree removed from the actual issues. But since Congress works that way, when it works at all, it seems to me the best hope for affecting the substance of decisions.

Congress is essentially a political institution and responds primarily to political stimuli. Rational arguments in such an institution carry little weight unless they are supported by political organization. Political organization can be mobilized around a national issue, but only with a great deal of effort. Usually, congressmen deal substantively and directly only with issues that are noncontroversial or with which they have dealt previously. If an issue is controversial and unfamiliar—as most important issues are—Congress will instinctively begin groping toward a procedural resolution.

Congress as an institution is conservative, cautious, and reluctant to initiate change. It responds to old stimuli more quickly than to new ones. When it opposes the executive, it is usually to protect some interest group or some aspect of the status quo. New initiatives on the federal scene rarely are a product of Congress. An individual member or a group of members may take the initiative; but Congress as an institution rarely does.

In earlier days when the executive was smaller and the issues Congress dealt with were fewer and less intricate, there was more balance between the two branches. That balance exists no more. The executive has grown and its agencies have become highly specialized. Congress must deal with all the issues. It has remained (except for some increase in staff) roughly the same size, even though the number of votes House members confronted rose from 159 in 1947–48 to 942 in 1977–78. Apart from the work load, Congress is much the same as Congress was; the executive is not as the executive was.

On the defense issues, as on many other subjects, the direct role Congress can be expected to play is limited. In the jockeying that goes on within the government over our defense policies, the actions Congress can take will be either too broad or too narrow to be very constructive—either adding 5 percent to the top of the entire defense budget or cutting the number of enlisted men working as servants for generals. The defense committees in Congress could be more effective, but because of their composition and outlook they will not be.

The failure of Congress to assume leadership in this and other areas is one reason for the great interest, and limited progress, in congressional reform. But reform, although a worthy goal in itself, is not likely to result in congressional leadership. The problem with Congress is its members: how they regard their job and how they make their decisions. It is possible, of course, that in time new people elected to Congress will bring with them new attitudes and that Congress will reassert itself. But that should not be counted on; the new members will find themselves in the same position as the old. They, too, will want to be reelected. They, too, will be subjected to conflicting pressures, will feel a lack of expertise, and will have little time to devote to any single issue.

Rather than try to make Congress into something it is not (i.e., an alternative to the executive branch as an initiator of new ideas), we should look realistically at what Congress is and search for ways to improve its performance. Congress is a channel for constituent concerns; this role could be improved by lessening the influence of special interests. Congress is a board of directors over government programs and policies; this function also could be strengthened by an increasing emphasis on oversight and investigation. Congress guards the procedures of government; and while it prefers procedure over policy, it could do better in this area if it consciously chose to *use* procedures rather than to hide behind them to avoid directly confronting an issue.

This may seem a pessimistic assessment of Congress' capacities, and perhaps it is. But, as the NEPA case demonstrates, manipulation of procedure can be a very powerful weapon. Right now it is a weapon that is understood instinctively by some members of Congress and not at all by others. It may not be the straightest arrow in the congressional quiver, but it is the one most easily brought into action.

14
Negotiating About Negotiations: The Geneva Multilateral Trade Talks

Robert C. Cassidy, Jr.*

I. INTRODUCTION

ARTICLE I, Section 8, clause 3 of the Constitution confers on the Congress the power to "regulate commerce with foreign Nations." At the same time, the president is the "sole organ of the federal government in the field of international relations."[1] Despite the problems presented by this awkward separation of powers, the United States has just concluded and implemented the most ambitious trade negotiation since the negotiation of the General Agreement on Tariffs and Trade in 1948.

Given the somewhat protectionist political climate in the United States arising from slow growth and persistent balance-of-trade deficits, the success of the Tokyo Round is somewhat surprising. Congressional approval of the legislation approving and implementing the Tokyo Round results—by massive majorities in both houses, after only thirty-four days of formal consideration—appears to many people to be astounding.[2]

To the extent the press noted this unusual event at all,[3] it tended to attribute the success of the enterprise to the skill of Am-

*The opinions expressed in this chapter are those of the author and do not necessarily reflect the opinions of the Office of the United States Trade Representative.

bassador Robert S. Strauss. While the results might well have been different without Strauss's considerable efforts, the success of the Tokyo Round is largely attributable to a "unique Constitutional experiment . . . [in] cooperation between the legislative and executive branches of the Government during a complex international negotiation."[4] This chapter will describe the evolution of this experiment.

To put the discussion in perspective, a brief summary of earlier experiments in coordination between the Congress and the president during international trade negotiations is in order. Beginning with the Trade Agreements Act of 1934,[5] the Congress has periodically delegated to the president authority to implement in domestic law the results of trade agreements insofar as they relate to tariffs. This system worked well until the Kennedy Round of Multilateral Trade Negotiations (1964–67) under the auspices of the General Agreement on Tariffs and Trade (GATT).

The problem that arose in the Kennedy Round did not relate to tariff changes but to antidumping procedures and customs valuation procedures. These issues were a novelty in GATT negotiations. The fact that they were considered at all reflects the success of previous negotiations in lowering effective tariff rates throughout the industrial world.

As tariff rates declined, the effects on international trade of national laws and policies other than tariffs, "nontariff barriers," became more apparent. The Kennedy Round agreements on antidumping and customs valuation represent the first serious attempt to expand the GATT system specifically to the significant problem of nontariff barriers. However, neither U.S. law[6] nor the U.S. Congress contemplated this kind of agreement resulting from the Kennedy Round. The result was that the undertakings relating to customs valuation were never implemented by Congress. Although the president entered into the Antidumping Code, the Congress adopted legislation, which became law, specifically requiring existing domestic legislation to prevail over the code.[7]

When preparations for a seventh round of GATT negotiations, the Tokyo Round, began in the late 1960s, the executive branch had to face in earnest the issue of nontariff barriers. They needed a procedure which would provide American negotiators and foreign governments some certainty that this time American commitments in negotiations would be fulfilled in a timely manner.

After an abortive attempt in 1969 and 1970[8] to obtain legislation for the Tokyo Round, the administration recommended the "Trade Reform Act of 1973" to Congress. Its fate is discussed below.

II. THE TRADE ACT OF 1974

A. THE ADMINISTRATION PROPOSAL

On April 10, 1973, Congressman Wilbur Mills introduced the legislation proposed by the Nixon administration as the legal basis for U.S. participation in the Tokyo Round. This bill, H.R. 6767,[9] would have delegated to the president the power to change existing law, by "order," to fulfill U.S. obligations under a nontariff barrier agreement.[10] Nontariff barrier agreements and presidential implementing orders would have been submitted to Congress for review only if the president determined that congressional action, in addition to H.R. 6767, was "necessary or appropriate" to give the agreement effect.[11]

In such a case, the president would have been required to notify Congress of his intention to seek congressional review at least ninety days before entering into the agreement. Presidential orders submitted for congressional review would have been "valid" unless the House or Senate, within ninety days after the order and agreement were submitted to the Congress, adopted a resolution stating that it disapproved the agreement. It was not clear that adoption of such a resolution under the bill would invalidate the international agreement.[12].

Although H.R. 6767 contained a subchapter captioned "Congressional Liaison," the bill did not contain a structure for congressional-executive consultations during international negotiations. The executive would have been required to supply information to Congress only after an agreement had entered into force.[13] The only provision that appears to have been intended to facilitate consultation during negotiations is the requirement that the president notify Congress of his intention to use the congressional review procedures in the bill at least ninety days before he enters into a nontariff barrier agreement.[14]

The Committee on Ways and Means never acted on H.R. 6767.

B. THE HOUSE BILL

After discussions between the administration, represented principally by officials from the Office of the Special Representative for Trade Negotiations (STR), and the members and staff of the Committee on Ways and Means, Congressman Al Ullman introduced H.R. 10,710[15]on October 3, 1973. This bill became the Trade Act of 1974.

Under Section 102 of the House bill, the president was permitted to enter into nontariff barrier agreements only after consulting with the Committee on Ways and Means and the Committee on Finance.[16] As in H.R. 6767, there was no requirement under the House bill that all nontariff barrier agreements entered into under the bill be submitted to Congress for review. However, the Ways and Means Committee clearly intended that the determination whether an agreement is to be submitted to Congress be made by the executive in consultation with the Committee on Ways and Means and the Committee on Finance,[17] rather than, as under H.R. 6767, by the president alone.

From H.R. 6767, the House bill incorporated the one-house "legislative veto" scheme, including the ninety-day notice requirement for nontariff barrier agreements and implementing orders submitted for congressional review.[18] The House bill clearly stated that both the trade agreement and the orders for its implementation would not take effect if either house were to adopt a disapproval resolution.

A significant feature of the House bill was the requirement in Section 161 that ten members of the House and Senate be accredited as official advisers to the U.S. delegations negotiating trade agreements.[19] The Ways and Means Committee added Section 161 to insure that there would be "continuing consultations" between the executive and Congress during international trade negotiations.[20] The concept of congressional advisers for trade negotiations was not new. Section 243 of the Trade Expansion Act of 1962[21] required four congressional advisers. However, the drafts-men of the administration bill decided not to include such a pro-vision because of fears of congressional meddling in a negotiation and the perception that the Kennedy Round advisers had little im-pact on the final, unsatisfactory fate of the Antidumping Code and customs valuation agreement.

The Ways and Means Committee clearly anticipated a more ac-tive congressional role in the Tokyo Round than did the adminis-tration. H.R. 10,710 required congressional-executive consultation before the president entered into a nontariff barrier agreement; implicitly required consultation to determine which agreements would be sent to Congress; provided Congress a veto over both the agreement and its implementation; and made members of Con-gress official advisers to U.S. trade delegations. As the Ways and Means Committee stated in its report on H.R. 10,710:

> Participation by Members of Congress as advisers to the negotiating delegation, and the consultations that will be required with respect to actions contemplated by the President under the authorities granted him by the bill, envisage a degree of consultations and oversight ac-tivity not previously considered under past extension of trade agree-ments authority.[22]

H.R. 10,710 passed the House on December 11, 1973. The pro-visions relating to congressional review and consultations were identical to the provisions in the bill when it was introduced.

C. THE SENATE BILL

The Senate took slightly more than one year to consider and pass H.R. 10,710. During that year President Nixon resigned. Congres-sional power relative to the executive was greater than at any time since World War II. The Senate Finance Committee took advan-tage of the executive's weakness to significantly modify the House bill. The statutory framework for congressional-executive consul-tation over trade negotiations contained in the Senate bill formed the basis for the "unique constitutional experiment" resulting in the successful conclusion of the Tokyo Round.

The first, and most important, amendment the Finance Committee made to the House bill was to substitute a positive approval procedure for the legislative veto of nontariff barrier agreements. The amendment was proposed by Senator Talmadge after discussions with the Finance Committee staff. The senator's major concern, which was shared by the staff, was that the legislative veto represented an abdication by Congress of its constitutional responsibility to make laws. Talmadge insisted that the usual constitutional pattern be followed. The president should request legislation to implement trade agreements that would then be passed or defeated by Congress.

The political implication of this change in procedures, which was clearly perceived by the senior members of the Finance Committee, was a significant shift of power to the Congress from the executive. Congress would determine the details of domestic implementation of trade agreements. It would not merely accept or reject a package presented by the president.

This new reality had a significant impact on the willingness of the executive to work with Congress during the trade negotiations as well as on the actual implementation of the trade agreements. Absent this assertion of congressional power, it is likely that congressional-executive interaction during the Tokyo Round would have been similar to the superficial and ineffective consultation carried on during the Kennedy Round. However, the reaction of the now more activist Congress to the results of the Tokyo Round would then probably have been more negative than it had been to the results of the Kennedy Round.

Although the committee agreed in principle to the Talmadge amendment in early June, it took five months to reach agreement on the details. The procedures, which were accepted by the House without significant change during the conference on H.R. 10,710, became Sections 102 and 151 of the Trade Act of 1974.[23]

The Senate bill, and the public law, retained the House bill's requirements that the president consult with appropriate congressional committees and that he notify Congress at least ninety days before entering into a nontariff barrier agreement.[24] The legislative veto was replaced by a procedure under which a nontariff barrier agreement does not "enter into force" for the United States unless the president submits an "implementing bill" and Congress, by a voting majority of both Houses:

(1) approves the agreement,

(2) makes changes or additions to domestic law necessary to implement the agreement, and

(3) approves a statement describing changes in administrative practice proposed to implement the agreement,

and the bill is signed by the president.[25] Administration demands for rapid congressional action on trade agreements were addressed by the creation of special procedural rules to accelerate congressional consideration of an implementing bill. The procedures are designed to result in a final congressional decision within ninety working days after an implementing bill is introduced. Important features of these procedures are automatic discharge of the implementing bill from committee after a set period, usually forty-five working days, and a limitation of floor debate to twenty hours. Most important, an implementing bill cannot be amended in committee or on the floor by either house.[26]

Although the positive approval requirement was the most significant amendment affecting congressional-executive consultation during the trade negotiations, the Finance Committee made an important modification to the House bill provision creating congressional advisers. The amendment requires the special representative for trade negotiations (STR) to keep both congressional advisers and designated members of the Finance Committee's and the Ways and Means Committee's staffs "currently informed" on the status of negotiations.[27] Under this provision, STR supplied the two committees with most position papers and reporting cables relating to the trade negotiations. As a result, the congressional committee staffs were able to carry on current and detailed discussions about the negotiations with both the administration and members of the committees.

III. IMPLEMENTATION OF THE TRADE ACT

Although the Trade Act of 1974 contains provisions governing congressional-executive consultation that are more elaborate than any previous legislation, it left a great deal to be implemented informally by both Congress and the executive branch. From early 1975 until late in 1977 there evolved a process of consultation that was generally satisfactory to both sides. It is probably fortunate that the trade negotiations moved very slowly during this period. As a result, both Congress and the executive agencies, particularly STR, were able to devote considerable time to developing the process as opposed to discussing substantive policy issues. In particular, personal relationships developed between individuals in STR and members and staff on the Hill. These relationships contributed importantly to the ultimate success of the process. Once the negotiations began to move quickly, in 1978, there was in place an operating system that could react quickly to unfolding events.

Before reviewing the different aspects of this system, it is important to understand how the Ways and Means Committee and the Finance Committee oversee a program when there is no legislation relating to that program before the committees. Both committees rely heavily on a few members who become "experts" on the subject. These members are usually on the subcommittee responsible for the program. Nonexpert members will typically pay attention to a program only when a specific problem of a constituent arises or when new legislation comes before the committee. Even the expert members rely heavily on the committee staff for guidance on all but the most general policy issues. The result is that the responsibility for oversight normally falls on the staff with an occasional intervention by a member.

A. INFORMATION

Section 161(b) of the Trade Act of 1974 (19 U.S.C. 2211) requires STR to keep congressional advisers currently informed. Early in 1975, the House and Senate committee staffs met with the special representative for trade negotiations, Ambassador Dent, to sign a memorandum of understanding implementing Section 161. Under this agreement, STR committed itself to supplying both committees in a timely manner with incoming and outgoing cables relating to the trade negotiations. The committees agreed to obtain appropriate security clearances for their staffs and to follow prescribed procedures for handling classified documents.

A formal agreement was considered necessary in light of State Department opposition to disclosure of internal executive branch communications. This opposition manifested itself in threats to invoke executive privilege and refusal to deliver certain "sensitive" cables to STR for fear they would be turned over to Congress. State eventually agreed to comply with Section 161 in light of the memorandum of understanding and a side agreement between the Department and STR. Under the side agreement, only cables between Washington and Geneva relating to the trade negotiations could be supplied to Congress. Cables from or to other posts were not supplied even though they related to the negotiations.

The information aspect of consultation worked fairly well. Somewhat to the surprise of executive branch officials, no cable supplied to the Congress between 1975 and 1979 was disclosed to any person without appropriate clearances.

The major congressional complaint was the week or so delay between the time a cable was sent from, or received in, Washington and its delivery to the committees. The committee staffs were occasionally disturbed by the fact that STR was obviously not sending all cable traffic relating to the trade negotiations. However, virtually all important cables were supplied to the Hill. Although committee members rarely asked to see cables, they were regularly used by staff as the basis for briefings.

A significant feature of the consultation process while the trade negotiations were in progress was that members of Congress and the committee staffs almost never made definitive statements for or against specific negotiating proposals put forward by STR. This conscious attempt by the Hill to avoid commitments did not prevent frequent discussion of details between STR and the committee staffs. It did require STR to rely heavily on the advice it received from its private advisory committees.

Those committees were established under the Trade Act of 1974.[28] They were composed of private citizens representing a broad array of industrial, labor, and agricultural interests. The committees were informed of current developments in the trade negotiations and provided guidance on specific STR proposals.

Despite congressional hesitance to give specific guidance, the dialogue between Congress and the administration left the trade negotiators with a clear idea of the political parameters within which they were working. It also gave the members of Congress some assurance that the negotiators were seeking results that were politically acceptable.

B. TRAVEL

Politics and economics aside, one of the most interesting aspects of international trade policy is the possibilities it presents for foreign travel. This lure was used effectively by both the members of Congress responsible for trade and by the STR to keep nonexpert members interested in the subject. The Ways and Means Committee and the Finance Committee sponsored one or more foreign trips each year for members to discuss trade issues with foreign officials and American negotiators in Geneva.

Both the members of Congress and the American negotiators, many of whom had never spoken with a member of Congress, apparently thought the trips valuable. On the congressional side, the members say that personal contact with foreign and American negotiators gave them a better understanding of the international political dynamics of the talks. Conversely, the American negotiators got a very clear view of the problems they would face when they returned to Congress with trade agreements.

In addition to travel by members, which was relatively rare, the committee staffers responsible for trade traveled to Geneva on a regular basis. This allowed them to verify information received in cables. It also exposed them to the day-to-day problems of the negotiators and vice versa.

While it is not possible to prove that the congressional presence in Geneva, either of members or staffs, was essential to the consultation process, both the executive and congressional participants believe it was one of the catalysts that made the system work. It permitted serious and relatively uninterrupted discussions of the domestic and international political issues in the trade negotiations. Furthermore, many American negotiators believe that allowing congressional representatives to discuss their concerns directly with foreign negotiators was infinitely more effective than mere reporting of these concerns by an American negotiator.

C. HEARINGS AND REPORTS

Formal hearings and reports by congressional committees during the trade negotiations were relatively rare.[29] The essential problem was that the negotiations were conducted in secret. The public could not comment on proposals about which it knew nothing. Those hearings that were held became forums for general trade policy complaints that had relatively little to do with the rather technical issues being negotiated in Geneva.

While the negotiations were in progress, members of Congress occasionally sought an indication of probable public reaction to the trade negotiations by speaking with members of the trade advisory committees described above. In general, however, most concerned members of Congress apparently assessed the political implications of the trade negotiations intuitively. The traditional means of oversight—hearings, investigations, and discussions with interested private groups—were found to be poorly suited to political assessment of ongoing international negotiations.

D. DOMESTIC LEGISLATIVE PROCEDURES

The elaborate procedural rules for considering implementing legislation under the Trade Act of 1974 left many essential issues unresolved. Who would draft the legislation? What committees would review the legislation? How and when would they review it?

The staffs of the Ways and Means Committee and the Finance Committee began to discuss congressional procedures early in 1978. Although they generally agreed that Congress had to control the process, no agreement on details was reached.

Beginning in April 1978, the Finance Committee staff spoke with Senators Long and Ribicoff about procedures. This resulted in a staff proposal (Attachment A) that was approved by the committee on June 23, 1978. The intent of these procedures was to provide the committee with an opportunity to influence the terms of the implementing bill *before* it was submitted by the president and became unamendable. In essence, the staff recommended that the committee consider administration proposals for the implementing bill just as though it was dealing with normal legislation.

The Finance Committee procedures were delivered to STR and the Ways and Means Committee. Although Ways and Means never formally adopted the Finance procedures, the two committees eventually followed the same pattern. STR officially acquiesced in the Finance procedures. Unofficially, however, they still hoped to carry on the bill drafting process without too much congressional interference.

Because of the STR reaction, the Finance Committee insisted on meeting with Ambassador Strauss on July 25, 1978, to reach agreement on procedures. Strauss acquiesced quickly. An exchange of letters between Senator Ribicoff and Ambassador Strauss confirmed their understanding. During a discussion with members of the Committee on Ways and Means and the Finance Committee in the White House on December 18, 1978, Ambassador Strauss repeated his commitment to the process proposed by the Finance Committee.

IV. CONGRESSIONAL CONSIDERATION OF THE IMPLEMENTING BILL

A. COMMITTEE MEETINGS

The president notified Congress of his intention to enter into trade agreements on January 4, 1979.[30] This was the ninety-day notice required under the Trade Act.[31] Shortly thereafter, the administration began sending detailed proposals for implementing legislation to the Finance and to Ways and Means. The committee staffs translated these proposals into the format both committees normally used when considering legislation. Under this format, current law is compared with the administration proposal and proposals of individual members of Congress, if any. In this case, the relevant provisions of the underlying trade agreement was described with each proposal.

At this point both committees came under considerable pressure to hold public hearings on the trade negotiations. Despite expressions of concern from STR, these hearings were held in February[32] and April 1979.[33] Unlike earlier hearings on the trade negotiations, these were useful to the members because witnesses focused on the issues that were the subject of negotiation in Geneva. This was possible because of the detailed description of the results of the negotiations that was published in the *Federal Register* as part of the president's ninety-day notice.

Both the Finance Committee and the Ways and Means Subcommittee on Trade began to hold executive sessions on administration proposals for implementing legislation in March 1979. In the Senate, the Agriculture Committee and the Commerce Committee also met to consider implementing legislation within their respective jurisdictions. In the House, the Ways and Means Committee considered all the implementing legislation.

The executive sessions were identical to markup sessions held on normal legislation except that they were closed to the public. Closed meetings were necessary because the administration proposals and the trade agreements were classified "confidential" by STR.

During the sessions, committee staff first presented the material. Then administration officials and members of the committee discussed the proposal until agreement was reached. Whenever disagreements arose, the committees directed their staffs to sit down with the administration to try and "work something out." In the rare cases where no agreement with the administration was possible, the committees voted on the question. More often than not, the administration lost those votes and some other proposal prevailed.

An indication of the success of the consultation process during the negotiations is the fact that STR was forced by Congress to renegotiate only one of the agreements brought back from Geneva. The Government Procurement Code, as originally negotiated, would have opened federal government procurement from minority-owned businesses to competitive bidding. At the insistence of Congress, this requirement of the code was deleted.

Although many administration officials initially viewed the committee sessions as hand-holding exercises, the results of which could be ignored, they eventually came to take the process very seriously and fought vigorously to sustain their position. This change in perception was due largely to the repeated statements by Ambassador Strauss that he would accept congressional decisions. It also undoubtedly reflected the serious approach of the committee members during the sessions.

The executive sessions continued until May. During that period, the United States entered into the trade agreements by signing a *procès verbal* in Geneva on April 12, 1979. In early May, Finance and Ways and Means met to reconcile their differences in a "nonconference" on the administration proposals for the implementing bill.

B. LOBBYING

Once the congressional committees began considering the proposals for implementing legislation, members of Congress began discussing the bill with various interest groups. Lobbying by those groups was severely handicapped by the secrecy surrounding the committee sessions. However, a number of groups pursued their concerns vigorously with varying degrees of success. As usual, the groups that had prepared long in advance usually did better than latecomers. The most active groups were the domestic steel industry, the domestic dairy industry, and a group of multinational corporations concerned largely about customs valuation. Conspicuous by their absence or late appearance were importers and consumers.

C. DRAFTING THE BILL

Beginning in March, administration representatives began meeting with committee staff in the offices of the Senate and House legislative counsels to draft an implementing bill consistent with the committees' decisions. This drafting group produced a comprehensive bill that STR then informally submitted to Congress on June 5, 1979. As a practical matter, this draft was more intensively reviewed by executive branch agencies than by Congress because it reflected congressional decisions.

Administration review of the draft resulted in only a few

278 THE TETHERED PRESIDENCY

changes. This may reflect fear of congressional reaction to significant changes in the draft. This fear was not irrational in light of the letter sent to President Carter by thirty-three members of Congress warning him against making any changes. The only change of significance was the deletion of an extension of the president's authority to reduce tariffs under Section 101 of the Trade Act without subsequent congressional`approval.[34] This deletion was made because of the numerous products Congress insisted on excepting from the tariff-cutting authority.

With minor changes, the president submitted the Trade Agreements Act of 1979 to Congress on June 19. It was introduced immediately, passed the Congress thirty-four days later, and was signed into law on July 26, 1979.

V. CONCLUSION

The separation of powers with respect to international affairs between Congress and the president has caused and continues to cause the U.S. government considerable problems in conducting international negotiations. The debates over the League of Nations Charter, the Antidumping Code, the Panama Canal treaty, and SALT II are a few examples of the kinds of controversy some people believe are inevitable under our constitutional system.

The negotiation of the Tokyo Round of Multilateral Trade Negotiations and passage of the Trade Agreement Act of 1979 demonstrates that the separation of powers, at least on international economic issues, does not necessarily result in destructive conflict between the congressional and executive branches of government. Congress formulated, and adopted in a timely manner, legislation that is consistent with the international agreements negotiated by the president. This represents both a major political feat and the success of a new institutional arrangement.

What were the features of the Trade Act consultation system that contributed most significantly to this success? First, discussions between Congress and the executive during the entire negotiations insured that neither the negotiators nor the Congress would be surprised by the end results. The negotiators had a reasonably clear idea of what they could and could not do in the context of domestic politics. The Congress had a reasonably good understanding of what was and was not possible in the international political context. The result was that extreme or unexpected actions by either side were almost impossible.

Second, the political process within the U.S. government, and particularly within the Congress, was managed by a relatively small group of people who were familiar with the issues. This familiarity was based on several years of experience. Furthermore, a community of interest developed between the responsible officials in Congress and in the executive, principally in STR. Although this certainly did not result in an absence of conflict between the two groups, it did create an alliance of sorts between them against critical ousiders in the Congress, executive agencies other than STR, and the public.

Third, each branch believed it maintained its constitutional prerogatives. The executive negotiated and Congress legislated. The key to this was probably the fact that the congressional committees focused on the domestic legislation. They took the international agreements as a given, except in the relatively minor case involving the Government Procurement Code. This was possible only because the committees were satisfied, as a result of the consultations during negotiations, that the agreements were generally acceptable.

An obvious question, which was asked frequently in Congress during its consideration of the Trade Agreements Act, is whether the Trade Act procedures are applicable to other kinds of agreements. The answer to this question is beyond the scope of my subject. However, a number of elements which were important to the success of the Trade Act process may be unique to the international economics area. These may also explain why the executive-congressional relationship on trade policy has evolved independently from that relationship on other international issues.

The Congress has an explicit constitutional power over foreign commerce that it does not have in other areas of international relations. Nontariff trade agreements usually require complex implementing legislation. Agreements in other areas usually come before Congress without implementing legislation. This increases the likelihood of congressional efforts to change the international agreement. When nontrade agreements do require implementing legislation, that legislation is often within the jurisdiction of a different committee from the committee with jurisdiction over the agreement. Trade agreements *and* their implementing legislation are controlled by the Finance Committee and the Committee on Ways and Means. Finally, the conflicts over trade agreements are based in economics. Economic conflicts are usually more easily resolved by compromise than are conflicts over national security or human rights, for example.

NOTES

1. *United States v. Curtis Wright Export Corp.*, 299 U.S. 304, 316-(1936).
2. H.R. 4537 was introduced on June 19, 1979, and passed the House of Representatives by a vote of 395 to 12 on July 11, 1979. 125 *Cong. Rec.* H 5690–91 (daily ed., July 11, 1979); it passed the Senate by a vote of 90 to 4 on July 23, 1979. 125 *Cong. Rec.* S. 10,340 (daily ed., July 23, 1979).
3. *New York Times*, July 24, 1979, p. 1; *Washington Post*, July 24, 1979, p. 3.
4. Senate Comm. on Finance, Trade Agreements Act of 1979, S. Rep. No. 93–249, 5 (1979).
5. Act of June 12, 1934, 48 Stat. 943.
6. Trade Expansion Act of 1962, P.L. 87-794, 76 Stat. 872.
7. P.L. 90-634, §201 (Oct. 24, 1968).
8. The Trade Act of 1969, H.R. 14,870, 91st Cong., 1st sess. (1969); The Trade Act of 1970, H.R. 18,970, 91st Cong., 2d sess. (1970).
9. The Trade Reform Act of 1973, H.R. 6767, 93d Cong., 1st sess. (1973).
10. *Id.* at §103.
11. *Id.* at §103(d).
12. *Id.* at §103(e).
13. *Id.* at §121.
14. *Id.* at §103(e) (1).
15. The Trade Reform Act of 1973, H.R. 10,710, 93d Cong., 1st sess. (1973).

16. *Id.* at §102(d).
17. House Ways and Means Comm., Trade Reform Act of 1973, H. Rep. No. 93-571, 41–42 (1973).
18. H.R. 10,710, 93d Cong., 1st sess., §102 (1973).
19. *Id.* at §161.
20. H. Rep. No. 93-571 at 42 (1973).
21. P.L. 87-794, §243.
22. H. Rep. No. 93-571 at 42.
23. P.L. 93-618, §§102, 151; 19 U.S.C. 2112, 2191.
24. *Id.* at §102(c), (e).
25. *Id.* at §102(e).
26. *Id.* at §151.
27. *Id.* at §161(b).
28. P.L. 93-618, §135; 19 U.S.C. 2154.
29. E.g., Hearings on Implementation of the Multilateral Trade Negotiations Before the Subcomm. on International Trade of the Senate Comm. on Finance, 96th Cong., 1st sess. (Feb. 21 and 22, 1979); Hearings on the Multilateral Trade Negotiations Before the Subcomm. on Trade of the House Comm. on Ways and Means, 96th Cong., 1st sess. (Apr. 23–27, 1979); Hearings on the Trade Agreements Act of 1979 Before the Subcomm. on International Trade of the Senate Comm. on Finance, 96th Cong., 1st sess. (July 10 and 11, 1979).
30. 44 Fed. Reg. 1933 (1979).
31. P.L. 93-618, §102(e) (1); 19 U.S.C. 2112.
32. Hearings on Implementation of the Multilateral Trade Negotiations Before the Subcomm. on International Trade of the Senate Comm. on Finance, 96th Cong., 1st sess. (Feb. 21 and 22, 1979).
33. Hearings on the Multilateral Trade Negotiations Before the Subcomm. on Trade of the House Comm. on Ways and Means, 96th Cong., 1st sess. (Apr. 23–27, 1979).
34. P.L. 93-618, §101; 19 U.S.C. 2111.

ATTACHMENT A
COMMITTEE PROCEDURES FOR CONSIDERING LEGISLATION IMPLEMENTING TRADE AGREEMENTS
APPROVED JUNE 23, 1978

The trade agreements will usually be drafted in sufficiently general terms to permit each country flexibility in implementation. The Trade Act prohibits amendments to implementing legislation submitted by the President. If the Committee wishes to negotiate the terms of the legislation with the Administration, then it must review the proposed bill *before* it is submitted (in fact, before the Congress adjourns in October).

Possible procedures.—The Committee may wish to review proposed legislation under the following procedures:

1. The Committee would hold closed executive sessions on a regular basis to review progress in Geneva and legislative proposals.

2. The Administration would submit detailed legislative proposals to the Committee as soon as possible (beginning early in August).

3. The Committee would in effect mark up these proposals, using a Committee resolution (or a series of resolutions) as the vehicle for these markups. The resolutions would consist of recommended drafting instructions for the implementing legislation. The resolution would in effect be a statement to the Administration of what the Committee would consider acceptable implementing legislation.

4. Other Committees (Agriculture, Governmental Affairs, Commerce) would follow similar procedures, with the Finance Committee staff acting as a Senate clearinghouse for all information related to the trade negotiations.

5. The Committee would hold a conference with the Ways and Means Committee to reconcile conflicts in the Committee resolutions, if any.

6. The Committee could direct the staff and the Legislative Counsel to draft the implementing legislation with the Administration.

15

Concluding Observations:
The Constitutional Dimension

Dean Norman Redlich

Tᴴᴇ ᴄᴏᴍᴘᴇᴛɪᴛɪᴏɴ between the president and Congress for a share of the role in determining foreign policy has a constitutional, as well as a foreign policy, dimension. Indeed, the untidy arrangements for the formulation and execution of American foreign policy, so ably analyzed in this volume, flow directly from a fundamental constitutional concept—separation of powers. Like that other uniquely American institution—separation of church and state—separation of powers allows potentially conflicting entities to flourish by keeping them apart. By dividing governmental power among three branches—legislative, executive, and judicial—the framers quite consciously sought to secure maximum political freedom by the apparently contradictory method of creating a strong central authority but providing that its powers would be exercised by three branches in a constant state of tension with each other.[1]

It was as if three missiles were launched into orbit, each attracted to, and repelled by, the others, each dependent on the others for existence, and each capable of destroying the others and also the entire system. Congress' power to legislate (in most instances requiring presidential approval) is largely dependent on the executive branch for implementation. Congress in turn can frustrate the executive by its control over the purse, its power to reject major appointments, and its ability to shape legislative programs including those involving the structure of the executive branch itself. The judiciary, whose power appears the least formidable of the three branches, has effectively secured the right to compel, or restrain, actions by the other branches, but it is largely dependent on the president for the execution of its orders. Its jurisdiction is subject to congressional control,[2] and Congress determines the salaries of judges (except that they cannot be lowered)[3] and has the ability drastically to affect their work load. Although Congress and the president theoretically are capable of rendering the courts impotent, the judiciary has evolved as the branch which ultimately decides the boundaries of each branch's powers, including its own. This does not mean that the Supreme Court decides the merits of all constitutional issues, but it does mean that the Supreme Court decides which of the branches should decide them. In the sense that the Court decides "who decides," it is indeed the final arbiter. But in the sense that there are wide areas where the Court, by either action[4] or inaction,[5] leaves the power of decision elsewhere, the judiciary effectively shares, but does not dominate, the allocation of constitutional powers.

The authors of this compendium have grappled with one of the most difficult separation of powers issues—that of foreign policy. If it appears difficult precisely to define, or limit, the powers of the president and Congress in the shaping and implementing of foreign policy, it is because neither the text of the Constitution nor almost two centuries of interpretation have provided answers to some of the most difficult questions involving the role of the respective branches. Not surprisingly, the authors have sometimes disagreed over when this absence of clear definition is a virtue, when a curse.

But the lack of clear answers to some of the most basic questions of power among the three branches is not confined to matters of foreign policy. With so many crucial questions lacking definitive answers, it might appear surprising that our constitutional scheme has survived at all. Perhaps the uncertainty flowing from shared power has forced the three branches to make the political accommodations which have preserved a form of government whose basic charter contains the elements of its own self-destruction.

To place the foreign policy issues in clearer perspective, it is helpful to review some of the other areas where the three branches of government coexist in tension, with many major issues unresolved except through the pressures of the political process.

THE PRESIDENT AND CONGRESS

Although the Constitution gives the president the power to appoint ". . . by and with the advice and consent of the Senate . . . Officers of the United States, whose appointments are not herein otherwise provided . . . ,"[6] this crucial executive power is shared with Congress. No clear line exists, for example, to mark the limit of Congress' power sharply to circumscribe the president's discretion by setting precise qualifications for an office.[7] On the question of the president's power to remove executive officers, the Constitution itself grants no specific power to the president to exercise this crucial lever of executive control. Indeed, except for the impeachment provisions, the Constitution is silent on the subject. The Supreme Court, in a series of cases, has drawn a fuzzy line between "executive officers," where Congress may not limit the president's removal powers, and "quasi-legislative" or "quasi-judicial" positions, such as members of regulatory commissions, where the president exercises such removal power as Congress confers.[8] Nor may we be certain of the president's power to remove "for cause," in those instances where the occupants do not serve at his pleasure. Politics, not law, resolves most of these questions concerning the president's powers of appointment and removal. Congress has only rarely attempted, other than through the confirmation process, to restrict the president's power to appoint,[9] and voluntary resignation by the office holder, or grudging acceptance of the occupant by the president, is the more likely result when a president confronts an official whom he would remove if he had the clear power to do so.

Even the most basic of presidential powers, to ". . . take care that the laws be faithfully executed,"[10] has proved difficult to define. In *Youngstown Sheet & Tube Co.* v. *Sawyer*,[11] the famous "steel seizure" case, President Truman sought to justify the seizure by claiming it was necessary in order to "execute" a group of laws passed during the Korean War, such as those involving the procurement of materials, wage and price stability, and the draft. In rejecting the president's claim, four of the six judges[12] who constituted the majority emphasized that Congress, in the Taft-Hartley Act, had rejected seizure as a method of resolving national emergency labor disputes, leaving open the possibility that in the absence of the Taft-Hartley Act, with its provision for the obtaining of an injunction (which the president had ignored), the Court might have sustained the president's actions. Since the three dissenters[13] supported the seizure in spite of this legislative history, the case hardly resolved the broader issues of presidential power.

If we are not sure how far the president may go in executing the laws, we are equally unsure of his powers to ignore or contravene Congress' wishes with regard to the implementing of its own legislation. Long before Presidents Johnson and Nixon created political furors by impounding appropriated federal funds, presidents had properly "executed" the laws by preventing waste in the expenditure of funds and by allocating appropriated funds over the period of the appropriation in order to avoid deficiencies.[14] When President Nixon used impoundment to circumvent legislative judgments by curtailing or eliminating programs, Congress responded by legislation sharply limiting the president's power not to spend appropriated funds.[15]

But the ultimate power of Congress to compel the president to spend money on a project or program which the president concludes is wasteful or inefficient will probably never be tested in court. The political processes will resolve such questions, as they have in the past. It would be unwise, however, to conclude that Congress has the constitutional authority to compel the execution of its laws in all instances. Justice Jackson, in his famous *Steel Seizure* concurrence, attempted to delineate the scope of the president's powers as they relate either to the silence or the expressed will of the Congress. He wrote, "When the President takes measures incompatible with the expressed or implied will of Congress, his power is at its lowest ebb, for then he can rely only upon his own constitutional powers minus any constitutional powers of Congress over the matter."[16] This analysis recognizes some residue of presidential power which could justify action, or inaction, even in the face of a contrary direction by Congress—another indication that in the area of separation of powers, the Supreme Court is reluctant to interpret the powers of the president or the Congress in such a way as to obliterate the role of the other. (The Court, of course, shows no such reluctance with regard to its own power ". . . to say what the law is.")[17]

This tendency of the Court to tread gingerly with regard to disputes between the President and Congress is demonstrated in the most celebrated "separation-of-powers" case of this century, *United States* v. *Nixon*.[18] In deciding that the president's privilege of confidentiality of communication must yield to the demands of "due process of law in the fair administration of criminal justice,"[19] the Court carefully limited its holding. Thus, it emphasized that it ". . . is not concerned with the balance between . . . the confidentiality interests and congressional demands for information. . . ."[20] Lower federal courts had indicated, in earlier Nixon tapes cases,[21] a greater receptivity to the president's claim of privilege when asserted against the Congress than against grand juries, and the Supreme Court did nothing to suggest a contrary result.

Even in the area where the president's claim of privilege was rejected—the administration of criminal justice—the Supreme Court limited its opinion to situations where the president was not asserting ". . . a claim of need to protect military, diplomatic, or sensitive national security interests."[22] Thus, while Nixon lost the case and his presidency, the Court left many questions unanswered: the scope of a president's right to withhold confidential information from the Congress, the full scope of presidential privilege in national security matters, and the question of whether the president's privilege extends to subordinate officials.[23]

Also unresolved is the scope of the congressional power of impeachment. Watergate triggered a widespread discussion[24] over the meaning of the standard in Article II, Section 4, limiting impeachment to "Treason, Bribery, or other high Crimes and Misdemeanors." President Nixon's resignation prevented a court decision not only on the question of whether the Articles of Impeachment charged him with offenses described in Article II, Section 4, but as a threshold matter, whether the Congress, rather than the Court, was vested by the Constitution with the final authority to decide the question.

And the Supreme Court has yet to rule on the constitutionality of the legislative veto, a frequently used mechanism of congressional control over executive actions. Professor Schwartz argues cogently in this volume in support of the validity of the legislative veto. The Court will undoubtedly be compelled to decide the question in the near future, at least in the domestic area. As yet it remains another important and unresolved issue in the constitutional tension between the president and the Congress.

THE PRESIDENT AND THE JUDICIARY

Here too, broad political realities rather than clear constitutional language, underlie important aspects of the relationship. The fact that the courts are totally dependent on the executive branch for enforcement of judicial orders creates a haunting question which has hovered over us from the start of the Republic. What happens if the president refuses to comply with an order, or refuses to enforce one? Was it an accident of history, or an example of John Marshall's brilliant judicial statesmanship, that his sweeping declaration, in *Marbury* v. *Madison*,[25] that the head of an executive department could be "sued in the ordinary mode of proceeding"[26] was only *dictum* and, therefore, was never tested? As is well known, the statute which gave the Court power to issue its writ to the secretary of state was, so Marshall held, unconstitutional because it enlarged the Supreme Court's original jurisdiction. But Marshall could very easily have sustained the statute and issued the order to Madison to deliver the judicial commission to Marbury.[27] One wonders how the history of the country would have been altered if the chief justice had forced this test of strength with the new Jefferson administration and issued his order, only to have it defied by the president. Many of our future liberties may well have hung in the balance while Marshall pondered his options during these critical months in 1802 and 1803.[28]

The Supreme Court has emphasized that it does not back away from its responsibilities because of a fear of noncompliance, a position which, of course, the Court must assert to preserve its moral authority.[29] But, surely, the fear that this country and its most precious freedoms would suffer grievous harm if a president defied a court order, or refused to enforce one, must influence both the president and the Supreme Court in certain areas. The refusal of federal courts to rule on the constitutionality of the Vietnam War may have reflected this concern although the result was framed in terms of "standing," or "justiciability," or "political questions."[30] And President Nixon surely knew that defiance of the order to turn over the tapes would have assured impeachment and removal from office.

CONGRESS AND THE JUDICIARY

The unresolved questions of power between the Congress and the courts derive in part from the text of the Constitution itself. Article III gives Congress the power to create the federal courts, and few today question that Congress can define the limits of federal jurisdiction which those courts exercise.[31] But how broad is this power? Can Congress withdraw certain types of cases, such as those involving school prayer, or the validity of a war? How broad is Congress' power to control the appellate jurisdiction of the Supreme Court? The text of the Constitution hardly provides an answer,[32] and the leading case of *Ex Parte McCardle*[33] is far from conclusive. In that case Congress only closed off one avenue of review to the Supreme Court, and, in upholding the law and refusing to exercise appellate jurisdiction, the Court carefully referred to the residue of appellate jurisdiction which Congress had left untouched.[34]

Congress has many ways to send messages to the judiciary. Salaries, appropriations for the work of the courts, the confirmation process, proposals to deal with alleged judicial misconduct,[35] jurisdictional and procedural legislation—all of these provide Congress with an opportunity to indicate its concern for substantive positions of the federal courts. However, the American people seem to appreciate that the judiciary must be permitted a wide area of independence, and any effort by Congress to use its constitutional powers to influence substantive positions would be politically unpalatable.

In a case which had all of the potentiality for a confrontation between the Supreme Court and the Congress, *Powell* v. *McCormack*,[36] the Supreme Court sounded a very loud trumpet, but carefully limited the scope of its order to avoid any conflict with the House of Representatives. Proclaiming once again its role as the final interpreter of the Constitution,[37] the Supreme Court rejected doctrines which would have enabled it to avoid the issue[38] and, instead, ruled that the House of Representatives had improperly excluded Adam Clayton Powell from the 90th Congress. Exclusion, ruled the Court, was limited to a failure to meet the standards set forth in Article I, Section 2 of the Constitution—age, citizenship, and residency. But the Court dismissed Powell's case against members of Congress[39] and issued its order to seat Mr. Powell to the Doorkeeper and Sergeant at Arms of the House. In view of the fact that Powell was already seated, having been elected to the 91st Congress, it was hardly a difficult order to comply with. Moreover, the Court declined to rule on two issues which might have created a confrontation with the Congress: Powell's claim for seniority and back pay.[40] Specifically put off to another day, and probably indefinitely, was the question of whether the Supreme Court could review a decision by the House to expel a member under Article I, Section 5, which provides that "each House shall be the Judge of the . . . Qualifications of its own Members . . ." and that "Each House may . . . with the Concurrence of two-thirds, expel a Member."[41] Like John Marshall, Earl Warren strongly asserted the Court's authority with regard to a coordinate branch of the government, but he did so in a way that precluded any challenge to the Court's authority.

We know, of course, that there may well be clear constitutional violations by the Congress which the courts will not remedy. If a nativity scene in a public school is an establishment of religion,[42] as I believe it is, "In God We Trust" on the coins of the United States might be similarly vulnerable, but "standing to sue" avoids the issue. A good example of this phenomenon is *United States* v. *Richardson*[43] which held that the plaintiff lacked standing to challenge the refusal of the government to provide detailed expenditures of the Central Intelligence Agency alleged to be a violation of Article I, Section 9, Cl. 7 of the Constitution which provides: "No Money shall be drawn from the Treasury, but in Consequence of Appropriation made by Law; an irregular Statement and Account of the Receipts and Expenditures of all public Money shall be published from time to time." Responding to the argument that ". . . if respondent is not permitted to litigate this issue, no one can do so," the Court said, "In a very real sense, the absence of any particular individual or class to litigate these claims gives support to the argument that the subject matter is committed to the surveillance of Congress and ultimately to the political process."[44]

SEPARATION OF POWERS IN FOREIGN AFFAIRS

Anyone who thinks that there are, or can be, definite answers to the questions posed in the preceding discussion does not understand the subtle dynamics of our constitutional system. It is within the framework of that system that the foreign policy issues raised in this volume should be viewed.

The foreign policy area magnifies the tensions created by our constitutional system because the governmental powers which are necessary to formulate and implement foreign policy are scattered all over our constitutional landscape.[45] The president executes the laws, is commander in chief, appoints and receives ambassadors, negotiates treaties, and probably has such "inherent powers"[46] as the gathering of intelligence (a subject which has provoked considerable controversy) and the negotiation of agreements. Congress has the power to declare war, to regulate interstate and foreign commerce, to appropriate money, to provide for the armed forces, and (through the Senate) to consent to treaties and the appointment of ambassadors and other key officials in the foreign establishment, most notably the secretary of state.

While the Constitution spells out the treaty power, it leaves open the question of the Senate's power to affect the substance of treaties through attaching reservations to its consent. Professor Meron, in his paper, indicates the complexity of that issue.

Are there limits to the president's power to bypass the Senate, and Congress entirely, by an executive agreement?[47] The few decided cases[48] indicate a broad presidential power, but, in practice, most agreements, and treaties, require some type of subsequent implementing legislation by the Congress and, therefore, political necessity dictates congressional authorization or approval, or presidential agreements.

Only recently, in *Goldwater* v. *Carter*,[49] has the Supreme Court decided that the president, without congressional approval, has the power to abrogate a treaty, although the majority reached that conclusion through differing routes. A plurality[50] concluded that the issue was a "political question" which the Court should not decide. Justices Powell and Brennan, concurring in the result, wrote opinions arguing that the plurality was misapplying the political question doctrine.

Vietnam, of course, provoked national debate over the competing war-making roles of the president and Congress, and the War Powers Resolution has not resolved the ultimate question of power, as was seen by the recent debate over the hostage rescue mission.

In sum, the foreign affairs area presents a picture which, in constitutional principle, is no different from other areas where powers are dispersed among the three branches. Probably the courts play a lesser role in the foreign affairs area, although, as *Goldwater* v. *Carter* demonstrated, the Supreme Court remains the ultimate arbiter, whether by ruling on the merits or by deciding that someone else has the power to decide.

We have lived by political accommodations and by unwritten rules, which had served us reasonably well until the Vietnam and Watergate eras, when the president broke some of these unwritten rules and the Congress responded.

Up to a point, the president has waged war, despite Congress' seemingly exclusive power to declare war.[51] Then came Vietnam, and Congress responded by imposing limitations on the president's powers, through the War Powers Resolution.

Up to a point, the president has the authority not to execute the laws of the United States. He can avoid waste, limit the rate of expenditures,[52] and as a practical matter use his budgetary control powers to influence legislative policy. But then came President Nixon's abuse of the impoundment power, and Congress responded.[53]

Up to a point, the president has gathered intelligence without complying with all of the procedures that would be required of a police officer. Then came burglaries, widespread and unauthorized wiretaps, and Congress responded, when politics dictated, by imposing limits of the president's authority to gather intelligence.[54]

Up to a point, the president can authorize clandestine activities abroad. Then came the Bay of Pigs, Chile, assassination plots, and Congress has responded by trying to create a CIA charter.

We really cannot be sure of the constitutionality of all of the president's actions, or of the congressional responses. We remain uncertain of the validity of the War Powers Resolution, the scope of the president's power as commander in chief, Congress' ability to limit the president's power to gather foreign intelligence, Congress' power to condition its consent to treaties, the validity of the legislative veto in the field of foreign affairs, the scope of the president's power to enter into executive agreements without congressional approval or authorization, or the ability of Congress to mandate expenditures for a weapons system which the President regards as ineffective. It would surprise me if these issues were to reach the Supreme Court. And if they do, I would expect that the

Court will exercise its power "to decide who decides," and then in practically all cases, the "who decides" will be another branch. There will always be a bow in the direction of *Marbury* but an everpresent recognition of the limitation of the judicial process and judicial power.

We can expect, then, that the political fight will continue for a larger share of the power in the conduct of foreign relations. The field is too uncertain and there are too many variables to allow us to devise precise rules to answer the unanswered questions which dominate this area. The authors in this volume themselves disagree sharply over whether the president is too weak, or too strong, relative to Congress.

Our democracy would clearly be in danger if we permitted a president, without constitutional restraint, to exercise the war-making powers which President Roosevelt believed were necessary to save Western Europe from Nazi domination during the period 1939–1941. Those who are critical of an expansive interpretation of presidential powers should remember that if our foreign policy had been conducted with congressional participation during that period, it is unlikely that England would have received 50 over-aged destroyers, or that our merchant vessels would have been armed, and escorted by destroyers, to fight off Nazi U-boats.

While we cannot have rules which permit a stamp of constitutional approval on what Roosevelt felt was necessary, neither can our democracy survive by adopting rules which assume that every president is a Nixon. Nixon may have taken advantage of the flexibility, but to deprive future presidents of freedom of action would impair our ability to function in the foreign area.

While there has undoubtedly been a shift in the direction of Congress in the post-Vietnam era, recent events in Iran and Afghanistan emphasize that, in any competition for power with the Congress, the president can take care of himself. He alone has the power to negotiate; Congress cannot hope to match the president's control of the bureaucracy, the flow of information, or his access to the media. Particularly in times of crisis, the president speaks for the country. But as many of our authors point out, if the president is to function effectively, he must recognize Congress' foreign policy role, derived from its constitutionally based powers.

How the power is divided may well depend less on questions of domestic politics or personalities and more on the nature of the world, the role of the United States, and the kinds of issues that will face the country. If, for example, trade and other economic issues become more important than strictly military considerations, Congress' participation becomes relatively significant. It is far easier for the president alone to decide the location of military bases than how to deal with the question of Japanese imports.

A polarized world, relying on one-to-one personal diplomacy, shifts power to the president. Such a world is a world of permanent crisis, and presidents thrive in such an atmosphere. A less polarized world will probably see a continuation of the turn toward Congress. Similarly, intelligence gathering, and covert operations, may appear far less important in a less hostile world. These are functions which are peculiarly within the province of the president. If diplomacy deals with jobs, energy, population shifts, and trade, Congress will be more involved. If, however, we revert to a world of large power confrontation, with renewed emphasis on the development of strategic weapons systems, intensive gathering of intelligence, aggressive use of covert operations, the president's role will be enhanced at the expense of Congress, notwithstanding Congress' control over the purse. There may be some well-publicized differences over weapons systems but they will represent a congressional flexing of muscle rather than a real sharing of power.

So, the messy situation will go on. But we should not shrug our shoulders in despair. Our untidy allocation of powers in the field of foreign affairs has problems and it has opportunities. At critical moments in history, the Supreme Court, in *Marbury*, the *Steel Seizure* case, and *Nixon* v. *United States* helped us resolve some of the difficult domestic separation of powers issue. Because such judicial intervention is unlikely in foreign affairs, political leadership becomes essential. Here is where our governmental system offers great opportunities because it provides many focal points for decision making. Unlike a parliamentary system, with powers centered at the apex of a party leadership, we have many points of entry into the process: through the executive branch with many positions of influence, and through congressional leaders and staffs which have become increasingly instituionalized. One has only to read the roster of the authors in this volume to realize how widely dispersed are the points of power in the foreign policy area, notwithstanding the paramount power of the president.

Thus, because the question of power in foreign affairs will be decided in the political arena and not in the courts, and because the executive and legislative branches are structured so as to allow such leadership to be exercised, the opportunities for creative political leadership are very great.

We must work toward a continuing dialogue between the president and the Congress in which the president asserts, "The president must conduct the foreign policy of this democratic republic, because other countries must have a fixed point for negotiation and because there can only be one chief executive in the formulation and execution of that policy. You, the Congress, can and should participate. I will share information. I will try to persuade, but I will be flexible. I will listen, and I will change my mind, but you must display the political leadership demanded by the responsibilities you seek and that I am willing to give you."

And the Congress should reply, "As long as you are honest with us, as long as we can participate in the process, and as long as you can show concern for our interests, particularly where our constituencies are involved, and as long as your policies are based on principles and goals worthy of this nation, we will allow you to play the dominant role which you seek and which our Constitution has fashioned for you in the formulation and execution of foreign policy."

It will take the highest order of political leadership for that dialogue to be meaningful. But in the conduct of this democracy's foreign affairs, should there be, can there be, any other way?

NOTES

1. *The Federalist Papers* No. 226 (A. Hamilton).
2. *Sheldon v. Sill*, 8 How. 441 (1850). See note 31 *infra*.
3. U.S. Const. art. III §1.
4. *Coleman v. Miller*, 307 U.S. 433 (1939).
5. *Holtzman v. Schlesinger*, 414 U.S.1304 (1973); *DaCosta v. Laird*, 405 U.S. 979 (1972); *Massachusetts v. Laird*, 400 U.S.806 (1970); *Mora v. McNamara*, 389 U.S. 934 (1967).
6. U.S. Const. art. II §2 cl. 2.
7. 2 B. Schwartz, *A Commentary on the Constitution of the United States* §183 (1963).
8. *Meyers v. United States*, 272 U.S. 52 (1926); *Humphrey's Executor v. United States*, 295 U.S. 602 (1935); *Weiner v. United States*, 357 U.S. 349 (1958).
9. *Buckley v. Valeo*, 424 U.S.1 (1976); 2 B. Schwartz, *supra* note 7, at §184.
10. U.S. Const. art. II §3.
11. 343 U.S. 579 (1952); See also, M. Marcus, *Truman and the Steel Seizure Case* (1977).
12. See opinions of Justices Frankfurter, Jackson, Burton and Clark. Justices Black and Douglas emphasized a lack of presidential power, rather than Congress' earlier rejection of seizure in emergency strikes.
13. Chief Justice Vinson, Justices Reed and Minton dissented.
14. *Antideficiency Act of 1950*, 31 U.S.C. §665(c) (1976).
15. *Impoundment Control Act of 1974*, 31 U.S.C. §1401 *et. seq.* (1976).
16. 343 U.S. at 631.
17. *Marbury v. Madison*, 1 Cranch 137 at 177 (1803); *United States v. Nixon*, 418 U.S., 683, at 703 (1974).
18. 418 U.S. 683 (1974).
19. *Id.* at 713.
20. *Id.* at 712 n. 19.
21. *Senate Select Committee on Presidential Campaign Activities v. Nixon*, 370 F. Supp. 521 (1974), aff'd, 498 F. 2d 725 (D.C. Cir 1974).
22. 418 U.S. at 710.
23. See, *Symposium: United States v. Nixon*, 22 U.C.L.A. 1 (1974), and P. Freund, *Foreword: On Presidential Privilege*, 88 *Harv. L. Rev.* 13 (1974).
24. See, R. Berger, *The President, Congress, and the Courts*, 83 *Yale L.J.* 1111 (1974); G. Gunther, *Judicial Hegemony and Legislative Autonomy: The Nixon Case and the Impeachment Process*, 22 *U.C.L.A. L. Rev.* 30 (1974); L. Pollak, *The Constitution as an Experiment*, 123 *U. Pa. L. Rev.* 1318 (1975); W. Van Alstyne, *The Third Impeachment Article:*

Congressional Bootstrapping, 60 *A.B.A. J.* 1199, (1974); W. Swindler, *High Court of Congress: Impeachment Trials 1797–1936*, 60 *A.B.A. J.* 420 at 424 (1974).

25. 1 Cranch 137 (1803).
26. *Id.* at 170.
27. See, N. Redlich, *The Supreme Court—1833 Term, Foreword: The Constitution—"A Rule for the Government of Courts, As Well As of Legislature"*, 40 *N.Y.U. L. Rev.* 1 (1965); W. Van Alstyne, *A Critical Guide to Marbury v. Madison*, 1969 *Duke L.J.* 1.
28. J. Marke, *Vignettes of Legal History*, 1 (1965).
29. *Powell v. McCormack*, 395 U.S. 486 at 549 (1968).
30. *Supra* note 5.
31. P. Bator, P. Mishkin, D. Shapiro, and H. Wechsler, *Hart & Wechsler's The Federal Courts and the Federal System* ch. IV (2d ed. 1973).
32. U.S. Const. art. III §2 cl. 2.
33. 7 Wallace 506 (1869).
34. *Id.* at 515; W. Van Alstyne, *A Critical Guide to Ex Parte McCardle*, 15 *Ariz. L. Rev.* 229 (1973).
35. I. Kaufman, *Chilling Judicial Independence*, 88 YALE L.J. 681 (1979).
36. 395 U.S. 486 (1969).
37. *Id.* at 549.
38. *Id.* at 518.
39. U.S. Const. art. I §6 cl. 1.
40. 395 U.S. at 550.
41. *Id.* at 507 n. 27.
42. *Citizens Concerned for Separation of Church and State v. Denver*, 481 F. Supp. 522 (D. Colo. 1979).
43. 418 U.S. 166 (1974).
44. *Id.* at 179.
45. See, L. Henkin, *Foreign Affairs and the Constitution* (1972); and A. Lowenfeld, Review 87 *Harv. L. Rev.* 494 (1973).
46. See, *United States v. Curtiss—Wright export Corp.*, 299 U.S.304 (1936); *Chicago and Southern Airlines v. Waterman Steamship Corp.*, 333 U.S. 103 (1949); *United States v. Brown*, 484 F. 2d 418 (5th Cir. 1973); But see, *United States v. U.S. District Court*, 407 U.S. 297 (1972).
47. See, L. Henkin supra note 22 at 176.
48. *United States v. Belmont*, 301 U.S., 324 (1937); *United States v. Pink*, 315 U.S. 203 (1942); *United States v. Capps*, 204 F. 2d 655 (4th Cir. 1953).
49. 444 U.S. 996, 100 S. Ct. 533 (1979).
50. Justice Rehnquist wrote the opinion, joined by Chief Justice Burger and Justices Stewart and Stevens.

51. See discussion in, L. Henkin, *supra* note 22 at 107, and excerpts from Sen. Rep. No. 797; 90th Cong. 1st Sess. (Nov. 20, 1967), in G. Gunther, *Constitutional Law Cases and Materials* 437–39 (9th ed. 1975).

52. *Supra* note 14.

53. *Supra* note 15.

54. *Foreign Intelligence Surveillance Act of 1978*, 50 U.S.C. §1801 *et seq.* (Supp. II 1978).